AND WE'RE ALL BROTHERS: SINGING IN YIDDISH
IN CONTEMPORARY NORTH AMERICA

To Geraldine Auerbach and Jennifer Jankel,

and in memory of Adrienne Cooper z"l (1946–2011)
Zol zi hobn a likhtikn gan-eydn.

And We're All Brothers: Singing in Yiddish in Contemporary North America

ABIGAIL WOOD
SOAS, University of London, UK
and University of Haifa, Israel

ASHGATE

Published by
Ashgate Publishing Limited
Wey Court East
Union Road
Farnham
Surrey, GU9 7PT
England

Ashgate Publishing Company
110 Cherry Street
Suite 3-1
Burlington, VT 05401-3818
USA

www.ashgate.com

British Library Cataloguing in Publication Data
Wood, Abigail, 1977-
  And we're all brothers : singing in Yiddish in contemporary
  North America. – (SOAS musicology series)
  1. Songs, Yiddish – New York (State) – New York – History
  and criticism. 2. Klezmer music – New York (State) – New
  York – History and criticism. 3. Music – New York (State) –
  New York – 21st century – History and criticism.
  I. Title II. Series
  782.4'262924-dc23

The Library of Congress has cataloged the printed edition as follows:
Wood, Abigail, 1977-
  And we're all brothers : singing in Yiddish in contemporary North America / by Abigail Wood.
      p. cm. – (SOAS musicology series)
  Includes bibliographical references and index.
  ISBN 978-1-4094-4533-3 (hardcover) – ISBN 978-1-4094-4534-0 (ebook) – ISBN 978-1-
  4094-7303-9 (epub) 1. Jews – Music – New York (State) – New York – History and criticism.
  2. Folk songs, Yiddish – History and criticism. 3. Songs, Yiddish – History and criticism. 4.
  Klezmer music – History and criticism. I. Title.
  ML3776.W66 2013
  782.42089'924073 – dc23
                                                                        2012039070

ISBN 9781409445333 (hbk)
ISBN 9781409445340 (ebk – PDF)
ISBN 9781409473039 (ebk – ePUB)

Printed and bound in Great Britain
by MPG PRINTGROUP

Contents

List of Examples

List of Tables

Acknowledgements

This book is about a thriving music community. I am grateful to all those in the Yiddish music scene who took the time to share thoughts and music with me during the course of my research, especially Michael Alpert, Adrienne Cooper *z"l*, Josh Dolgin, Sruli Dresdner, Itzik Gottesman, Deborah Karpel, Frank London, Chana Mlotek, Zalmen Mlotek, Binyumen Schaechter, Beyle Schaechter-Gottesman, Andreas Schmitges, Miryem-Khaye Seigel, Lorin Sklamberg, Sophie Solomon, Deborah Strauss and Jeff Warschauer, and Josh Waletzky. I would also like to thank the librarians and archivists who made materials available to me (some of whom also schlepped my endless book orders), including Gila Flam at the National Library in Jerusalem, Herbert Lazarus and Yeshaye Metal at YIVO, and Faith Jones and the other staff of the Dorot Jewish and Performing Arts divisions of the New York Public Library. I am also grateful to Lloyd Wolf for generously allowing me to use his image of Adrienne Cooper for the cover of this volume.

Any project of this scope would be an impossible undertaking without the contribution of information, advice, support, hospitality, friendship and enthusiasm by many individuals. Those who helped me along the way are far too numerous to list; however, the following deserve special mention: Gitta Bechshøft, Jeanice Brooks, Lorele Cahan-Simon, Brukhe Caplan, Ari Davidow and members of the Jewish-music mailing list, Gina Genova, David Halperin, Marion Jacobson, Faith Jones and Winnifred Tovey, Alex Knapp, Katie Light, Billy Meyers and Nahma Sandrow, Edwin Seroussi, Helen and Ben Styles, Rhiannon and Christopher Thompson, Ilana Webster-Kogen and all those at home on Kibbutz Ganei Shemesh. I am grateful to Simon Mills and Phil Alexander for typesetting musical examples.

This book grew out of my doctoral dissertation. I am grateful to my wonderful supervisor, Ruth Davis, for her support, good advice and kohlrabi salad, to my academic advisor David Rowland for helping me to stay in the business, to Christ's College and the Music Department at the University of Cambridge for providing me with a rich intellectual environment in which to begin my research career, and to my colleagues at Southampton for supporting me as I juggled finishing my dissertation with the demands of a lectureship.

The financial support of a number of institutions enabled me to carry out this research. The initial stages of work were supported by a doctoral award from the Arts and Humanities Research Board. Without generous travel grants from the Arts and Humanities Research Board, Christ's College, Cambridge, the Faculty of Music, Cambridge University, and the Faculty of Arts, Southampton University, vital research overseas could not have taken place. Further scholarships from YIVO and the Levy-Plumb Fund, Christ's College, allowed me to attend the 2001

Uriel Weinreich Summer Program in Yiddish Language and Culture at Columbia University, New York, and a Youth Scholarship allowed me to attend KlezKanada, August 2001. Since I arrived at SOAS in 2006, I am grateful for the generous support of Geraldine Auerbach, Jennifer Jankel and the Jewish Music Institute. Finally, in 2008 YIVO's Heifetz and Kramen scholarships enabled me to complete my archival research in New York.

I am indebted to those who provided valuable feedback on earlier versions of this work, including Rachel Beckles Willson, Phil Bohlman, Nicholas Cook, Kevin Dawe, Rachel Harris, Mark Kligman, Vivi Lachs, Mark Slobin, Lindsey Taylor-Guthartz, Owen Wright, several anonymous reviewers, and to my colleagues at SOAS for their ongoing advice, support and insightful conversations. Of course, all errors are mine alone.

Heartfelt thanks to Laura Macy, Emma Gallon and Philip Stirups at Ashgate for steering this book so smoothly through the publication process, and to Jonathan Hoare for his meticulous proofreading.

Finally, I would like to thank my family, Dunja, Roy, James, Melanie, Reuben, Lilia and Evie Wood, for their love, good humour and continued support across already more than a decade of research and three continents. You all taught me to ask good questions; I hope that the intellectual curiosity you have always encouraged and shared with me shines through some of the following pages.

Introduction

One of the most vivid manifestations of East European Jewry was the folksong. The Yiddish Folksong was a mirror of their life; it reflected reality and dreams, joy and sorrow, love and longing – with a wealth of musical forms. The terrible tragedy of the Holocaust, with the destruction of hundreds of communities and the death of millions of Jews, put an end to all singing … What is left? Where can one go? (Gorali, Almagor and Bick 1970, preface).

Un mir zaynen ale brider	*And we're all brothers*
Un mir zingen freylekhe lider.	*And we sing happy songs.*
Un mir haltn zikh in eynem	*And we stick together*
Azelkhes iz nito bay keynem.	*Like nobody else.*
… Un mir zaynen ale shvester …	*And we're all sisters*
Azoy vi Rokhl, Rus un Ester.	*Like Rachel, Ruth and Esther.*
Un mir zaynen ale freylekh	*And we're all gay*
Vi Yoynoson un Dovid hameylekh.	*Like Jonathan and King David.*

(From 'Ale brider' [All brothers], Klezmatics, adapted from a popular Jewish-socialist folksong based on a poem by Morris Winchevsky. Klezmatics, *Shvaygn=Toyt*, 1988.)

Both addressing a contemporary, transnational audience for Yiddish song during the latter part of the twentieth century, the extracts cited above seem poles apart. For Gorali, Almagor and Bick, eternally silenced songs serve as a metaphor for ever-silenced communities, indexing the irreversible, absolute destruction of vernacular Yiddish culture in Eastern Europe, along with its speakers, in the Holocaust. By contrast, the Klezmatics, at this time a fairly new klezmer band taking a break from the New York club scene in 1988 to play the Heimatklänge festival in Berlin and to record their first album, *Shvaygn=Toyt*, append a redemptive, even playful, narrative of rebirth. 'In making this record', proclaim the liner notes, 'these musicians in effect rode the German rails again, this time trumpeting Jericho. And that alone is worth writing home about' (Klezmatics 1998, liner notes, under pseudonym Allolo Trehorn).

The resurgence of East European Jewish music in North America during the latter decades of the twentieth century, exemplified here by the Klezmatics, seems indeed to have been 'worth writing home about'. The last quarter of the twentieth century and the early years of the twenty-first saw a steady stream of new recordings in Yiddish: newly composed songs, well-known singers performing 'nostalgic' favourites, American popular songs translated into Yiddish, theatre songs, and even a couple of forays into Yiddish hip hop. Yiddish songs also form a substantial part of the repertory of many contemporary klezmer bands; folk songs, socialist songs and theatre songs are interwoven with new material, testifying not only to the enduring appeal of older material but also to continuing creative activity.

Indeed, after a few decades of relative decline, by the end of the twentieth century, Yiddish song was firmly back in the Jewish-American soundtrack. In his coffee-table book *Jews/America/A Representation* (1996), French anthropologist-photographer Frederic Brenner presents a portrait of Jewish America in the form of 731 snapshot pictures, each precisely four centimetres square, entitled 'inventory june 1993–september 1995 (arranged alphabetically)'. Pictures of kosher food products, a Disney yarmulke, Jewish bumper stickers, newspaper cuttings and various items of Judaica sit side by side with advertisements, computer graphics, a Jewish dentist, Holocaust memorials, synagogues, underwear, El Al duty-free, religious items, pornography, the Talmud, a badge with the slogan 'Kiss Me, I'm Jewish'. Notwithstanding the limitations of the photographic medium, music receives ample representation in Brenner's portrait. CD covers pepper his collection of images – 'Fiddler on the Roof' (no. 82), Cantor Joseph Malovany (no. 90), Bob Dylan (no. 96), Simon and Garfunkel (no. 308), a 'Jewish Party' compilation (no. 391), Shlomo Carlebach (no. 564), the Miami Boys Choir (no. 703) … and the Klezmatics (no. 659). Fifty years after the Holocaust, then, a klezmer band with a gay sensibility and New York attitude, whose vocal numbers are nearly all in Yiddish, found itself among the icons of American Jewish culture, playfully juxtaposed between the cool and the kitsch.

Brenner presciently places the Klezmatics within a grid of images which the reader must herself parse. Cool or kitsch? It's up to the beholder; I am reminded of Gary Tomlinson's Geertzian observation that relationality itself, the cultural web we construct to understand music, is also a fiction of the historian (Tomlinson 1984). The complex, floating intentionalities of music lend themselves easily to such fluid interpretation. In recent years, contemporary Yiddish song and its protagonists have been invoked in a startling array of scholarly contexts: held up as exemplifying musical revival, post-Holocaust cultural politics, the transformation of language use, radical alterity and a new generation of American Jewish identities (see, for example, Slobin 2002a, Gruber 2002, Shandler 2006, Barzel 2004). Notwithstanding its relatively few practitioners, contemporary Yiddish song seems remarkable for its public visibility, tenacity, creativity and for seemingly contradicting many of the other trends of American Jewry identified by sociologists (assimilation, Zionism, moves towards the Orthodox right, organised synagogue movements). Indeed, at the height of this interpretative whirlwind, in his recent book *Klezmer America* (2008) Jonathan Freedman cites Yiddish music as a metaphor for the re-making of American Jewish culture itself. However abstract his musical reference may be, it is clear that the resonances of these musical activities are felt much more widely than the community of those who directly engage in them.

The present volume seeks gently to prise open, and to untangle this discursive web, exploring how Yiddish song became such a potent medium for musical and ideological creativity at the twilight of the twentieth century. The scope of a complete portrait of Yiddish song in post-Holocaust North America would be far beyond a single volume; instead I hone in on a single time and space to present an episode in the flowing timeline of a musical repertory – New York at the dawn of the twenty-first century, outlining some of the trajectories that Yiddish song and its singers have taken to, and beyond, this point.

Initially, this study responded to an apparent gap in the ethnomusicological map. The majority of surveys of Yiddish song came to a halt at the Holocaust, the symbolic end-point of an embedded, vernacular Yiddish culture in Central and Eastern Europe.[1] A growing cluster of scholars, led by Mark Slobin, had begun to address the revival of East European Jewish instrumental repertories among a new generation of North American musicians, under the loose heading of 'klezmer revival'.[2] While many authors mentioned songs along the way, the overwhelming focus of 'klezmerology' on instrumental music seemed to me not fully to account for the centrality of Yiddish-language vocal music in the repertories of many of the same ensembles.[3] Further, far from the 'end to all singing' of Gorali et al., song also pervaded the activities of a wider creative community focused on the Yiddish language, from stage productions to home singalongs, from language lessons to a stream of newly published songbooks. Lying further outside the professional klezmer scene, these wider contexts for contemporary Yiddish vocal music were virtually absent from the academic literature.[4]

As I began to trace the eclectic pathways of Yiddish song repertories through the late twentieth century and into the twenty-first, it became clear that beyond musical repertory and performance, as a textual medium song was also particularly implicated in ideological work, serving as a medium for the negotiation of complex social transactions, and helping to create, sustain and challenge the discursive networks within which contemporary Yiddish musical practice is constituted. Yiddish song is a repertory about which imaginative discourse abounds. Songs

---

[1]   Ruth Rubin's *Voices of a People* (1979) is to date still the only general monograph concerning Yiddish song. Other recent book-length studies dealing wholly or partially with Yiddish songs have also tended to emphasise past or culturally 'other' contexts for Yiddish songs, including Holocaust songs (Flam 1992), early twentieth-century folklorists (Gottesman 2003), popular songs of Jewish immigrants in America (Slobin 1982 and Heskes 1992) and Lubavitcher Hasidim (Koskoff 2001). A parallel strand of enquiry has focused upon the collection and publication of songs themselves, ranging from popular publications to folkloristic volumes documenting material collected from the elderly and Holocaust survivors, or republished from earlier collections, to the reissuing of old recordings, including archival field recordings held in the Former Soviet Union. Recent scholarly studies include Bohlman and Holzapfel's comparative study of songs with German and Yiddish variants (2001) and Slobin's edition of collections by folklorist Moshe Beregovski (1982). These studies, too, however, focus primarily on historical material.

[2]   The terminology of 'klezmer' and 'revival' is addressed at greater length in Chapter 3.

[3]   In his groundbreaking survey of the klezmer revival, Mark Slobin acknowledges this omission (2000, 7–8).

[4]   A notable exception is Jacobson's thesis (2004) on Yiddish folk choruses.

and singers are slotted into histories of Yiddish culture, bringing diverse threads together into unified narratives. These stories have themselves become cultural tropes: songs and the words that discuss them are enmeshed in a joint discourse that in itself stands as a self-portrait encapsulating the ideological projects of contemporary Yiddish culture.

Lonely Planet: Yiddish(land)

First, some orientation is necessary. The concept of a language-defined genre called 'Yiddish song' is itself a rather recent invention reflecting late nineteenth- and early twentieth-century European ideologies of *Volkskunst*. As eloquently documented by Itzik Gottesman, early twentieth-century folklorists used song as a means to picture the Yiddish nation as equal to its European counterparts (2003); as I will suggest in Chapter 2, this conceptual genre has lost none of its rhetorical power, but rather continues to be reimagined in a variety of guises.

Further, any discussion of contemporary Yiddish song is inseparable from the wider context of Yiddish. The word 'Yiddish' is itself polyvalent: in English, 'Yiddish' is used as a noun referring to the Yiddish language; in Yiddish, by contrast, it is an adjective meaning 'Jewish', and carries substantial cultural resonance. 'Yiddish' stands for the cultural and ontological world of the Eastern Ashkenazic Jewish community, encompassing values, norms and expectations, set in contrast to the cultural world of non-Jewish neighbours.

As a product of Jewish diaspora, the Yiddish language has always indexed minority status; since the Holocaust it has become a minority language even within the Ashkenazic Jewish world itself.[5] Growing from Middle High German roots, Yiddish was for many centuries the language of the Eastern Ashkenazic Jews. The structure of the Yiddish language reflects the migration of this Jewish population eastwards from the Franco-German borderlands to Central and Eastern Europe. Written from right to left in the Hebrew alphabet, the grammar and a large proportion of Yiddish words are Germanic, but its richly diverse vocabulary also draws from Hebrew and Aramaic, the tongues of the synagogue and Jewish study, and from the Slavic languages in whose territory Yiddish speakers resided. Further, throughout the large part of Central, Eastern and Southeastern Europe over which the Jewish population spread, the Yiddish language also exhibited regional variations in accent and dialect.

A third meaning of 'Yiddish', however, is equally important to the present discussion: the place of Yiddish in contemporary Jewish-American life. The term 'Yiddishland', while it appears in no Yiddish dictionary, has been used for over a century to imagine 'a virtual locus construed in terms of the use of the Yiddish

---

[5]   For detailed studies of the history of the Yiddish language, including its decline in the mid-twentieth century and its place in North America up to the early 1990s, see Fishman (1981 and 1990).

language, especially, though not exclusively, in its spoken form' (Shandler 2006, 33).[6] This label is, nevertheless, implicitly either utopian or ironic: even at the height of Old-World Yiddish culture, Yiddishland never existed. Notwithstanding frequent reference to discourses of nationalism, Yiddishland has none of the formal attributes that serve to legitimise a modern nation-state – government, embassies, airports, a Lonely Planet guide and, of course, a *land*.

Neither can this identification rely on linguistic fluency. According to a 1999 report published in the *New York Times*, Yiddish was used daily by about 700,000 people worldwide, in large part in strictly Orthodox Hasidic communities, whose high birth rate suggests that within a generation daily use of the Yiddish language in America may even grow in absolute terms.[7] Outside ultra-orthodox communities, the use of Yiddish as a vernacular has declined enormously since the mid-twentieth century. Nonetheless, as Yiddish scholar Uriel Weinreich already remarked in the 1970s, 'the measurement of the present knowledge of Yiddish, and its novel place in the Jewish cultural economy, requires tools far subtler than those of ordinary censuses' (1971, 789). Counterpoised against the decline in Yiddish fluency has been a surge of interest in Yiddish as 'heritage', reflected in the widespread growth in popularity since the 1960s of Yiddish-related books, music recordings and other cultural products, allowing the non-fluent reader to gain access to Yiddish language and culture, and in the simultaneous rise of adult Yiddish education. Jeffrey Shandler observes that, 'as fewer American Jews speak or read Yiddish, its symbolic value here has escalated. Many who profess a profound, genuine attachment to Yiddish also admit they do not really know the language; moreover, they do not see their lack of fluency as interfering with their devotion to Yiddish' (2000, 98).

In his recent extensive study of this quintessentially Jewish-American phenomenon, Shandler describes this relationship with the Yiddish language as 'postvernacular'. It is worth quoting his definition at length:

> As it implies, the term *postvernacular* relates to Yiddish in a manner that both is other than its use as a language of daily life and is responsive to the language having once been a widely used Jewish vernacular. Postvernacularity is, therefore, a relational phenomenon. It always entails some awareness of its distance from vernacularity, which is usually contemplated in terms of retrospection – even as vernacular Yiddish continues to be maintained by Jewish communities around the world. What most distinguishes postvernacular Yiddish

---

[6] The epithet Yiddishland is frequently used by insiders to refer to the Yiddish cultural world. This usage is discussed further below. In addition to Shandler's *Adventures in Yiddishland* (2006), the use of this word has frequently been discussed in *Mendele*, an Internet newsletter for Yiddish literature and language; see volume 8.055 (1998) for a summary and also Moderator's notes to vols 8.001 (1998) and vol. 9.056 (1999) (*Mendele* is archived at http://www.ibiblio.org/pub/academic/languages/Yiddish/mendele/).

[7] *New York Times*, 3 September 1999.

is its semiotic hierarchy; unlike vernacular language use, in the postvernacular mode, the language's secondary, symbolic level of meaning is always privileged over its primary level. In other words, in postvernacular Yiddish the very fact that something is said (or written or sung) in Yiddish is at least as meaningful as the meaning of the words being uttered – if not more so (2006, 22).

For those who choose to opt into Yiddish today, then, Yiddish is not just a language; neither, however, does it represent the fully functioning, normative Jewish cultural world it occupied in Eastern Europe. While Yiddish is frequently spoken among the fluent, the lingua franca of Yiddishland is American English, albeit seasoned liberally with various fragments of Jewish, European and Slavic languages. Rather than purely residing in the language, then, the essential qualities of Yiddish culture are embraced by an inclusive term, 'yiddishkayt'. Like the term 'Yiddishland', 'yiddishkayt' is a consensual, popular term, its meaning stretching beyond the translation 'Jewishness; Judaism' given by Weinreich's dictionary (Weinreich 1977, 206). Perhaps better translated 'Yiddishness', this term is used by insiders to invoke a shared cultural territory, illustrated here in Irving Howe's popular-nostalgic history of Jewish immigration to America. Howe observed:

> Like other important terms in cultural discourse, *Yiddishkeit* [*sic*] has no single, agreed-upon meaning … As I use the term here, *Yiddishkeit* refers to that phase of Jewish history during the last two centuries which is marked by the prevalence of Yiddish as the language of the east European Jews and by the growth among them of a culture resting mainly upon that language. The culture of *Yiddishkeit* is no longer that of traditional Orthodoxy, yet it retains strong ties to the religious past. It takes on an increasingly secular character yet is by no means confined to the secularist elements among Yiddish-speaking Jews. It refers to a way of life, a shared experience, which goes beyond opinion or ideology (1976, 16).

This popular, consensual concept of yiddishkayt encompasses a flexible web of narratives. Drawn from the rich history of the Yiddish-speaking world, a canon of imagery serves as a hermeneutic frame for today's Yiddish culture, serving to define an Ashkenazic Jewish alterity. In the wider American Jewish world, such imagery may be limited to a stereotyped, sentimental picture of rural European Jewish life, epitomised by *Fiddler on the Roof*, superimposed on a historical background of immigration, Jewish assimilation and the Holocaust, factors which in their very different ways contributed to the end of vernacular Yiddish culture as a normative way of life. Among the Yiddish cognoscenti, however, this common core of imagery is widened to a textured understanding of the history, literature and cultural capital of Yiddish-speaking communities worldwide.

Nevertheless, notwithstanding this historical frame of reference, at the turn of the twenty-first century, for those with eyes to see, Yiddishland is a real, tangible place, here and now. A thriving contemporary, North America-centred subculture coalesces around a network of institutions involved in the teaching and promotion of Yiddish culture. If not definable by language or spatial borders, today's Yiddishland is created by interpersonal networks based around shared cultural reference points. Many of these are the legacy of the rich Yiddish cultural life that thrived among Jews emigrating from Europe to North America in the late nineteenth and early twentieth centuries. Most prominent among the institutions remaining active today is YIVO – Yidisher visnshaftlekher institut (Yiddish Scientific Institute) – dedicated to the preservation and study of Jewish, especially Yiddish, cultural material. Founded in Berlin, with headquarters in Vilnius until the Nazi invasion, YIVO moved its headquarters to New York in 1940; since 2000 it has formed part of the Center for Jewish History in downtown Manhattan. Other cultural institutions of today's Yiddishland include Yiddish-language publications, among them the weekly *Forverts* (Forward) newspaper and the *Tsukunft* (Future) journal, a number of Yiddish radio programmes, and cultural organisations including the Folksbine Yiddish theatre and the Arbeter Ring (Workmen's Circle), an organisation dedicated to Jewish community, Yiddish culture and social justice. Newer organisations testify to a renewal of interest in the Yiddish language and culture among a younger generation: Yugntruf (Call to Youth), an organisation of Yiddish-speaking and Yiddish-learning young adults, was founded in 1964 in New York City, and continues to develop new projects encouraging the use of Yiddish as an everyday language; the Yiddish Book Center in Amherst, Massachusetts, has since 1980 served as a central point for the collection and distribution of written Yiddish materials.

These more permanent institutions have fixed addresses on the ground, visible to the ordinary streetmap user. Many further Yiddish cultural activities, however, take place in borrowed spaces, which become Yiddishland for an hour, a week or a month, their exact locations often determined by convenience: apartments, cafés, universities, hotels. These institutions and events are connected not only by a shared concern for Yiddish, but, equally importantly, by the community they support. The web of today's Yiddish cultural community encompasses individuals literally scattered all over the world; the majority, however, are based in North America, the most prominent cluster of these within New York City. This geographical clustering reflects patterns of immigration: New York was the point of entrance into the USA for many East European Jews.

Within this symbolic landscape and wider Yiddish cultural community fall the trajectories of contemporary Yiddish song. In defining a corpus of song for discussion, I interpret the term 'Yiddish' broadly, considering song that is explicitly connected with an East European Jewish musical heritage, most – but not all – of which is sung in Yiddish. This material represents a broad range of musical strands, from commercial popular song to folk song and paraliturgical melodies. While diverse in style, these repertories overlap in musical material, derive from the same aesthetic and cultural world, and, more significant to the present discussion, tend consensually to be incorporated by musicians today under the same musical umbrella.

Song plays a prominent role within the institutions of Yiddish community life: a regular column in the *Forverts* by YIVO music archivist Chana Mlotek traces the origins of songs sent in by readers; folklorist Itzik Gottesman's music slot on the weekly Yiddish radio show 'Forverts Sho' (Forward Hour) presents songs new and old. Live performances of Yiddish song in New York City range from intimate downtown meetings attended by a small crowd fluent in Yiddish, to sell-out gigs at mainstream venues; during a fieldwork visit to the city in April 2003, the Yiddish performances on offer numbered more than one per day.

While contemporary Yiddish musical activity is by no means confined to the East Coast, two institutions were instrumental in drawing together a core of musicians in New York City during the late 1970s. President Carter's Comprehensive Training and Education Act (CETA) included an artists' project; under the auspices of the American Jewish Congress, this provided employment for a number of individuals to research and perform Jewish music. This project coincided with the beginnings of a revival of interest in Yiddish music, drawing a number of musicians to YIVO, which offered both resources and funding for work on Yiddish music and culture, as well as an annual summer programme teaching Yiddish language, literature and culture. Together, the CETA projects and YIVO not only enabled a younger generation of musicians to pursue individual interests in Yiddish music, but also provided a forum for individuals to meet, bolstering the widely documented phenomenon known as the 'klezmer revival', a renewed engagement with Yiddish music beginning in the mid-1970s and continuing today.[8]

Under the umbrella of the klezmer revival, since the mid-1980s the Yiddish music scene has spawned its own network of institutions, particularly in a number of annual music camps, attended by hundreds of musicians, amateur and professional. Although relatively few people involved in Yiddish music had grown up with the Yiddish language and culture in their homes, the Yiddish Folk Arts Institute, a week-long programme better known as KlezKamp, was formed in 1985 'to offer musicians, singers and Yiddishists a place to learn, exchange, and create Yiddish music in a challenging intergenerational environment' (Sapoznik 1999, 228). KlezKamp has been held every year since, becoming a major international event, and a number of other camps have sprung up in its wake.

This growing community of knowledge is particularly important as the network of camps and events which constitute the Yiddish music scene itself becomes a primary context for Yiddish cultural life, challenging the linguistic focus of Shandler's 'vernacularity'. It is a small world: glancing at the liner notes of new Yiddish CDs and the staff lists of camps, the same names appear time and time again. While passive participation – listening to Yiddish music – may be a relatively mainstream activity among American Jews and wider audiences, the number of people who are actively involved in, or seriously engaged with, the Yiddish musical tradition – whether as professionals, amateur musicians or committed

---

[8]   See Kirshenblatt-Gimblett (2002, 134) for further discussion of institutional support of the Yiddish music scene.

listeners – is small, and proudly so: violinist Sophie Solomon aptly summed up the core of the scene as 'more niche than niche'.[9] The events and institutions within which the wider Yiddish music scene is enacted provide an important forum for friendships and professional relationships to form and acquaintances to be renewed, within what is fundamentally a distributed community: the economics of the world music scene mean that outside a festival context it would not be viable for a number of bands to be in the same space simultaneously, even if based within the same city. Festivals and camps reverse this scenario, building a context for Yiddishland to catch up on its own news, and temporarily forming a community where performance can be geared towards the insider with an assumed level of cultural literacy (if not high, then higher than among the general public).

Terminology, of course, plays a vital role in imagining and negotiating Yiddish cultural networks. In choosing terms of reference for my wider discussion, I attempt to mirror the consensual usage of those involved in Yiddish music today, maintaining a plurality of discourse. I use the terms '*community*', '*world*', and '*scene*' interchangeably to describe the landscape of felt interpersonal networks described above. I add qualifiers to these nouns, however, to indicate overlapping yet distinctive modes of engagement. I use '*Yiddishist*' *community/world/scene* to indicate activity primarily focused on the Yiddish language and culture; within this context, song frequently forms a component of wider linguistic or cultural activities.[10] By contrast, '*Yiddish music*' *community/world/scene* indicates activity primarily focused on music, where the Yiddish language and wider cultural forms may take a secondary role. In reference to repertory, I use *Yiddish music* to refer to all music of Eastern Ashkenazic origin, and *Yiddish song* to specify vocal music. In popular usage today, however, the term *klezmer music*, which originally referred specifically to Eastern Ashkenazic instrumental music played by professional musicians, has come to be a synonym for Yiddish music. Here I use the term '*klezmer*' *community/world/scene* when my comments are connected specifically to the 'klezmer revival', to be discussed in greater depth in Chapter 3.

Frameworks

Those who choose to sing in Yiddish today are hardly a uniform group of people. They include both amateurs and professionals; those with a rich fluency in Yiddish culture and those wishing to explore European Jewish roots; those who grew up speaking Yiddish and those, both Jewish and non-Jewish, who simply feel attracted to the language and its music; the religious and the defiantly secular. Neither is their repertory homogenous: the available canon of Yiddish song reflects the gamut of Yiddish cultural life, from rural Old-World folk song to theatre music,

---

[9]   Sophie Solomon, interview with the author, London, 16 December 2002.

[10]   See Goldsmith (1998), for a historical outline of the Yiddishist movement.

from spiritual Hasidic melodies to revolutionary songs from Russia, from poetic art song to translations of popular twentieth-century Americana. Further, the most acclaimed artists and projects in recent years tend deliberately to straddle borders and subvert generalisations, challenging preconceptions of their audiences.

Rather than attempting to paint a comprehensive picture of Yiddish song today, then, I follow Lila Abu-Lughod's proposal of 'ethnographies of the particular' (1991). Suggesting that cultural theories tend to overemphasise coherence, she proposes avoiding generalisation in favour of local and specific actions manifested in the words and actions of their protagonists. I aim here to allow individual voices to speak, gradually building a multifaceted picture of the 'scene'. This approach is also catalysed by the epistemological problems implicit in considering urban communities that do not conform to the conditions, geographical and otherwise, which have conventionally been used to describe the ethnographic 'field'. Such problems have been noted in recent theoretical writings: Vered Amit writes that 'episodic, occasional, partial and ephemeral social links pose particular challenges for ethnographic fieldwork' (2000, 14–15); she cites specific methodological challenges concerning the study of such dispersed and/or fragmented social networks including, for example, the observation of 'practices that are enacted here and there, by one or a few' (2000, 15).

The musical community I describe here does not encompass the whole of the Yiddish-speaking world. Indeed, it largely exists in mutual isolation from the largest group of speakers of Yiddish today, the strictly Orthodox Hasidim, with whom it shares a language but differs significantly in cultural and aesthetic goals. Jeffery Shandler notes that '[the] implicit endorsement of Yiddish as the Hasidic vernacular of choice should not be mistaken for Yiddishism, which the *haredi* [strictly Orthodox] community typically regards with great suspicion'; he suggests further that Hasidim 'are suspicious of efforts to cultivate Yiddish for its own sake. Instead, they value Yiddish both as a traditional vehicle of Hasidic lore and for its new role – one that has emerged in the post-Holocaust era – of distinguishing Hasidim from other Jews' (2002, 27). While the high population growth rate in the Hasidic world has certainly ensured the survival of spoken Yiddish for at least another generation, at the same time the strictly Orthodox world continues to move to the religious right in its thinking, and has little contact with the non-Orthodox Yiddish world.[11]

The physical geographies of this study are also complicated. In building a framework within which to map the dispersed Yiddish music scene, I begin from Fog Olwig and Hastrup's statement that, 'generally, we may define the field, not primarily in terms of a locality, but as the field of relations which are of significance to the people involved in the study' (1997, 8). The intersecting musical lives of a core group of American Yiddish musicians, and the Yiddish cultural scene in New York City form a core thread running through the following chapters. As they participate in a transnational imagined community and a contemporary

---

[11]   See Shandler (2002), and Chapter 5, below, for discussion.

cosmopolitan world music scene, these mobile musicians might at first glance seem to undermine any sense of geographical focus, travelling both within North America and beyond. Nevertheless, the scene that I describe is distinctly American, and notwithstanding other significant areas of Yiddish activity in the USA, New York City continues to be a centre of gravity for contemporary Yiddish musicians, both because of its Yiddish history, and because it is home to a critical mass of cultural hubs, meaning that musicians and audiences have gravitated there.

Paradoxically, as new Yiddish music began to spread overseas, far from decentring New York and the USA, the centrality of these physical locations was further underlined by the 'guest star' status accorded to American musicians at performances and festivals. Alongside participating in local European scenes, a number of European musicians studied under these teachers and made virtual pilgrimages to New York City, KlezKamp and the YIVO Yiddish summer programme in order to be part of the 'real thing'.[12] The internal development of independent klezmer scenes in many locations in Europe is outside the scope of the book; while engaging in various degrees of conversation with the music described here, these scenes operate against a vastly different cultural and linguistic backdrop and invoke very different discourses, which have been widely rehearsed in recent literature (see Gruber 2002, Saxonberg and Waligórska 2006, Ottens and Rubin 2002 and others). Nevertheless, in Chapter 4 I do consider the roles played by performing and teaching in Europe in the personal and creative narratives of several New York-based musicians.

The following discussion also reflects my own journeys through field and archive research undertaken during ten years of engagement with the Yiddish and klezmer music scenes. My fieldwork began with a five-month visit to New York City (April–August 2001), followed by further visits during 2003 and 2008. During this time, I studied Yiddish language, literature and culture full-time for two months on the YIVO/Columbia University summer programme, made use of the extensive library holdings of the YIVO Institute, the Jewish Theological Seminary and the New York Public Library, and immersed myself in the substantial Yiddish cultural life of the city. I became a member of the Yidisher filharmonisher folkskhor – the Jewish People's Philharmonic Chorus (JPPC), a choir singing exclusively in Yiddish – for a summer season, including performances both in the city and in upstate New York, and attended meetings of *svives* – small groups convened regularly around members' shared wish to improve their command of the Yiddish language. I also attended a variety of Yiddish concerts and other cultural events, and spent much time with friends and acquaintances met via a shared interest in Yiddish culture. During and following my fieldwork, I participated in a number of summer schools: KlezKanada, Klezmer Wochen Weimar and KlezFest London, where I later became a regular staff member. Alongside formal interviews, I frequently draw on material from teaching sessions: moments of spontaneous

---

[12]   Cologne klezmer band, A Tickle in the Heart, document such a process in their album *Klezcats* (2003).

individual or group discussion and introspection which often arose during lectures and workshops provided important insights.

My fieldwork was not based on static cultural immersion. Participation, at least to some degree, is prerequisite for entry to the Yiddish music community, a field with no national or even spatial borders otherwise to negotiate. My identity, then, as a fieldworker was more a matter of intention than substance. Occasionally this intention was made evident: I was listed as 'ethnomusicologist' on the lists of participants for various festivals, and my research interests were clear both in formal communications and in informal conversation whenever anyone asked who I was and what I 'did'. Far from placing me as an outsider with respect to the community, however, this tended to elicit respect and a sense of worth: I was among the relatively small number of people who were committed to a 'day job' engaging with Yiddish music and culture. Like others involved in the community, I shared in the ups and downs of Yiddish cultural life: participation in the heightened experience of festivals, then bidding farewell to friends with whom one has shared intense musical experiences. Emotional e-mails exchanged during the 'down' period of readjustment to the Yiddish diaspora added to the wealth of experiences that constitute belongingness in and understanding of the Yiddish cultural world today.

Further, whereas informants in an ethnographic field study are often implicitly assumed to be distant from the academic world, within the Yiddish music community, research, either formal or informal, is a way of life. Several important builders of Yiddish culture are also respected academics, presentations of research are common at Yiddish culture festivals, many of those whose work I discuss – while not currently engaged full-time in academic work – have some background in ethnomusicology, and still more spend a lot of time doing activities well known to the ethnomusicologist: interviewing, listening to historic recordings and so on. Neither is it unusual for an individual's entry into the community to come via this activity: particularly in my own generation, very few members of the community learned to speak Yiddish outside an academic environment. In turn, as my own role widened from student to performer and teacher, I gained wider insights into the high value accorded to the retention of Yiddish culture in wider cultural circles.

Within this interpersonal, geographic and methodological framework, I begin to unpack the discursive web illustrated by the quotations with which I began. Two stories tend to stand side by side in framing the vast changes Yiddish culture underwent during the second half of the twentieth century, and in bridging the gaping, raw abyss left by the Holocaust. First, narrating the declining trajectory of the Yiddish language has itself become a metaphor for wider losses. As Jeffrey Shandler observes, '[the] trope of recounting the decline of Yiddish in postwar America as an ambivalent sign of cultural loss has continued though the turn of the millennium' (2006, 18). Shandler tellingly observes that this narrative became so pervasive that even prominent Yiddish poets such as Glatshteyn and Sutzkever had to defend their choice to write in Yiddish against the charge that the language was moribund (2006, 19).

Second, counterposed against these narratives of decline is a widespread tendency to see contemporary Yiddish cultural activity as a counterexample, celebrating instances where this narrative of destruction seems to be undermined. Shirli Gilbert notes that discussions of music making during the Holocaust have been dominated by redemptive narratives, framing music as a vehicle for heroism and resistance. In other words, she says, 'music not only affords the victims a certain retrospective moral victory, but also restores *for us* a certain measure of closure and meaning to the events' (2005, 5). While the events discussed here stand an ocean and several decades apart from the Nazi ghettos and camps, such redemptive narratives – sometimes expressed consciously, sometimes indirectly – are deeply embedded in the discussion of contemporary Yiddish culture, and continue to inflect the way in which it is described. Just like the stories recounted by Gilbert, imagining a vital Yiddish present – postvernacular or otherwise – is an interpretative step towards closure and meaning.

The suffusion of imagery of loss and rebirth in both academic and popular literature on contemporary Yiddish culture testifies to the enduring usefulness of these narratives as a means to engage with the past. Nevertheless, the strength of this discursive landscape has tended to restrain the recognition of wider parallels with late twentieth-century cultural processes. Here, then, I set out to shed light on these processes of historical narration: not to delegitimise this potent mode of engaging with the past, but rather to recognise the impact of our discursive framing on the narratives that we legitimate. Care is needed in order not to conflate recognition of the tough – and often un-speakable – historical, emotional and processual circumstances within which contemporary Yiddish music is grounded, with a wider aesthetic ideology suggesting that the contemporary interpretation of Yiddish materials is itself governed by impenetrable artistic or abstract sensibilities. Engaging with the process of historical framing serves to open up a conversation that allows contemporary Yiddish music to take its place as a product not only of Jewish-American history, but also of wider late twentieth-century aesthetic processes. In calling attention to these processes, I follow the lead of Mark Slobin, Barbara Kirshenblatt-Gimblett and other scholars of the first klezmer generation, together with a growing group of scholars of Jewish music, among them James Loeffler and Klára Móricz, who have recently explored the wider cultural, historical and ideological environments within which the aesthetics and ideologies of Jewish music played out during the long twentieth century.

Today, the trajectories of Yiddish song lie between popular, literary and art cultures; between the processes of revival and aesthetics of the contemporary; between vernacular and postvernacular; between diaspora and settled community. If the landscape of American Jewishness has received almost obsessive scholarly attention in recent years, more neglected have been its encounters with the (post-) modern and the global, and the roles played by changing media networks that have rendered an intensely intimate subculture visible and have facilitated the formation of new, dispersed social networks. Further, for a movement that places great attention on its own relation to history – often constructed in somewhat static terms

– there has been little recognition of the rapidity of change in twentieth-century American conceptions of Yiddish culture themselves. The subjective antiquity of a timeless rural past masks a flux of outlooks and attitudes that – together with the institutions that support them – have often barely lasted a generation at a time.

Here, then, I tease apart the internal discourses of the Yiddish music scene, seeking to understand the social transactions and cultural economies in which today's Yiddish song repertory is embedded. I consider Yiddish song and the narratives within which it is embedded as a fluid and changing discursive space where multiple imaginings of the Yiddish past collide with ideological and aesthetic choices, respond to contemporary currents in the Jewish and wider worlds, and conjoin with expressions of community, shared space and embodied, emotional practices. These processes operate simultaneously across multiple media and in an array of cultural 'places', from small events shared by a handful of people to CDs released by bands active on the transnational world music scene. Some of this ideological work is explicitly recognised by practitioners, yet other elements emerge in the act of performance, alternately reinforcing and challenging the dominant narratives of miraculous rebirth, 'heritage' and 'revival' invoked by scholars and performers alike.[13] Michael Herzfeld and others usefully invoke the term *social poetics* to describe this 'confluence of stereotypes, their use in social interaction, and their necessarily unstable evocation of competing histories' (2005,16).

To illustrate this 'necessary instability', let us return to the Klezmatics example cited at the opening of this chapter. The restorative notion of American Jewish musicians 'riding the German rails again' draws upon a rich seam of West-East travel narratives, framing the post-Holocaust return of American Jews to Central and Eastern Europe.[14] Yet the Klezmatics' performance is traversed by other discursive fault-lines. As musicians, the Klezmatics here participate in a transnational commodified music scene, where their exoticised status as 'radical' Jewish Americans translates into financial incentive. At the same time, the strength of the American Jewish/German and performer/consumer dichotomies evidenced by their invitation to the festival is disrupted by their choice to sing 'Ale brider'. While Winchevsky's text invokes close familial relations as a metaphor for a Jewish romantic nationalism, the Klezmatics' updated text, evoking feminism and gay rights, simultaneously evokes fluency with and distance from the author's cultural context. In performance, the song's melody, however, literally forces the reappropriation of utopic socialism: the participation of the audience in the refrain (marked by the quintessentially Yiddish vocable 'oy') raises the potential that the 'brider' to which the text refers might include all those present.

---

[13]   For an example of the 'revival' paradigm coupled with a focus on instrumental music obscuring the ideological positions of contemporary klezmer musicians, see Kirshenblatt-Gimblett (2002, 140–44).

[14]   See Chapter 4 for discussion.

Together, these discursive strands allow for the expression of different kinds of imaginaries, which exist together in a complementary rather than conflicted relationship. Such relationships constitute the space in which music is created, and in which, in turn, histories and narratives emerge from music. Art and its context are mutually constitutive, and musicians move through this conceptual space via different trajectories, whose expression couples aesthetic and ideological choices. Within this framework, sound worlds and authenticities are negotiated, whether located in songs, singers, sound or narrative. This is also an experiential space that mediates emotional engagement and response, and frames encounters with history. Narratives work in tandem with, rather than as a replacement for, emotional and experiential discourse.

In the remaining chapters of this book, I work through these spaces and trajectories. Part I considers the creation of contemporary frameworks for Yiddish culture during the final decades of the twentieth century in the response to the decline of traditional regimes of fluency. Chapter 1 focuses on the roles played by song in the New York Yiddishist community. Here, song functions as a tool for entering, enacting and sustaining a shared cultural space; it is a device for structuring symbolic events, and its use helps us to trace the trajectories of institutions whose function has transformed as they have adapted to the process of change in the meanings and functions of Yiddish.

Chapter 2 turns to Yiddish song as a cultural artefact. Songs and repertories are not only practices but are also 'things' that exist in objectified form and tell multiple Yiddish histories. In this chapter, via a survey of the activities of Yiddish folklorists during the second half of the twentieth century, I consider songbooks as embodying Yiddish narratives, and the creation of core canonic repertories as a means in which the Yiddish past has been negotiated in published form.

Part II turns to Yiddish song as a contemporary musical practice, focusing on the klezmer revival, the most prominent context in which the repertory is performed today. Despite its omission from many standard accounts, song has played a core role in the modern klezmer repertory since the revival began in the mid-1970s. Chapter 3 focuses upon the challenge faced by klezmer musicians to create a contemporary communicative framework for Yiddish song, suggesting that this musical movement points to regimes of communication and fluency more complex than Shandler's vernacular/postvernacular distinction.

The next pair of chapters – 4 and 5 – turn to the fringes of Yiddish cultural space, considering Yiddish song as a point of transcommunal encounter. Chapter 4 follows American musicians to Germany and Central Europe, lands which are stained with the legacy of the Holocaust but yet where klezmer music has recently achieved unforeseen popularity. Through conversations, textual accounts and songs, I explore the ways in which different musicians have processed their personal encounter with these spaces. Chapter 5, by contrast, considers how contemporary musicians of the secular Yiddish music scene have turned to the local – but distant – strictly Orthodox Hasidic world for material, engaging with profound differences in ideology and musical aesthetics between the two communities.

Finally, Chapter 6 looks forward to the ways in which a new generation is engaging with the challenges of Yiddish creativity. Techniques of sampling and bricolage allow an alternative approach to linguistic and cultural fluency, reading the Yiddish soundscape in a way that privileges the listening ear rather than an essentialised language or repertory, challenging conventional formulations of musical 'revival'. In an epilogue, I consider how these changing frames within which Yiddish song has been reimagined – as linguistic performance; as material, printed canon; as a musical-aesthetic praxis; as a shared soundscape – contribute to new formulations of 'locality' and intimacy in the Yiddish music scene.

PART I
Contemporary Frameworks
for Yiddish Song

Chapter 1

Becoming Yiddishists

As I turn back to an old file of research materials, I happen upon one of the few digital snapshots that have survived a decade of displacement since my first field trip to New York City in 2001. It is a silent, fuzzy stop-frame picture of a warm July evening in Riverside Park in Manhattan. About 20 people are singing, sitting on the grass in a rough circle. One strums a guitar. The remnants of a picnic are scattered around, and some of the group clutch photocopied song sheets. The group encompasses at least five nationalities, some six or seven decades of ages, and religious affiliation from non-Jewish to observant Orthodox. I recognise some of the figures: today several hold doctoral degrees in Yiddish subjects, one is a rabbi and another an actor and singer. The little girl with braided hair kneeling at the side is now a confident stage performer. At the time, however, many were at the beginning of their Yiddish journeys.

The snapshot of musical becoming was taken at an event organised by Yugntruf – Youth for Yiddish. Seeking to expand the contexts in which young people could meet and speak Yiddish in an informal environment, Yugntruf had recently inaugurated a programme of '*svives*' (lit. 'surroundings'), small groups of young Yiddish-speakers, who met weekly in different New York City locations in order to create a Yiddish-speaking environment. This particular evening was a special event: the Upper West Side *svive* invited the students of the YIVO-Columbia University Yiddish summer programme to join them for the evening. Here, beginning students, struggling to speak after only four days of Yiddish lessons, would have a first opportunity to sit alongside native Yiddish speakers and long-time Yiddish language devotees.

Picnic aside, the evening's activities focused on song. The group sang a cross-section of well-known Yiddish favourites. 'Ale brider' (All brothers), based on a poem written by Morris Winchevsky, illustrates the ideals of brotherhood and equality central to turn-of-the-century Jewish socialism. This song, rapidly folklorised in its time and popular ever since, lends itself to the creation of new lyrics: while Winchevsky's text emphasises traditional themes: 'Un mir zaynen ale brider, un mir davenen fun eyn sider … Frum un link fareynikt ale, vi der khosn mit a kale, vi der khumash mit di rashe …' (And we're all brothers, and we pray from one prayer-book … Religious and leftists are all united, like groom and bride, like the Pentateuch with Rashi's commentary …), some of those at the picnic added more recent verses written by New York klezmer band the Klezmatics, cited at the opening of this volume: 'Un mir zaynen ale shvester, azoy vi Rokhl, Rus un Ester … Un mir zaynen ale freylekh, vi Yoynoson un Dovid hameylekh' (And we're all sisters, like Rachel, Ruth and Esther … And we're all gay, like Jonathan and

King David).[1] On an upbeat note, the singing session ended with two Russian-Yiddish numbers: 'A glezele lekhayim' (A little toast), a Soviet Yiddish song whose melody derives from an early twentieth-century Yiddish theatre song, and 'Geven a tzayt' (Once there was a time) a 1970 translation by Yiddish singer Teddi Schwartz of Gene Raskin's lyrics 'Those were the days', itself a contrafactum to another popular Russian song.

The purpose of Yugntruf's *svives*, however, is not only recreational; rather, the meetings are an expression of rigorous devotion to language study, creating a space where, for an hour or two, Yiddish is no longer *post*vernacular. This picnic was no exception: those present studied the texts of three further songs in small groups, using the texts as a basis for the discussion of idioms and of Yiddish culture. Some worked on vocabulary – how could words learned from the song texts be used in everyday Yiddish? How did the imported Anglicisms in 'Di grine kuzine' (The greenhorn cousin) reflect the immigrant experience? Jokingly testing the group's knowledge of traditional Jewish observance, a young Orthodox man wondered whether anybody noticed an impossible juxtaposition in the religious practices comically portrayed in the song 'Der rebe elimelekh' (Rebbe Elimelekh). At the same time, other students enjoyed playing with three children from a local Yiddish-speaking family. Despite the linguistic aspirations shared by the group, such young native speakers were rare enough to be a novelty: by now fluent Yiddish transmitted in a family context was uncommon enough to be a remarkable exception to the rule.

This snapshot neatly introduces the roles played by song among those seeking to acquire a fluent command of Yiddish in New York today. The majority of those who identify with Yiddish language and culture are not specialist musicians, and most contexts for song are combined with other activities: the theatre, social events, education or commemoration. Song is constitutive of community: an enjoyable, sociable activity, and is a structural element that can be used and re-used in creating contexts for the performance of language. Singing is in itself a reason to get together, and a means of performing common purpose once gathered. In performance, songs become a concretised manifestation of culture and community.

If today's Yiddish culture is little spatialised within conventional frameworks and borders, it is nonetheless strongly felt as a kind of 'counter-space', a Yiddishland that is in part defined by its transformation of mundane, everyday spaces. In his 1967 essay 'Of other spaces', Michel Foucault labels such spaces 'heterotopias': places that contradict the geographies of everyday life; real spaces

---

[1]   Vivi Lachs observes that Morris Winchevsky's poem, called 'Akhdes' (Unity), published in the *Arbeter Fraynd* in 1890, was in fact intended as satire: Winchevsky, a socialist, anti-religious, anti-capitalist, invokes unity tongue in cheek, in the knowledge that the Jewish world is not united. This political reference was lost when the song was popularized in the klezmer revival 'leaving a happy-clappy song which would have made Vinchevsky roll his eyes' (Personal communication, 19 December 2012).

that enable a 'simultaneously mythic and real contestation of the space in which we live'; places which in themselves are enfolded a juxtaposition of incompatible sites. Heterotopias occupy a peculiar position of duality: they are both open and hidden, both isolated and penetrable. They exist in analogy with the outside world but are at the same time distanced from it.

Song functions as a door into heterotopic instantiations of Yiddishland. As a repertory, Yiddish song facilitates the imagining of Yiddish worlds, provides a tangible connection to multiple Yiddish pasts, and serves to help define a community of knowledge – but through song as practice, singers actively (re)locate this community in time and space. Focusing on North American institutions, this chapter explores these twin processes of becoming Yiddishists and constituting Yiddish cultural spaces. First, via group singing during a summer Yiddish language programme, I consider the interplay between linguistic and cultural literacy; as a component of the latter, educators ascribe a dual role to song: a linguistic text and an entrance point into Yiddish 'citizenship'. Second, I focus on a cross-communal Holocaust memorial event as a manifestation of a past-rooted, community-oriented Yiddish culture. Here, songs serve as a structural device for a shared event, but also enable multiple, participatory depictions of the nature of Yiddish community. Finally, I turn to communal singing at KlezKanada, a specialist Yiddish music camp of rather recent creation, but in which participatory singing, set in contrast to the instrumental music for which most participants arrived at the camp, serves as a marker of community, enabling embodied cultural experience, and pointing to possible Yiddish futures.

Song in Yiddish Education

Of several summer schools providing intensive university-level Yiddish teaching, the Uriel Weinreich Program in Yiddish Language, Literature and Culture – offered by the YIVO Institute of Jewish Research in conjunction with various higher education institutions (in recent years, Bard College, New York University and Columbia University) – is the longest running and most prestigious. The programme took its first class of students in 1968; to date, well over a thousand students have graduated the programme, many of whom play active roles in today's Yiddish cultural community.

At its inception, the primary motivation of the YIVO summer programme was an academic one: to train researchers to use Yiddish resources, an attempt to counter the decline of the Yiddish language of the mid-twentieth century. However, from the outset the programme's goals expanded beyond formal language acquisition to encompass a wider cultural agenda. 2001 programme director Yankl (Jeffrey) Salant writes:

> Priceless treasures that could immeasurably enrich the field of Jewish social science – and by the same token – the general domain of social science – remain

to a large degree unutilised. For these treasures in the form of institutional records, minutes, books, epistolary collections, diaries, newspapers and journals are mostly in Yiddish, an adequate knowledge of which is uncommon among American researchers. To remedy this situation, YIVO has planned and worked out the program now conducted jointly by Columbia University and YIVO'. The above, excerpted from an article in *Yedies fun yivo/News of the YIVO* issue #106, March 1968, describes the founding motivation for the Uriel Weinreich Program in Yiddish Language (Literature and Culture were added to the name three years later).

Conceived as a starting point for high school seniors who would continue their Yiddish education in college, the Uriel Weinreich program was first launched under the directorship of Dr. Marvin Herzog and sponsored by the Atran Foundation as an 8 week, non-credit elementary course with an enrolment of 25. With morning classes in Yiddish language taught by Mordkhe Schaechter and James Matisoff and an afternoon program including Yiddish folksongs and excursions to Yiddish places of interest, the first year was a success leading organically to much growth and evolution over the years (2001, 6).

By 2001, when I took part in the Intermediate II class, enrolment in the programme had grown to 68 students and four levels of instruction. The programme still catered for researchers: a large proportion of the participants were university students, many of whom – including myself – were tackling Yiddish-related doctoral theses. Others came for a variety of reasons, from high school students hoping to become involved with the Yiddish theatre to Judaica librarians who worked with Yiddish material; from seniors wishing to refresh childhood knowledge of the language, to those who knew no Yiddish before they set foot in the classroom yet simply felt drawn towards the language and culture. Most students came from North America; however, countries as diverse as Poland, Germany, Korea and Japan were also represented.

Emphasis continued to be placed upon the acquisition both of language skills and of cultural knowledge. Like in many similar language programmes, song was used both to teach vocabulary and idioms, and as the basis for wider acquisition of Yiddish culture. Morning grammar and literature classes were followed by an afternoon cultural programme; the 1968 syllabus of Yiddish song and outings now supplemented by workshops in dance, theatre and translation, seminars and films. Linguistic and cultural immersion was encouraged, many students taking the opportunity to live together on campus in a Yiddish-speaking environment. It is not surprising, then, that Yiddish songs turned up not only in song classes but also in many other guises during the summer programme.

The formal context for singing during the summer programme, a weekly afternoon song class, was a well-attended and popular activity. During the 2001 session, these classes were taught by Adrienne Cooper, a former director of the summer programme and former assistant director of YIVO, and a prominent Yiddish singer. Like the majority of the summer programme, her classes were taught in Yiddish, though translations of songs were also given. On the first Wednesday afternoon of the course, a large group of students gathered for the opening session. Since at this point beginning students had only two days' experience in the Yiddish language, Cooper taught the first two songs by ear, choosing texts containing a great deal of repetition.

The first was 'Shlof, shlof, shlof' (Sleep, sleep, sleep), a folk lullaby, in which a list of objects are rhymed with parts of the body:

Shlof, shlof, shlof	*Sleep, sleep, sleep*
Der tate vet kumen fun dorf	*Daddy's coming back from the village*
Vet er brengen an epele	*If he brings a little apple*
Vet zayn gezunt dos kepele	*Your little head will be healthy.*

In later verses the rhyming pair *epele* (little apple) / *kepele* (little head) becomes *nisele* (little nut) / *fisele* (little feet), *yoykhele* (little soup) / *boykhele* (little tummy) and so on. The low tessitura and narrow pitch span of the song created an easy entry to the singing group for those less confident of their voices; the words were illustrated by Cooper with simple hand gestures, easing the acquisition even of the limited vocabulary required. Further, beginning with a lullaby was a symbolic statement: in the absence of linguistic transmission in the home, the summer programme (or its song class) is the virtual cradle of a new kind of Yiddish fluency, a symbolic restoration to participants of a 'lost' childhood. Within a disrupted linguistic society, learning children's songs at least allows this childhood to be redeemed, enabling an illusion of cultural fullness.

By contrast, the second song Cooper taught, 'Esn est zikh' (Eating happens effortlessly) is of Hasidic origin, associated with the Lubavitch movement:[2]

Esn est zikh,	*Eating happens effortlessly,*
Trinkn trinkt zikh,	*Drinking happens effortlessly,*
Vos zol men ton	*What should one do*
az es lernt zikh nisht?	*when it's hard to study?*
Esn est zikh,	*Eating happens effortlessly,*
Shlofn shloft zikh,	*Sleeping happens effortlessly,*
Vos zol men ton	*What should one do*
az es davent zikh nisht?	*when it's hard to pray?*

---

[2]   This song appears on an early recording issued by the Chabad-Lubavitch Hasidic movement (Zalmanoff 1961), and also appears in Chabad's own printed collection of melodies (Zalmanoff 1985, no. 109), both reproduced in full online at: http://www.chabad. org/multimedia/media_cdo/aid/140699/jewish/Essen-Est-Zich.htm (last accessed 20 February 2012). Cooper's version is closer to the recorded version than the notated melody reproduced here. The author of this website identifies this song as a 'Chassidic folksong' rather than a melody specifically linked with the Lubavitch dynasty. For wider discussion of Lubavitcher repertory and musical practices, see Koskoff (2001).

This song taught further simple vocabulary (to eat, to drink, to sleep), and reflexive structures (the construction *esn est zikh* translates literally as, 'to eat eats itself'). The song, however, also clearly refers to the traditional religious culture of its origin. Unlike the simple lullaby with which the class began, this song has a more substantial three-section melody with internal modulation; the two parts of the song are followed by an untexted melody, a typical feature of Hasidic music. The rising arched shapes of the melody and delayed return of the tonic reflect the yearning of the text; those hoping for confirmation of stereotypical 'Yiddish' melody contours might also have been pleased by the recurrence of the augmented second interval as the melody moves between A minor and E *Freygish*.[3]

Helped by the expressive potential of the combined melody and words, Cooper encouraged all present to relate the song to their own experience – frustration when a supposedly simple activity just won't work. Encouraging everyone to sing with conviction, she urged all to get in touch with their 'inner Jew', that part inside – even for the non-Jews present, she emphasised – where this text resonates. This formulation pointed to the complex negotiation between Jewish and inclusive language when translating Yiddish culture for a wider audience. As the language of an ethno-religious minority, the Yiddish language assumes a Jewish frame of reference. While the words of this song and its association with Hasidism did not easily lend themselves to a translation outside a Jewish framework, here Cooper's deliberate insistence on inclusivity pointed again to a new kind of community: connection to the Jewishness expressed in Yiddish culture is open to all through language, a democratic Yiddish heterotopia through which happenstance entrance by birth might be replaced by a formative shared educational experience.

In later sessions, a popular series of songbooks (Mlotek 1972, Mlotek and Mlotek 1988, 1995) provided source material; covering wide ground these books serve music festivals and language programmes alike as a collected shared repertory.[4] Introducing songs in a sing-along format, Cooper taught half a dozen new songs during each session. In a later interview, I asked her how she chose material when teaching. She explained:

> It depends. If it's in the [YIVO] summer programme, I'm picking in order to reinforce the language teaching, and so you want both to show people a good time, show them the variety of genres and kind of music that there is, but also reinforce the language skills that they're developing, so you're not taking them to certain places where the challenges are too difficult … What always interests

---

[3]   See Slobin (1980) and Móricz (2008, 23) for discussion of the augmented second interval as an ethnic marker in Yiddish music. Horowitz (1993) provides an outline of Yiddish modes.

[4]   Compiled by YIVO music librarian Chana (Eleanor) Mlotek and her late husband, Yosl (Joseph), these three books, giving text, transliteration, capsule translations, melody and chords for each song, have become widely regarded as the 'staple' collections of Yiddish songs since their publication. These collections will be discussed further in Chapter 2.

me is meeting people at the level of their own cultural competence, so they're not being infantilised, and they're being spoken to as whole people – intellectually interesting, sensually interesting, you know, songs that they can relate to. I'm not interested in fetishising *khasides* [Hasidism], or, you know, certain kinds of experience that I think have less to do with who they are. So I want them both to have a personal experience that they can relate to, have their language skills reinforced, and have a jolly time! [laughs]. Or a sad time, or whatever. I know that there have been years where I've taught much sadder songs and I have much more clarity now about the range of things that people can learn without going to that place.[5]

Again, Cooper's comments link the dual function of songs as repertory and experience outlined at the beginning of this chapter: songs are explicitly linked to language teaching, but at the same time, are a vehicle to allow students to have a meaningful, embodied experience of singing.

A contrasting song workshop session was presented by Binyumen Schaechter, a native Yiddish speaker and Yugntruf activist, son of prominent Yiddish linguist and long-time summer programme instructor Mordkhe Schaechter, and one of a handful of parents outside the strictly Orthodox world choosing to raise his three children in Yiddish. Among his many activities as a professional musician, Schaechter conducts the Yidisher filharmonisher folks-khor (Jewish People's Philharmonic Chorus), a New York Yiddish choir, and has convened various Yiddish children's ensembles. On this occasion the group sat round a piano to sing. Following a selection of children's songs, Schaechter taught three modern Yiddish songs, all written by his aunt, poet Beyle Schaechter-Gottesman. Here were songs presented as material directly from the life of a Yiddish-speaking family; this 'normal' language transmission by now the exception rather than the rule. Several members of the extended Schaechter family were directly involved in aspects of the publication of Beyle Schaechter-Gottesman's songbook *Zumerteg* (Summer days) (1990), and one of the songs in this collection honours Binyumen's own bar-mitzvah ('Tzu Binyumeles bar-mitzve').

Singing on the summer programme was by no means confined to song classes: songs also played an important part in the teaching of grammar and literature. A morning's classes would often end in a song, such as 'Az nisht keyn emine tsuzamen mitn gelt' (Without faith as well as money), a religious Yiddish song working through an alphabetical list of traditional Jewish virtues. Again, the structure of the song is repetitive, easy to learn yet introducing a core vocabulary. This song teaches the student a list of Yiddish words of Hebrew origin, a vocabulary used widely in Yiddish to express key Jewish religious-ethical concepts. Each Hebrew word is coupled with a Yiddish verb starting with the same Hebrew letter (the pairs are shown in bold in the following excerpt):

---

[5]   Adrienne Cooper, interview with the author, Lantier, Quebec, 25 August 2001.

Az nisht keyn **emine** tsuzamen mitn gelt,	*Without faith as well as money,*
Vos-zhe **arbetstu** af der velt.	*What's the point of working?*
Az nisht keyn **bine** tsuzamen mitn gelt,	*Without understanding as well as money,*
Vos-zhe **broykhstu** di gantse velt.	*Why do you need the whole world?*

In literature classes students were encouraged to find and sing songs by the poets being studied; at other times song choice reflected ideology more than pedagogy – the class sang along to a recording of 'Vaserl' (Stream), a song written by Rukhl Schaechter and Paula Teitelbaum in the 1970s in folk-pop style, comparing the Yiddish language to a frozen stream, which in time will thaw and flow again. While the texts formed the basis for language exercises, the message was clear: songs not only are an aid to language learning, but also help one to internalise and to perform a Yiddishist message: traditional Jewish life, Yiddish literature and song and the survival of the language itself are all bound up together. Outside the classroom, this message seemed to take hold. Yiddish and klezmer CDs were passed around the summer programme hall of residence, and those keen on singing found plenty of informal opportunities to engage their interest, from gatherings with a guitar outside the classrooms during a break to impromptu close harmony in the resonant space of an empty classroom.

This culture of informal, creative singing came to fruition in the *siyem ha-zman*, the graduation ceremony on the final day of the summer programme. On the morning of 3 August 2001, students and teachers – joined by a considerable number of family, friends, a representative from the *Forverts* newspaper and other interested members of the Yiddishist community – gathered in the auditorium of the Center for Jewish History on West 16th Street for a programme whose blend of pageantry, high culture and parody echoed a longer Yiddish history of skits, *purim shpiln* and other theatro-musical expression.

The programme began with Yiddish-language speeches, which again reinforced the vision of the programme as a cultural intervention, not just a language class. It is telling that in the account that appeared in the *Forverts*, the former is expressed as a primary motivation: at the beginning of the twenty-first century, Yiddish is a growing field of university study – yet this alone does not ensure the continuity of contemporary Yiddish culture.

> Eugene Orenstein [a summer programme teacher and keynote speaker at the *siyem*] expressed his hope that the students from the summer programme would become consumers and even creators of Yiddish culture, and not just academics who need Yiddish for their research ('Siyem ha-zman fun der yivo/columbia zumer-program' [Graduation ceremony of the YIVO/Columbia summer programme], *Forverts*, 10 August 2001, 15, translation mine).

Orenstein's hope certainly seemed to be fulfilled that morning, and in a substantial part through the medium of song. As customary, before the presentation of certificates to the graduating classes, the students presented a programme of

Yiddish-language entertainment on stage. Of the 13 items in the programme, seven were completely or partly sung, and covered a wide range of themes: a comic theatre duet portrayed a fighting couple; a female close-harmony group presented 'Mayn rue platz' (My resting place), by the worker-poet Morris Rosenfeld; and student Zalmen Hoffman evoked an emotional response with his rendition of 'Mayn shvester Khaye' (My sister Khaye), a recent setting by Israeli singer Chava Alberstein of a poem by Binem Heller, in which the author laments the loss of his young sister, burned by the Nazis in Treblinka.

Also included were a clutch of self-translated items, from a Yiddish version of 'Somewhere over the Rainbow' performed by a beginner student, to a short operetta which adapted *Porgy and Bess* to a synthesis of themes from Yiddish history and literature. An intermediate class adapted 'Let's Call the Whole Thing Off' to call for the unification of Yiddish dialects, and a group calling itself the *Dorfsmentshn* (Village people), translated the 1970s gay anthem 'Y.M.C.A.' into a summer programme anthem 'Y.I.V.O.', receiving an enthusiastic response from the audience. Here, if the summer programme was a route into Yiddish acculturation, ludic and macaronic translation both forms a 'rehabilitation' of the link to the outside world, which becomes playfully reappropriated as Yiddish, and also permits access to familiar cultural ground which might be more accessible to students than the Yiddish cultural world they so recently entered. In-jokes, of course, serve to underline the distance between the heterotopic world and outside society; however, the parodic format in which these were expressed allowed students to connect to wider strands of Jewish humour.

Yiddish Education: Song and Cultural Literacy

While speculations about the future of Yiddish in America might seem to have reached a crisis point as the oldest representatives of a full, living European Ashkenazic culture reach the end of their lives, the use of song to enable a postvernacular generation to acquire an embodied fluency in Yiddish language and culture is not new. Rather, the YIVO summer programme in its current format is the latest manifestation of a string of institutionalised secular American Yiddish education initiatives that developed through several generations during the twentieth century. Well before the Nazi Holocaust decimated Yiddish culture in Europe, American immigrants saw the classroom as a space in which to (re)imagine the East European Jewish cultural heritage, and a context in which it could flourish.

The first American Yiddish educational efforts were supplementary schools aimed at children from Yiddish-speaking families, run by organisations such as the Workmen's Circle (Arbeter Ring), a secular Jewish mutual aid organisation founded in 1900 to pursue socialist ideals.[6] In 1910 an Educational Committee was formed, which organised activities ranging from lecture tours to Sunday schools

---

[6] For further discussion of Yiddish socialism and socialist education in New York, see Michels (2005, particularly chapter 4).

to book publishing; cultural activities including choral groups were also part of the organisation's remit (Michels 2005, 180). In fact, the Workmen's Circle's first supplementary schools, created in 1906, were taught in English, with no Yiddish or Jewish studies at all. After a brief failed attempt in 1908, it was not until 1910 that Yiddish was introduced into the curriculum, in part a reaction to other, rival schooling options (Michels 2005, 211). At this early stage, language and culture did not need to be educational priorities. In an unpublished survey of educational programmes undertaken by the Workmen's Circle, Joseph Mlotek notes that until the mid-1930s, there was little mismatch between the linguistic and cultural experiences of pupils inside and outside the schools:

> The home and environment of the student of the WC school, from the years of its founding until the middle of the 30's, was a Yiddish-speaking one. Not only did the pupil hear Yiddish spoken all around him, but the home, to some extent, acted as a complement to the ideological atmosphere which the school attempted to create. The song which was taught in the school was sung at home by the parents; every important topic taken up in the school, was echoed in the environment with which the child was associated outside the school. The holidays of his environment were the same holidays of the school. On the walls of the schools were suspended the portraits of Marx, Engels, Lasal, Tolstoy and some Jewish writers. On May 1st the pupils of the WC schools marched through the streets together with their parents and their parents' workers organizations. There could always be found a Yiddish newspaper in the home, a Yiddish work of fiction or popular science – on physics, chemistry, etc. (1954, 8).[7]

Instead, the earliest supplementary Yiddish school programmes prioritised political content. Mlotek continues:

> If thought was at all given to the ideological education of the children, it was only directed at acquainting them with the political beliefs, with socialist principles. Such became the aim of the first socialist Sunday schools of the WC, which were created in New York, in 1906. Jewish studies were not taught in the Sunday schools. In *Der Fraynd*, official organ of the [Sotsyalistisher farband], the aim of the Sunday schools is described thus: 'The object of parents with radical convictions should be to give their children an education, which is not in conflict with their opinions. They should see to it that – from their early childhood – their children become imbued with radical thinking' [*Der Fraynd*, January 1912]. (Mlotek 1954, 4; correction by Chana Mlotek, email correspondence, 27 August 2012).

---

[7]   Commenting on this extract, Chana Mlotek differed with her late husband's essay, noting: 'In the 30s, when I went to Shule, there were no pictures of Marx, Sacco and Vanzetti, but pictures of Peretz, Mendele and Sholem Aleichem and others. We didn't learn about the Socialist leaders either' (e-mail correspondence, 27 August 2012).

Between 1910 and 1915, the educational goals of the Workmen's Circle were vigorously debated at the organisation's annual conventions. Although in 1915 the majority opposed a specifically Jewish – or Yiddish – educational mandate, from 1918 onwards the organisation founded a string of Yiddish-speaking supplemental schools, which children would attend several times a week after public schools. These schools quickly flourished; according to Tony Michels, by 1924 there were 65 such schools nationwide with 12 in New York alone (2005, 214, 216).

Nevertheless, even if Yiddish was still spoken in many homes, the end of open immigration from Europe to America in the early 1920s brought a halt to the mass influx of Yiddish speakers. It was clear even in the 1930s that educational intervention was needed if Yiddish fluency was to be preserved in the new generation. An excerpt from a 1930 booklet celebrating five years of Workmen's Circle summer camps shows how the role of passing on the language was already being relocated from the home to the classroom, which had in turn become a vehicle for Jewish cultural, rather than socialist ideological, education:

> We are still asked: 'Why should our children's camp be run in Yiddish? Would it not be better if the talks, the singing, the discussions of the children would be conducted in English?' The people who ask these questions know that the Yiddish-American child understands English better than Yiddish, and that it would therefore be more familiar and easier if the work in our camp should be carried on in English. ... For those children who have attended a Workmen's Circle School, the Yiddish language is only a continuation of what they had before. For those who have not attended a school, the learning of the Yiddish language is one of the 'new things' they are taught at camp, one of the new things that call forth new ideas and thoughts. The language is a necessity for both the first and second group. During the few weeks that the children spend at camp, they become acquainted with Yiddish culture – with Yiddish stories, names of Yiddish writers, incidents of the workers' movement, biographies of people who fought for the freedom of mankind, and Yiddish folk-songs. All this helps directly or indirectly to give the children some idea of our Yiddish life in general and the Yiddish workers' life in particular. In camp more work can be done in a few weeks than a year's work in a 'schule' [supplementary school]. ... In this short period the children spend more time with the teachers and counsellors and they can therefore get more from the work and from the cultural-social activity that is carried on in camp. When a child learns some Yiddish folk-songs or workers' songs and when he becomes acquainted with Peretz, Ash, Scholom Aleichem, Marx, Lenin, Gompers, Meyer London, Sacco and Vanzetti, he only begins to take part in the wonderful work that goes on in camp (*Workmen's Circle Camp* commemorative booklet, Arbeter Ring, 1930, 8–9).

Over the following decades, this linguistic decline continued. By 1954, when Mlotek analysed the results of a major survey of Workmen's Circle school parents, over three quarters of the schools' pupils were the child of at least one American-born parent, and answers to a questionnaire distributed to some 3,000 families suggested Yiddish was no longer the primary language of most school parents.

The Workmen's Circle schools and associated summer camp were by no means the only American Yiddish educational enterprise operating during these decades. The Sholem Aleichem Folk Institute ran a parallel stream of supplementary schools, and, from 1923 to 1979, the Boiberik secular Yiddish summer camp.[8] Boiberik, frequented by Yiddish writers and activists in addition to cohorts of children, was a particularly fertile ground for Yiddish creativity. It is worth quoting the breadth of Boiberik's musical activities at length, since while contexts for Yiddish education have changed substantially, the basic format of pageantry, newly-composed popular-art songs juxtaposed with Hasidic *nigunim* and parodies, has been bequeathed to future generations of Yiddish learners. Chana Mlotek recalls:

> Camp Boiberik had a very rich music program, in which all campers and staff participated:
>
> First there were the weekly *Shabes* [Sabbath] programs, with special beautiful Shabes songs. There were slight variations in the programs (certain songs were eliminated) during the years, but most Boiberikaner recall them, and these can easily be recorded. The music was written or adapted by Lazar Weiner, from the liturgy, with some music by Joseph Achron and others. The texts were believed to have been written by Leibush Lehrer, the longtime director and guiding spirit of camp.
>
> Every season had a '*Mit-sezon*' pageant, devoted generally to a theme in Jewish history, e.g. Bar Kokhba, The Cantonists, Hannah Senesh, Dr. Herzl, etc. with music and dance, in which the whole camp participated. I have a few scripts in my files, from the years when I was the singing teacher of camp. Each year camp learned a different Hassidic *nign* (Leibush Lehrer and his brother Lipa were very fond of *nigunim*; some appear in Ch. Vinaver's Anthology of Jewish Music; one I included in a holiday anthology; also Sidor Belarsky recorded a few). ...
>
> The closing celebration of camp was the unique *Felker Yomtev*, a beautiful pageant that Leibush Lehrer conceived, of all the nations of the world coming together to celebrate peace. The Felker Yomtev cited the message of Isaiah, and had its symbol of a white dove that brings peace to the world. (And he had his vision many years before the creation of the UN!) Each group became a nation, dressing in the country's costume, with its own song and dance, and with a *toyer* (a stageset representing the country's landscape and architecture). There were, in addition to the nations, a nation *Yidn* (the Biblical Jews) and *Boiberikaner* (the nation of Boiberik). Certain songs were repeated every year, and every

---

8   Itzik Gottesman, 'A Short History of Camp Boiberik', http://boiberik.media.mit.edu/history.html (accessed June 2012).

Boiberikaner knows these. Some words were changed after the establishment of Israel. The songs of the individual nations were beloved and many are recalled and can be traced and recorded, but this will also require time and effort.

In the earlier years other songs were also learned. I, for instance, recall 'Freyd fun erd' (Ay s'iz gut), 'Tshimbarabasaba'. Other Boiberikaner may recall others.

Many parodies were written in Boiberik, and were a source of fun. Some were written by Lehrer, others by talented campers and counselors. Many Boiberikaner will recall them. We sang them at campfires or on Kindertog (a day when counselors dressed and acted as children, and when Lehrer received a hazing). Some words were of a high calibre. I once heard a snippet of a parody of Oklahoma written by Uriel and Gaby Weinreich and Amik (Abe) Brumberg. These parodies should definitely form part of the Boiberik Songbook (Chana Mlotek, letter to 'Sam', February 1988. Joseph and Chana Mlotek Archive, YIVO, New York. Reproduced with permission).

Established in response to geographical and cultural dislocation, and struggling to maintain cultural and linguistic literacy among the American-born generation, it is perhaps not surprising that the Yiddish secular school system and summer camps described above lasted only two, perhaps three, generations before they too fell victim to changing patterns of American Jewish life. By the end of the twentieth century, in line with wider trends in the community, emphasis had moved to elective adult education. Indeed, Bernard Dov Cooperman observed that, according to the results of the 2001 National Jewish Population Survey, university-based Jewish studies programmes had become the main source of general post-bar/bat mitzvah Jewish education outside the strictly Orthodox world (2006, 137).

Part of this wave of adult education, like its predecessors, the YIVO summer programme represents a continuing effort not only to increase participants' competence in the Yiddish language but also to encourage its students to become involved in the fabric of creative contemporary Yiddish culture. Such involvement requires familiarity with the language itself, coupled with competence within the world of associations surrounding it. If Jeffrey Shandler's *Adventures in Yiddishland* shows that in the case of Yiddish, cultural engagement widely became decoupled from linguistic fluency, the reverse is also true: in a 'postvernacular' community, cultural literacy must actively be taught if it is to be acquired. Although some may critique the extent to which education is implicated in the creation and sustenance of 'national' cultures (see Herzfeld 2005, 10), the possibility for formal education to intervene beyond linguistic fluency is widely acknowledged. For example, as the basis of his manifesto for proposed reform to the American education system *Cultural Literacy: What Every American Needs to Know*, popular educationalist E.D. Hirsch used the term 'cultural literacy' to describe:

the network of information that all competent readers possess. It is the background information, stored in their minds, that enables them to take up a newspaper and read it with an adequate level of comprehension, getting the point, grasping the implications, relating what they read to the unstated context which alone gives meaning to what they read. ... To grasp the words on a page we have to know a lot of information that isn't set down on the page (1987, 2–3).

By way of illustration, consider the following passage. The booklet accompanying the Klezmatics' 1992 album *rhythm + jews* opens with a passage by Canadian Jewish author Michael Wex, entitled 'From the Memoirs of Yisroel (Israel) Wex, Yeshiva Beatnik', from which the following is an excerpt:

> I bopped my *shokl* on the off-beat by Purim of my junior year, intoned my Torah with the fifths all flattened every Monday, Thursday and oo-bop-a-Shabbes. Nine times through *On the Road*, and I still didn't get it – if getting drunk and driving too fast was the wave of the future, then the Yiddish papers were hip, as hep to the *shlep* as they come – but I wasn't going to argue with success. Beth Jacob girls wanted to beat my bongos, and compared to a plain old yarmulke, my new black beret was the bendin', solid-sendin', the all-offendin' – you *know* where I'm comin' from – END. I swung with my undergarment-fringes, flipped my sidelocks – those Little Bo-*peyes* – into beat generation sideburns while scatting my daily Talmud to A Night in Tunisia. I was driving the rabbis insane ... (Wex 1992).

The passage is in English – but the comical world of the protagonist, a *yeshiva bokher* (student in a traditional Jewish religious academy) growing up alongside 1950s rock and roll, makes little sense to a reader unfamiliar with Torah, Talmud, yarmulkes, Shabbes, Beth Jacob girls, *peyes* and Purim. To appreciate this passage it is not necessary precisely to be able to define what the Talmud is, nor ever to have read it; it is, however, necessary to experience the humour of the juxtaposition of the worlds of Hasidism and rock and roll between which Wex's language darts.

Song plays an integral role in Hirsh's cultural literacy: the titles of some 44 songs, from 'America the Beautiful' to 'You Are My Sunshine' appear in his list of 'what literate Americans know' (1987, 152–215). These songs not only represent a shared repertory consisting of individual 'items' of cultural knowledge, but in their subject matter also make reference to wider American history and culture.

An analogous conception of song as an integral component of Yiddish cultural literacy can be seen in the literary material included in postwar Yiddish textbooks. Uriel Weinreich's *College Yiddish* (1949, since republished several times), still the text most frequently used among beginners, includes 12 songs, presented together with melodies, and a short section in English on Yiddish folk songs. These songs span well-known folk or folk-like songs, songs for both the Jewish holidays Purim and Khanuke and for secular celebration, a Hasidic *nigun*,[9] and finally, the 'Partizaner-himen', Hirsh Glik's Partisans' Hymn, written during the Holocaust and today often used as an anthem of remembrance. Similarly, a further 12 songs with melodies are included in Mordkhe Schaechter's intermediate textbook *Yidish tzvey* (Yiddish II) (1986/1995). In this more advanced textbook, as might be expected, the songs receive deeper attention in terms of language and idiom. Other intermediate textbooks, including David Goldberg's *Yidish af Yidish* (Yiddish in Yiddish) (1996) and Khanan Bordin's *Vort bay vort* (Word by word) (1999) include a substantial number of songs. In the latter two books, however, the texts – some for little-known songs – are presented alone, suggesting a focus purely on language acquisition. This contrasts with the emphasis on active cultural participation implied by the presentation of songs 'ready to sing' with their melodies in Weinreich's and Schaechter's books, a standpoint reflecting the ethos of the YIVO summer programme, perhaps to be expected given both authors' close connection with the programme.

Cultural literacy, then, is not an abstract educational goal, but rather has a reciprocal relationship with community. Cultural literacy allows an individual to participate in a community, it plays a role in defining community, and through community cultural literacy is shared, learned and expressed. Although the group of people involved in contemporary American Yiddish culture is in no way homogenous, shared Yiddish cultural literacy, including songs, is a strong point of commonality. In song, the Yiddishist community becomes a densely populated Yiddishland, linking itself to a chain of past and future Yiddish speakers not only through the content of the songs, but also through the act of singing, shared across time and place.

Remembering the Past

While the vocal performances at the graduation ceremony of the YIVO summer programme – the *siyem ha-zman* – focused on the future of Yiddish culture and new acquisition of cultural literacy, participation in Yiddish today also necessarily means engagement with the Yiddish past and the dark shadow of the Holocaust. Just as the Yiddishist community comes together to celebrate the future of Yiddish, so the commemoration of loss also forms an integral part of the cycle of the New York Yiddish calendar. Throughout the Jewish world, Yom ha-Shoah (Holocaust Remembrance Day), is marked on or near 19 April, the anniversary of the Warsaw Ghetto Uprising.[10]

---

[9] *Nigun* (plural: *nigunim*): literally 'melody', often refers to wordless Jewish religious songs, particularly those of the Hasidim. See further discussion in Chapter 5.

[10] While always marking the Warsaw Ghetto uprising, Yom ha-Shoah may be observed according either to the Gregorian or to the Hebrew calendar. Since the actual Hebrew date of the uprising (14 Nisan) falls immediately before the Passover holiday, in 1953 the Israeli

On 19 April 2001, I attended a Yom ha-Shoah programme organised by the Arbeter Ring (Workmen's Circle). The event was sponsored by some 13 other Jewish and Yiddishist organisations, which together represented the participation of the wider Yiddish body politic. The programme, entitled 'Yugnt (Youth) Hymn: Children's Voices and the Holocaust', was held at the CUNY Graduate Center, a large building on Fifth Avenue in central Manhattan. The commemoration began at 6:30 p.m.; arriving a few minutes beforehand, I found almost all the places in the large auditorium, which seated some 500 people, were taken. Those present ranged from children, running around at the back of the auditorium, to the elderly, including several Holocaust survivors. On the stage sat a large choir – the combined members of the Workmen's Circle Yiddish Chorus and the New Yiddish Chorale – totalling about 50 singers, dressed in black and white. Placards in Yiddish exhorted us to remember the six million.

The audience was buzzing, and an elderly lady was shouting in a thick Yiddish accent. It took the chairman a few minutes to quieten the audience and to persuade everyone to take their seats. The proceedings opened in Yiddish: though two speakers later spoke in English, a good deal of material was in Yiddish and was not translated. A candle-lighting ceremony marked a formal start to the proceedings. Six candles on a table at the front of the stage were lit by Holocaust survivors – some of whom were so shaky they could barely climb the steps or hold the candle – and by children of survivors. During this ceremony, Margot Leverett (clarinet) and Zalmen Mlotek (piano), two well-known professional musicians specialising in Yiddish music, played background music. While this was a secular event, the formal conduct and the symbolism of the opening candle-lighting ceremony lent a religious tone to the occasion. The candles and those who took part in the ceremony remained on the stage throughout.

Yiddish songs formed a substantial part of the programme. Notably, through song the evening incorporated not only variations in musical texture (choirs, soloists, instrumentalists) and in genre but also a cross-section of members of the Yiddish musical community, from young to old, from amateur musicians to top names from the professional Yiddish performance scene. Family links among the performers testified to an active continuation of Yiddish traditions: at least three families were represented by two or more generations, and children from three Yiddish *shuln* (Yiddish secular schools) participated in the programme.

Towards the opening, the choir sang arrangements of three well-known numbers: 'Ani maamin' (I believe), 'Dremlen feygl' (Birds are drowsing) and 'Unter di khurves fun Poyln' (Under the ruins of Poland). The first is a Hebrew song sung by Polish religious Jews in Warsaw, Lublin, Lodz and Bialystok, early victims of Nazi aggression; it subsequently became popular among all Jews of East European origin (see Rubin 1979, 457). The text of the second, written in the Vilna ghetto, is a contrafactum to an older Yiddish song, here portraying the

---

government fixed the Hebrew date of 27 Nisan for commemorations, falling in late April or early May. In 2001, 27 Nisan corresponded to 18 April.

lullaby of a stranger to an orphaned child. The third sets a poem written after the Holocaust by Yiddish poet Itzik Manger, in which the protagonist mourns a blond-haired girl, buried under the ruins of Poland.

Solo songs were also included in the programme. Under the heading 'Voices of a Family', Noah Yucht (mandolin), his son Philip (guitar) and his granddaughter Tovah (voice) performed two Yiddish songs: 'Makh tsu di eygelekh' (Close your eyes) and 'Shtil di nakht' (The night is quiet). Later Adrienne Cooper, accompanied by Margot Leverett and Zalmen Mlotek, sang 'Mayn shvester Khaye' (My sister Khaye). Like 'Unter di khurves fun Polyn', the text of this song was written after the Holocaust, by poet Binem Heller. His poem was recently set to music by Israeli singer Chava Alberstein as part of her cycle of new song settings of verse by twentieth-century Yiddish poets 'Di krenitze' (The well), recorded with the Klezmatics in 1998; this version quickly entered the contemporary Yiddish song canon.

Well-known songs were balanced with less familiar material. Twelve children, aged between six and 13, pupils of the Pripetshik school and the Midtown and Westside *shuln* (Yiddish secular schools) of the Arbeter Ring performed excerpts of *Lyalkes* (Puppets). This Yiddish children's operetta, telling the story of a puppeteer and his animated puppets who eventually become free, was first performed at the Medem Sanatorium, near Warsaw, Poland, in the 1930s. The children performed the complete operetta, directed by Binyumen Schaechter, in March 2001 at the Sholem Aleichem Center in the Bronx, and excerpts on three later occasions including this one. Wearing appropriate costumes for their characters, all the children sang solos in this staged performance; those participating included two of Schaechter's own children and their cousins.

The programme, which also included lengthy speeches, lasted nearly two hours. The evening closed with two songs which act as anthems of Holocaust remembrance among the Yiddishist community. First, in keeping with the theme of 'youth', the choir sang the 'Yugnt-himn' (Youth hymn), the song from which the programme took its name. Solo verses were sung by ten-year-old Elisha Mlotek, son of the choir's director Zalmen Mlotek. This song, written in the Vilna ghetto by songwriter Shmerke Katsherginski and set to music by Basye Rubin, was dedicated to the ghetto's youth club, and was performed by the youth choir at its meetings. While the verses allude more specifically to life in the ghetto, the refrain proclaims radical optimism in the face of adversity: 'Yung iz yeder, yeder, yeder ver es vil nor, yorn hobn keyn batayt, alte kenen, kenen, kenen oykh zayn kinder fun a naye fraye tzayt' (Everyone who wills it can be young – years have no meaning. Elders can also be the children of a new, free age) (Katsherginski 1948, 325).

Finally, all present stood to sing 'Zog nit keynmol' (Never say), also known as the Partisans' Hymn, the Yiddish text of which was printed in the programme. This song, again proclaiming optimism in the face of adversity, was written by Hirsh Glik, a member of the literary group 'Yung vilne' (Young Vilna), and in 1943 became the anthem of the United Partisan Organisation. It was not just this adoption of the song, but also its subsequent wide use, which have contributed to its status today. Ruth Rubin writes:

> Of all the songs of the ghettos, the one which spread like wildfire, almost from the moment that it left the poet's pen, was the marching song by Hirsh Glik .... With almost magical speed it was caught up by all the concentration camps and by the time the war was over, it was being sung by Yiddish speaking Jews the world over and by a score of other peoples as well (1979, 453).

Just 22, Glik was killed in 1944 in battle against the Nazis, having escaped from the Estonian concentration camp that he was sent to upon the liquidation of the Vilna ghetto. Today, above all other songs, this song serves as an anthem of Holocaust remembrance, and is treated with respect similar to that given to a religious text. The Partisans' Hymn is the first song in the 1948 collection of Holocaust-era songs published by Katsherginski, and, underscoring its importance, the text is printed twice the size of the other songs in the book. In printed literature, the phrases 'Zog nit keynmol' (Don't ever say ...) and 'Mir zaynen do!' (We are here!), which appear in the first verse of the song, frequently serve as a referent for Holocaust songs in general, for example furnishing the title of Mlotek and Gottlieb's 1983 collection *We are here!*.

> Zog nit keynmol az du geyst dem letztn veg,
> Ven himlen blayene farshteln bloe teg.
> Kumen vet nokh undzer oysgebenkte sho,
> Es vet a poyk ton undzer trot: mir zaynen do!
> ('Partizaner-himen' opening verse. Katsherginski 1948, 3)
> (Never say that you're walking your last road / When leaden heavens eclipse blue days / Our longed-for hour will yet come / Our tread will drum out: we are here!)

There was no applause at the close of the programme. People left quietly, some humming the tune to themselves, others recognising and seeking out friends.

Yiddish Song and the New York Yiddishist Past

Titled 'a memorial program', the Arbeter Ring's Holocaust memorial programme represented, like similar programmes in Jewish communities worldwide, a response to the shared need of survivors, their descendants and other members of the community, to gather together to mark Yom ha-Shoah. Nevertheless, while the date itself is shared by Jews worldwide, there is no one blueprint or liturgy for planning such a commemorative event. Rather, the need to commemorate, coupled with the absence of a fixed agenda, allows each community to create a format unique to itself.

The structure of the Arbeter Ring programme recalls the formal pageantry of other American Yiddish occasions, including the yearly Boiberik productions described above by Chana Mlotek, and the YIVO summer programme graduation. These highly ritualised events help to structure the shared calendar of this community rooted in secular, cultural Judaism, and provide another means of linking the Yiddishist community across place and time. Their prominence also relates once again to the important role Yiddish education assumed as culture bearer in the USA. In her study of the New York Yiddish choral movement, Marion Jacobson observes that 'the Yiddish schools were also instrumental in developing secular celebrations of Jewish holidays, which became widespread in movement-affiliated families' (2004, 81). New or adapted events, like the Passover 'cultural seder' first held in Arbeter Ring schools in 1923, quickly became adopted more widely. Mark Mlotek recalls the important role played by these events in structuring a shared communal Yiddishist life:

> For us who grew up in a Workmen's Circle home and community, the traditions and rituals for celebrating holidays or life events (births, deaths, weddings, etc.) became second nature. We (and I mean almost everyone in the community) sang the same songs, read the same poems, commemorated the same special events on our secular calendar, and, accordingly, could celebrate any of the holidays or life events by ourselves or in each other's homes. Examples of the foregoing include: lighting candles on Chanukah while singing *borukh ate zingt der tate* (father sings: blessed be Thou), singing *zmires* on Friday night, singing the *Bundishe Shvue* at funerals, participating in May Day and Labor Day events, commemorating April 19 (the anniversary of the Warsaw Ghetto uprising) every year (2006, 268).

The consistency of the format of Yiddish Holocaust commemoration events across at least four decades is striking. Marion Jacobson notes:

> Beginning in 1946, the secular movements initiated collective, institutionalized official public performances in response to the Holocaust. The year 1963 saw the first Warsaw Ghetto Resistance Organization Commemoration, organized by a group of survivors who wished to establish a dignified but non-sectarian observance of the Holocaust. These 'Holocaust memorial' concerts were accompanied by the lighting of six candles representing the six million Jews who perished in the ghettos and camps. Yiddish choral music was a key part of the celebrations, and it was incorporated into the highly orchestrated programs of speeches, candle lighting and readings. It is striking to note that among the Holocaust songs that emphasized martyrdom and pathos, the memorial organizers and choruses tend consistently to select the numbers that emphasize resistance and heroism; the 'Partizaner Him[en]' [Partisans' Hymn] always

concludes that program; and the audience rises to sing it with the performers (2004, 186–7).[11]

The structure that Jacobson describes includes elements common to many Jewish Holocaust memorial programmes – candle lighting, readings, music and speeches, together with elements identified with the secular Yiddish movements – Yiddish choral music and the Partizaner Himen. Nearly 40 years on, the 2001 event described above illustrates how solidly this basic format became codified, even though pathos and martyrdom were now no longer so consistently avoided. Within this framework, the selection of changing content every year affords the New York Yiddishist community a flexible space not only to commemorate the past, but also to articulate its own relationship with that past. The wider loss of the Jewish community is particularised, contextualised within the experiences of this community and of those individuals who take part in the programme. In doing so, the impact of the Holocaust is not relegated to past events, but rather recognised in its continuing consequences for survivors, their families and the community itself. While the reverential atmosphere and the memorial candles burning on the stage at the 2001 event did not allow attention to stray from the victims of the Nazis, the programme did not simply re-tell or historicise the story of the Holocaust. Rather, this story was embedded within the wider framework of the history of Yiddish-speaking Jewry in New York. This merging of East European and American Jewish histories expressed the coexistence of past and present within the lives of those present. The shattering devastation of the Holocaust was articulated within and alongside the continuing expressions of Yiddish culture in the United States.

Song played a prominent role in the structure of the occasion, enabling these layers of meaning to be embodied on a variety of levels. Among the performers, Yiddish choirs and Yiddish secular schools – with their long history attached to American Jewish secular organisations including the Arbeter Ring – appeared alongside families and individuals prominent in the Yiddish music scene. The event as a whole was arranged so that musical performance alternated with the spoken elements of the evening (opening remarks by the chairman, the candle lighting ceremony and two featured speakers). The song texts, then, provided a direct counterpart to the spoken selections. The two speakers focused primarily on the present, on their own relationship to the Holocaust as the children of survivors, several decades removed from the events themselves. Similarly, the candle-lighting ceremony drew attention to the here and now, to the relationship of survivors with the past. By contrast, the sung selections represented words brought directly from the past, written either before or during the Second World War (with the exception of two later, explicitly commemorative songs).

---

[11]   See Werb (2008, 406) for a description of a 1946 pageant in Lodz on the theme of the 'Nazi ordeal and Jewish resistance' which also concluded with the 'Partizaner Himen'.

Discussing a very different Holocaust commemoration ceremony, held in Israel by survivors of the Lodz ghetto, Gila Flam notes the use of songs as an expression of collective memory:

> Today the stories and songs of the ghetto endure as a mandate to the world at large – and the Jewish world in particular – to remember and to commemorate. To remember these songs is to recall the ghetto dwellers' struggle for survival (1992, 170).

At the Arbeter Ring event, songs enabled the performance of words of individuals who did not survive the Holocaust, such as Hirsh Glik, and the memorialisation of a living Yiddish culture that was destroyed: a world not only where poets wrote weighty texts, but also where children performed a fairy-story operetta.

The Yiddish choruses involved in the programme provide another tangible bridge between the New York Yiddishist past and present. The handful of Yiddish choruses active today trace their origins to the huge boom in popularity of Yiddish choral singing among American Jewish socialists in the 1920s and 1930s: some choruses had hundreds of members. Today membership of the choruses remains intergenerational, older alumni of Yiddish secular schools mixing with younger singers caught up by the enthusiastic tide of the Yiddish revival. As Jacobson has discussed, choirs are a particularly compelling metaphor for community: 'the chorus, with its four more-or-less "balanced" parts – is a utopian fantasy of the collective at its most joyous, sensuous, primal, and orderly best' (2004, 371). While the repertory of these choruses still largely focuses on workers' songs and choral arrangements of folk songs, Holocaust songs additionally form a significant part of their concert repertory, indicating the broader relevance of this material to the Yiddishist community today. Of some 25 songs in the working repertory of the Jewish People's Philharmonic Chorus during the spring-summer 2001 season, three were Holocaust-era songs; similarly, Holocaust songs appear amongst other material on Di Goldene Keyt's album *Mir zaynen do tsu zingen!* (We're here to sing!) (1997), one of only a few commercial Yiddish choral recordings.

Symbolically, the final song of the programme was a fully participatory moment. The 'we' of the exclamation 'We are here!' served a twofold meaning. First, the use of the first person identifies the choir with the partisans who are the protagonists of the song, the fight of the partisans analogised to, and affording historical urgency and legitimacy to the struggle to stem the decline of Yiddish. Second, however, the phrase is re-read into the present, proclaiming that Yiddish and its speakers are still here. The joining together of the voices of audience and choir broke down the barrier between stage and audience, past and present, bringing all in attendance together in an act of performance, and unifying the group as a manifestation of the Yiddishist community itself. If the songs performed during the Arbeter Ring programme in themselves, then, stood for a collective past, the act of their performance stood as an articulation of the wider Yiddishist community in New York today.

New Yiddish Spaces

> By recontextualising Yiddish culture, KlezKamp has itself become a context (Sapoznik 1999, 271).

If today's Yiddish culture is strengthened by shared cultural literacy and by enacting links to a shared Yiddishist past, its contemporary vitality is nonetheless dependent on the continued recreation of new contemporary contexts for the expression of Yiddish cultural life. In recent years, the most prominent of these new contexts have been a clutch of Yiddish music camps established since the mid-1980s. The first, the Folk Arts Institute, which became a prototype for other such gatherings, quickly became known by the nickname KlezKamp.[12] Originally under the auspices of YIVO, the first KlezKamp was held in 1985, in the Paramount Hotel in the Catskill Mountains in upstate New York, the heart of the so-called 'borscht belt'. While Yiddish music was – and continues to be – foregrounded among camp activities, like the language programmes discussed above, KlezKamp intended to contextualise this within a place to participate in, to experience and to learn about Ashkenazic culture. One of the camp's founders, Henry Sapoznik writes:

> The original idea of the Folk Arts Institute was to offer musicians, singers, and Yiddishists a place to learn, exchange and create Yiddish music in a challenging intergenerational environment. It also came to serve as payoff for students who had completed YIVO and Columbia University's rigorous six-week intensive summer Yiddish language program. For one week, these students would be able to use the language they learned with some of the leading lights of Yiddish music and folk art culture – and have a great time (1999, 228–9).

More popular than anyone might have expected, not only has the annual KlezKamp continued and grown, but it has been joined by a host of spin-off festivals, both in North America and in other parts of the world. What role do these festivals play in the Yiddish cultural community? Drawing on Walter Benjamin, Michael Taussig describes festivals as times of 'licensed transgression involving excess consumption and excess giving, of squandering and letting go' (1995, 370). According to Taussig, this richness and excessive consumption triggers the creation and experience of a rich memory landscape: voluntary memories are joined by involuntary memories triggered by the saturated sensory environment, linking individual and collective pasts in an experiential whirl. At Yiddish music festivals, it is the outside world that is let go: music camps are a consummate form of heterotopia, secluded places of intensely enacted community life where physical distances between participants are virtually eliminated while the conceptual distance from the outside world is heightened. Set apart from the outside world, Yiddish culture becomes a lived norm, and ordered timetabling affords structured

---

[12]   For further discussions of KlezKamp, see Sapoznik (1999) and Slobin (2000).

shared experiences. The concentrated production and consumption of music during these festivals creates a rich sensory environment, encouraging repeated experiences of emotional engagement and musical entrainment which occur on a much less frequent basis in 'normal life'. These experiences build a bank of community experiences, encapsulated and (re)experienced in the sensory act of musical production. The ripples of these events pan into the future: recorded teaching sessions provide material to work on back home, emotional peaks are relived in conversation, and their energy is channelled into the beginning of new musical projects – a kind of recharging of creative batteries.

In a more tangible way, festivals play an important role in the transmission of repertory, as reflected in the material performed by younger Yiddish musicians today. Itzik Gottesman notes, 'I like to hear a new folksong during my research. And if I can pass it on, I give it to Meyshke [Michael Alpert]. He's the one who spreads them around – he has learnt songs from me which he's then taught to others'.[13] Through teaching and performing at several different Yiddish music workshops each year, professional singers have an effective means to 'spread songs around', working intensively with groups of singers for several days, as well as leading sing-along sessions. Since the same material will frequently be taught to several different groups over the summer, a dispersed community of knowledge is built up among those who might not attend the same classes, but will meet in other Yiddish musical contexts. The anthems of Yiddishland – songs popularised via song classes and recordings and sung ubiquitously at music camps and Yiddish cultural get-togethers – form the mainstay of today's shared Yiddish vocal repertory.

Creating a Contemporary Music-rooted Community: KlezKanada

One of the largest annual Yiddish music camps is KlezKanada, held at the secluded Camp B'nai Brith, a Jewish summer camp in the Laurentian Highlands, some 60 miles north of Montreal, Quebec. By 2001, when I took part in the camp, KlezKanada was in its sixth year, and had over 350 registrants. Its physical location notwithstanding, the camp was dominated by the New York Yiddish scene: of the 37 teaching and performance staff, 22 were New York-based.

On arrival at the campsite all participants were 'tagged' with a bright plastic bracelet, a visible though temporary emblem of Yiddish cultural affinity, although in practice the isolated location and the packed timetable prevented the likelihood of many people wandering onto or off the site. A pervasive Yiddish cultural atmosphere came to life well before arrival at the campsite. Arriving two hours early at Montreal's Dorval Airport, from where the KlezKanada bus was to leave, I sat down with my heap of luggage and was shortly jolted out of my daydreams by a voice speaking Yiddish. As more and more musicians turned up, the

---

[13] Itzik Gottesman, interview with the author, New York, 9 April 2003. Translation from Yiddish mine.

airport became a hive of activity – conversation flowing in Yiddish, English and sometimes a mixture of both. Old friends were greeted, new people met; books and recordings were exchanged – and singing started, an intensive atmosphere that would continue day and night until the end of the camp the following Sunday afternoon.

Camp B'nai Brith occupies many acres of forested, hilly land at the side of an attractive lake; the spacious, outdoor layout of the site provided ample space for impromptu musical jam sessions to operate without too much interference. The camp itself has a distinctly Jewish identity: there are two synagogues, the kitchen is kosher, and the names scrawled on the bunks and buildings testify to a generation of Jewish sojourners. The prevalent Israeli Hebrew camp culture, however, occasionally provoked outbursts of self-conscious alterity by committed Yiddishists. On a tour of the campsite, a member of the camp's young staff pointed out, using an Israeli Hebrew pronunciation, 'This is an area called *Khaverim* (friends)'. Immediately, a passing musician shouted back 'We speak Yiddish! We say *Khaveyrim*!', moving the accent from the last to the penultimate syllable.

Participants at KlezKanada ranged from children to the elderly, and from beginners to professional musicians well established on the klezmer scene. To cater for such a diverse group, a substantial programme of workshops, classes, lectures on Yiddish cultural topics and performances ran in parallel sessions. While the primary focus of KlezKanada is instrumental music, Yiddish song also formed a prominent part of the programme, taught by five well-known figures: Michael Alpert, Adrienne Cooper, Zalmen Mlotek, Theresa Tova and Jeff Warschauer. Three masterclasses for experienced singers were offered; a further workshop explored the connection between Yiddish song and klezmer melody, and a choir was also formed. For those who did not wish themselves to perform, the lecture series included several sessions on Yiddish song. Needless to say, the performances given during the week, both at the staff concerts and at the open 'KlezKabaret' sessions also featured much singing in Yiddish.

The camp structure combined participation with more formalised learning. Workshops challenged participants to build up lasting skills over the course of the week, and individuals' efforts paid off – a young clarinettist, struggling throughout the week with the technical demands of klezmer was able to play a solo centre-stage with her dance band by the final night. Participants were encouraged to bring tape recorders to review material at home, and many sat recording concerts, hoping to pick up new tunes. Peysekh Fishman led Yiddish classes, teaching customs for the approaching High Holidays alongside the Yiddish language. Learning was participatory, the older participants in particular furnishing reminiscences for their often younger teachers.

From this whirl of activity, two contrasting events illustrate how outside the formal performance programme, the participatory performance of Yiddish song was used to build communal cultural activities that encouraged widespread participation. These events were, as advertised on the programme, *Lomir Zingen Zmires* (Let's sing zmires), held on Friday, after dinner, and *Shabbes Shpatsir*

(Sabbath walk), held on Saturday afternoon. Both were participatory and inclusive, open to, and indeed participated in by, a large number of camp participants, reaching across borders of age and professional/amateur musicianship.

That both these events took place on Shabbes, the Jewish Sabbath, is not surprising: Shabbes is a day on which Jewish community, both religious and family, is traditionally enacted. While the majority of KlezKanada participants were not religiously observant, Shabbes was markedly set apart from the other days of the week both in terms of the programming offered and by the participants themselves. In keeping with traditional Jewish law, which prohibits playing instruments on the Sabbath, no instrument classes were held on that day. On Friday evening, towards sundown, participants gradually changed clothing – most women put on skirts and most men a yarmulke. Services, both traditional and progressive, were held for those who wished to attend, and a room was set aside for candle lighting.[14] There followed a traditional Friday night dinner, the everyday food of the week replaced by holiday fare, set on white tablecloths: wine, challah, chicken soup, gefilte fish, roast chicken …. My list ends at this point, not because dessert wasn't served, but because I, like many people there, never saw any. The *zmires* had begun.

Lomir zingen zmires … (Let's sing zmires)

> *Zmiros* are indeed a baffling Jewish creation: religious drinking songs for the holy, communal postprandial sing-a-long (Loeffler 2001).

The singing of *zmires* on Shabbes is a peculiarly Ashkenazic custom.[15] 'In plainest terms', writes James Loeffler, 'the *zmiros* custom consists of the singing of metrical, hymn-like songs with liturgical-poetic texts at the table during and after the three celebratory meals of the traditional Jewish Sabbath: Friday evening, Saturday midday and Saturday late afternoon' (2001). While the term '*zemer*' appears in the Bible and other early rabbinic works, the roots of the Sabbath *zemer* tradition lie in the liturgical poetry (*piyyut*) of late Antiquity, which began to appear around the seventh century. Loeffler identifies the roots of the present Ashkenazic *zmires* tradition, however, in the medieval period, when the pietistic movement Hasidei Ashkenaz (the pious of Ashkenaz) embraced the idea of communal singing after meals on the Sabbath. Gradually three groups of *zmires* achieved prominence and were printed in most prayer books: eight for the Friday evening meal, eight for the Sabbath noon meal, and nine for the end of the Sabbath; the texts of these date from the tenth to the sixteenth centuries.

Today, *zmires* are still widely sung within traditional Jewish communities: the Artscroll prayer book commonly in use among American Orthodox Jews prints three

---

[14] Traditionally, the women in a Jewish household light candles at the beginning of the Sabbath.

[15] '*Zmires*' is plural; singular: *zemer*. Loeffler's alternative spelling stems from a different transliteration of the Hebrew root.

such sections of *zmires*, containing five, five and four texts respectively (Scherman 1987). While texts of the traditional *zmires* are in Hebrew and Aramaic, a corpus of Yiddish texts evolved later, some of which, along with Hebrew and Aramaic *zmires*, have been embraced and performed by contemporary Yiddish musicians.[16]

In the large KlezKanada dining hall on Friday night, participants sat at round tables, about ten people to a table. Waiting between courses of the meal, a handful of people began to sing 'Sholem aleichem' (Peace to you) – traditionally the first *zemer* of Shabbes, sung before the Friday night meal – to a popular modern rhythmic melody by Shmuel Brazil, the head of an orthodox *yeshivah* in Queens, New York. From then on, the singing continued, centred on a table where a group of KlezKanada faculty sat. Soon more participants began to gravitate to this area, gathering around the table. Others, including children, danced at the other end of the dining hall. One song flowed into the next, without a break; those who chose to lead songs had the job of forcing the inert tide of singers into a new melody, occasionally shouting out lyrics to try to keep the singing on track.

With so many musicians present, the singing was supplemented by improvised harmonies. Emulating the behaviour at a Hasidic *tish* (religious celebration), those at the table hit it with their hands, giving a strong rhythm (enough to cause more than one glass to break), and passed around a bottle of Scotch. Alcohol was hardly needed to sustain the mood however – the intensity of the singing combined with the physical closeness of participants created a saturated sensory experience. The singing of 50 or so people in a resonant hall made the kind of exciting, full sound in which individuals are subsumed, the emotional intensity of the moment grounded both in the intense sensory experience and in its perceived authenticity.

As the evening drew on and the dining hall closed, those who wished to continue to sing moved to another room, in which the burning stubs of a hundred or so Sabbath candles were flickering, going out one by one as they burned down. As the evening drew on, the repertory moved from traditional Hebrew *zmires* to other material: klezmer tunes sung as wordless *nigunim*, and several well-known Yiddish songs with religious themes, including 'Az nisht keyn emine' (Without faith …), 'Zol zayn Shabbes' (Let it be the Sabbath) and 'Shnirele Perele' (Little string of pearls). Most of the melodies chosen during the evening shared a rhythmic, repetitive structure, suited to group singing; the three or so hours of constant, relentless outpouring of song was evidence of just how wide a shared repertory existed among participants. As the original leaders of the singing grew tired, others began to take a leading role. Gradually singers left, cold and exhausted; around midnight, the singing wound to a close and those remaining departed, some walking back to their cabins, others heading to a bonfire promising a few more hours' music under the clear, starry Canadian skies.

---

[16]   Recordings include London et al., *Nigunim* (1998) and *Zmiros* (2001). See Loeffler (2001) for discussion of the development of Yiddish *zmires*. See also Chapter 5 for further discussion of these projects.

Shabbes shpatsir (Sabbath walk)   This unrestrained outpouring of zmires enacted a centuries-old Ashkenazic tradition – even if, outside the camp, this tradition might be followed by few KlezKanada participants on a regular basis. By contrast, the 'Shabbes shpatsir' the following afternoon represented a very different use of historical song material. This event, masterminded by theatre director Jenny Romaine and folklorists Itzik Gottesman and Emily Socolov, was conceived as a one-of-a-kind ethnographic tourist trail, in which 'scenes' from the past would be recreated by KlezKanada participants in front of others. The surreal nature of this production was enhanced by an 'advertising campaign' featuring, among other things, an endorsement from the eighteenth-century Rebbe Nakhmen of Breslov, a Hasidic figure well known for his music. In her initial proposal for the event, Romaine described it thus:

> We will capitalize on the chaos of paths, and folks waiting for dinner, waiting for shows to start, etc. People of all ages will learn simple tasks, and get an ethnographic briefing. Like a giant game of ethnographic twister for 400 people with good content. Something we all make together. Also, bi-lingual. We thought processions would be presented like (slightly odd) tourist attractions on a dirt road. Very clear signs and directions. Easy participation for people.[17]

The theme of the '*shpatsir*' was 'how Jews walk'. Not only did the 'tourists' have to walk between locations on the site during the 'show', but each of the performances itself involved walking. Led along the mud track that formed the main road at the camp by Jenny Romaine, the first stop for the 'tourists' was by a clump of trees. Romaine proclaimed via a megaphone to the assembled masses what they were going to see, then folklorist Itzik Gottesman, in the guise of an eccentric professor, elucidated the historical context. Meanwhile, hiding in the trees were a group of 'young maidens', representing girls walking together in the woods on Shabbes. Led by Adrienne Cooper, the singers included women and staff members from the KlezKanada song workshops, costumed, in the creative spirit of community theatre, in gypsy-style shawls which had previously been used as table coverings for cabaret sessions. A band of mandolin players recruited from another KlezKanada workshop accompanied the singing; moving through the trees in a stylised fashion, they sang 'Sorele in vald avek' (Sarah away in the woods), and 'Brontshele' (Brontshele), two songs in which a young woman contemplates love.

Next, the 'tourists' encountered a group of 'Hasidim' carrying sticks – rather surprisingly joined by a techno DJ – in another wooded area. Here, Romaine intended not only to illustrate a 'scene' of the past, but also to use sound creatively to illustrate the words of a song text. She writes:

[17]   Jenny Romaine, e-mail communication, 23 October 2001.

An informant told Itzik [Gottesman] that on *Lag B'omer*[18] he and his *cheyder*[19] friends used to go out in the woods and process behind their teacher, sing that song (usually known as an anti-hasidic song) and carry swords (sticks) and bows and arrows made of branches. The nice lady (Reena Katz) spinning disks was the *ruakh* [spirit]. The spirit sung about in the lid [song] 'Oy vey rebenyu ikh shtey un tsiter' [Oh, Rebbe, I stand and shiver].[20]

Finally, at a junction in the path, a group of teenagers recreated a procession of *Di Bin* (The Bee movement), a Yiddish scouting movement formed by Uriel Weinreich in Vilnius. The members trooped into formation, recited *Di Bin*'s code of conduct, and sang their theme song in Yiddish, as well as their strange chant ('BRAVA LAKA BOOM-KOVED!').[21]

Jeffrey Shandler has compared Yiddish festivals to tourist destinations, the attendees ostensibly adopting the role of tourists in their own cultural domain (2006: 136). Via a self-conscious self-tourism standing on the border of parody, this theatrical recreation of scenes from the Yiddish cultural past allowed participants access to historical material usually considered to be the realm of folklorists. The living representation of scenes usually encountered through the written word in a history book blurred the distinctions between experience, theatre and ethnography. While the singing of *zmires* represented the direct enactment of tradition, the *Shabbes shpatsir* emphasised the experience of particular, detailed events, seen through a self-conscious window of imagination and historical distance.

A Context for Contemporary Yiddish Culture

These activities serve to illustrate the role played by Yiddish music camps in enabling a new generation of students to acquire an embodied fluency in Yiddish culture. While the events described earlier in this chapter took place in New York City, KlezKanada represents a broader context, in which members of the New York Yiddishist community join with a larger scene, including the active Yiddish cultural communities of Toronto and Montreal, in a shared 'other space'. The structure of the week creates an illusion of cultural cohesion and nondisrupted traditions. Here there was no question of having to go to work, go shopping or go to the cinema on the Sabbath; for those for whom family traditions of Yidishkayt had fallen by the wayside, here was the real thing – candles waiting to be lit; *zmires* led by those who knew exactly what to sing and when; *havdalah*, the ceremony concluding

---

[18]   Lag b'Omer is the 33rd day of the Omer (18th Iyar in the Jewish calendar), a day on which customs of abstention kept during the Omer period (from the second day of Passover until Shavues) are abandoned. Traditionally, children would play with bows and arrows on this day.

[19]   Religious Jewish primary school.

[20]   Jenny Romaine, e-mail communication, 24 October 2001.

[21]   The chant is meaningless, but *koved*: honour, glory.

the Sabbath, conducted by Michael Wex in a resonant Ashkenazic Hebrew today little heard outside the strictly Orthodox world; dance sessions led by Michael Alpert and Zev Feldman – and far more, saturating the senses, with events usually found distributed across a family calendar condensed into one week. Whatever background an individual arrived from, and whatever their specialism, during the week they would be pulled into a contemporary representation of traditional Yiddish cultural life.

A poignant moment during the final late-night cabaret illustrated the importance of this heterotopic, saturated cultural space to participants whose lives may otherwise be remote from Yiddish cultural centres. A young singer and ardent Yiddishist from Minnesota, Miryem-Khaye Seigel was used to performing to audiences whose acquaintance with Yiddish was passing, if even existent (she recalls a telephone call from someone who mistakenly believed she sang in Hindi). Having been encouraged by friends to perform, and having fought her way onto the performance order amid throngs of others eager to take part, Seigel sat alone at the keyboard, and, in Yiddish, introduced a song of her own composition. She then sang, the words of the song relating the importance of Yiddish to her.

The well-crafted words of the song illustrated Miryem-Khaye's linguistic competence, but her presence on stage, at the heart of a community who listened silently, with not a few misty eyes, signified something more: the culmination of a process of becoming. Here was not just a performer, but a fluent new cultural creator, the embodiment of a continuing Yiddish present. The ovation that followed her song genuinely surprised her: for once, her audience not only understood her words in the literal sense, but also identified with her achievement.

***

As annual fixtures in the calendar of the wider Yiddishist community, the three events discussed in this chapter participate in shaping the contours of a heterotopic Yiddishland. They also illustrate some of the diverse activities and pathways through which participants might enter and sustain this Yiddishland. Here, singing in Yiddish encompasses more than just performance of an externalised identity: if language classes and dictionaries supply the nuts and bolts of linguistic fluency, song is a medium for *becoming* Yiddish. As a participatory medium, song draws participants to reimagine themselves as cultural insiders. Participation opens a space for training and re-forming the self, for embedding Yiddish into bodily habitus (see Mahmood 2005, 158). Song allows a re-envisioning of self, a way to insert oneself into a culture, vicarious *becoming* through uttering a lullaby, through singing in a choir representing the Yiddish body politic, or through stepping out of everyday life into a new Yiddishland.

This cultural becoming both creates cultural continuity and enables people to be part of that continuity. Like the Greek chorus, upon taking up these voices, the singing community literally embodies the 'voices of a people', becoming inseparably merged with that people, both past and present. It is to another forum for the imagination of that people, that I now turn. Framed by narratives that aim to bridge the passing generations, Yiddish songbooks reimagine the same voices as a historical canon to be mediated via material, printed narratives.

Chapter 2
Narrating a Canon

THERE IS A NEED 'TO PRESERVE'! THERE IS A NEED TO 'REMEMBER OUR ROOTS'! THERE IS A NEED 'NEVER TO FORGET' the Jewish memories of our BOBES and ZEDES (grandmothers and grandfathers)! Only if WE TEACH OUR YOUTH ABOUT THE 'YIDDISH CULTURE' OF THE PAST, can we secure a rich heritage for the 'JEW OF THE FUTURE!' (Zim 1984, preface).[1]

Introducing a songbook whose cover shows a sepia image of a Jewish couple walking through an unidentifiable Central European town between houses and a ghetto wall, their eyes averted from the reader's gaze, compiler Sol Zim urges the reader to take Yiddish song into their own hands, his wayward capital letters driving home the urgency of the task. While songbooks are generally conceived as inert vessels for the transmission of repertory, considering them primary sources reveals the substantial role this literature has played as a medium for the post-war encounter with Yiddish culture. If creativity in traditional Yiddish culture consensually ended with the Holocaust, during the post-war decades folklorists nonetheless unanimously asserted that Yiddish song, now presented as a historical canon, held continued relevance for contemporary audiences.

Here, I consider twin processes of canonisation: folksong collection and the publication of a corpus of Yiddish songbooks, between 1945 and the present day. This discussion falls into three sections. First, it explores the development of a rhetoric of unbridgeable historical distance in post-war collections of Yiddish song. The destruction of European Yiddish culture in the Holocaust came to be understood as a final end-point of creativity in Yiddish culture. While the explicit articulation of a point of no return developed among folklorists working immediately after the Holocaust, it also consolidated and reinforced the romantic nationalist discourses of earlier folklorists who had held song to be emblematic of a receding normative, traditional Yiddish culture, a worldview that has underpinned popular conceptions of the repertory from the late nineteenth century to the present day.[2]

The second part of this chapter turns to the cultural objects themselves: songbooks. With the dislocation between cultural material and its audience came a need to create narratives to frame Yiddish repertory within a wider context of

---

[1] Capitalisation and punctuation original.

[2] Herzfeld helpfully uses the term 'structural nostalgia' to describe cases where nostalgia is transmitted between generations (2005).

symbols and meanings. Here I explore the narratives of Yiddish cultural history around which three recent song collections are structured. I suggest that in including such material the compilers of popular songbooks not only act to inscribe a contemporary canon of Yiddish songs, but also participate in the shaping of wider collective memories of Yiddish culture. In doing so, they frequently write against the diversity inherent in the repertory they present, and sometimes against the plain meaning of their texts. Yet, in privileging the paradigm of memory over historiography, and in reinforcing popular tropes of nostalgia, these accounts echo a collective history that has arguably had much greater impact on the popular imagination than standard historiographic accounts.

Folklorists and Yiddish Song: Nationalism and Preservation

The early history of the collection and publication of Yiddish songs is closely intertwined with wider practices of folklore collection in Europe. As Matthew Gelbart documents, 'by the 1820s and 1830s, almost every country in Europe east of Germany was finding its own folk roots, hand in hand with political and linguistic nationalist movements and revivals' (2007, 229). This turn to folk music, wedded strongly to political nationalism, was accompanied by scholarly debates about the nature of 'folk' music (2007, 10, 24).

While Jewish scholars had been associated with wider folklore initiatives, and Jewish melodic materials had been cited by Russian nationalist composers during the mid to late nineteenth century, the collection and publication of Yiddish songs began rather later. Indeed, until the early years of the twentieth century, with few exceptions, folklorists, Jewish and non-Jewish alike, continued to question the independent existence of Jewish folk music.[3] Nevertheless, during the early decades of the twentieth century, bolstered by new forms of Jewish political nationalism, folklorists' engagement with Yiddish song rapidly mushroomed. This flowering of scholarly activity was in most cases relatively short-lived, curtailed both by changing ideological landscapes and by the fragile situation of European Jewry: the perceived fragility of Yiddish folk traditions was underscored by the anti-Jewish pogroms that began in Imperial Russia in 1881, by the beginning of massive Jewish emigration to the United States and elsewhere, and by the consequent rupture of geographical and family units. Notwithstanding this turbulence, however, this work left behind a substantial printed legacy together with numerous early recordings. The majority of those working on Yiddish folk music were themselves Jewish; nevertheless, these collecting projects fitted into the wider frame of folkloric studies in Central and Eastern Europe, representing a broad range of ideological and methodological perspectives. A number of scholars

---

[3]   See for example Loeffler (2010a, 36, 56–7 and 2010b, 390); for earlier examples see Loeffler (2010a, 67). Gottesman (2003) connects scholarly interest in Yiddish folklore to the recognition of Yiddish as an independent language.

including Itzik Gottesman, James Loeffler and Mark Slobin have recently reviewed this early folkloristic material; in the discussion that follows, I summarise some key nodes of activity.

Among the earliest voices connecting folksong with Jewish national identity were Yoysef-Yehude Lerner (1847–1907) and Joel Engel (1868–1927). Having collected folk materials in Odessa, in 1889, Lerner published an essay on Yiddish folksong, which sought to prove that the Yiddish language was capable of lofty and profound thoughts (Gottesman 2003, xvii–xix). Meanwhile, Joel Engel participated in an intellectual Moscow circle with Peysekh Marek, who together with Shaul Ginzberg published the first major printed collection of Yiddish folk songs (St Petersburg, 1901). This collection documented only song texts, but Marek continued to work with Engel, whose interest lay particularly in melodic inflection. Following this affirmation of the value of study and dissemination of Yiddish music, Engel was eventually to set up the St Petersburg Society for Jewish Music in 1908; a Moscow chapter was founded the following year. The Society both promoted the study and performance of Jewish music and published articles, arrangements of folk songs and works by Jewish composers. In 1912, Engel conducted the Society's first folklore expedition, joined by Sholem An-Sky and later replaced by Zinovii Kisselhof; unfortunately, much archived material was lost during the following wars and Revolution.[4]

Meanwhile, debates about the nature of Yiddish folk song, and which 'folk' song collectors should represent, consumed significant scholarly ink. Lerner and Engel's scholarly approach imagined 'folk song' as largely created by an anonymous 'folk' over a substantial period of time (see Gottesman 2003, xviii). Nevertheless, this view was counterposed by other consensual uses of the word 'folkslider' (folk songs), most famously by Mark Warshawsky, an amateur songwriter whose Yiddish songs had rapidly risen to popularity and had become folklorised among Jews in the Pale of Settlement (Loeffler 2010a, 75–7; Gottesman 2003, xviii). Warshawsky's labelling his material 'folk song' was endorsed by popular Yiddish writer Sholem Aleichem, who supported him in the Yiddish press.

Similar debates were also couched as methodological critique. At the same time as Joel Engel and others collected folk music in Europe, Yehuda Leyb Cahan collected songs from East European immigrants in London and New York; the first two volumes of his work were published in 1912. Itzik Gottesman suggests that Cahan 'introduced the notion of *ekhtkayt*, authenticity, into Yiddish folkloristic discourse' (2003, xxii). Reviewing two recent publications of Yiddish song in 1913 under the pseudonym L. Vilenski, Cahan commented pointedly that

---

[4]   See Loeffler (2010a, chapter 2) and Gottesman (2003) for extensive discussion. For earlier discussions of Russian Jewish musical research in the early twentieth century, see Beregovski's essay 'Jewish folk music' (1934; published in translation by Slobin 1982). Slotnick (1976) provides an overview of Soviet Yiddish scholarship during the period 1924–48; her article is critiqued by Mlotek (1978).

the collector of folk songs, or of whatever kind of folkloric material, gets the necessary mastery only after years of study of his subject. Furthermore, he must have great patience and endurance (Vilenski [Cahan] 1913, 356. Translation mine).[5]

Here, this 'necessary mastery' refers not to specific field or analytical techniques, but rather to the collector's ability to judge the folkloric content of material, based on an essentialised category of 'the folk', an idealised population specifically excluding professional or educated individuals. Cahan strongly criticises a recent collection by Noah Prilutski for including songs by the likes of *badkhonim* (wedding poets) and scholars, 'which do not come from the folk tradition in which genuine folksong was shaped' (Vilenski [Cahan] 1913, 361); he even dismisses material gained from an oral tradition if it is found to be based upon theatrical couplets or folk-like songs of known authorship. Later, a similar debate between Lazare Saminsky and Joel Engel concerning the nature of 'genuine' Jewish folk song raged in the St Petersburg press. The polemic continued from 1915 until 1923, the year in which the Society for Jewish Folk Music eventually disbanded.[6]

While, as Loeffler and Gottesman demonstrate, Yiddish song came to occupy a central place for folklorists concerned with Yiddish nationalism, it occupied a more ambivalent place in the work of Abraham Tzvi Idelsohn, a composer and folklorist who sought to create a new category of Hebrew music according to Zionist ideals. Born in Latvia, and later working in Palestine and the USA, Idelsohn initially adhered to the principle of *shelilat hagalut*, the rejection of diaspora culture. Nevertheless, he eventually included substantial Yiddish material in his monumental *Thesaurus of Hebrew Oriental Melodies* (published 1914–32).[7] Slightly later, a further significant corpus of printed and recorded material was collected by Moshe Beregovski, a student of Ukrainian folklorist Kvitka. Despite Stalinist pressure, he undertook numerous field trips between 1929 and 1947. Concerned with problems of transcription and the interrelationship of Jewish material and other co-territorial folk musics, Beregovski produced carefully notated transcriptions. Documenting instrumental music as well as Yiddish songs, his work was of particular interest to klezmer revivalists; two volumes of his collections were reissued with English commentary by Mark Slobin and others (Slobin 1982, Slobin et al. 2001). During the 1990s his archive of wax cylinder recordings was rediscovered at the Vernadsky National Library in Kiev; some have been reissued in digital form by the library.[8]

---

[5]   The inclusion of this review in Max Weinreich's 1952 collection of Cahan's studies reveals Cahan's pseudonym.

[6]   Extracts of this debate are reproduced by Saminsky (1934). See also Gottesman (2003, xviii).

[7]   See Loeffler (2010a) and Cohen (2010) for discussion.

[8]   See Beregovski (1982), Slobin (1986), Braun (1987), Adler (1995) and Zaltsberg (1999) for further discussion of Beregovski's life, work and collections.

While Yiddish folk culture was already perceived as needing preservation by pre-war song collectors, the Second World War marked a turning point in the attitudes of folklorists towards Yiddish material. The Holocaust left not only obliteration, but also an imperative to remember. Survivors became the custodians of a whole cultural world, and the primary task of the folklorist became the collection of all possible material from them. The sudden loss of carriers of the tradition and the destruction of the cultural context in which it flourished fired a new sense of urgency in this mission, compounded still further by the deaths of numerous folklorists along with the culture they studied, and by the destruction of archive collections. These changed circumstances prompted three main ideological changes relating to Yiddish song as a repertory, which I will explore in turn.

Yiddish Song as a Unified Repertory

The first principal change in general attitudes to Yiddish song after the Holocaust was the consensual expansion of the 'folk' represented by the Yiddish song canon to include the full compass of the Yiddish cultural world and all examples of Yiddish song. Debate about the relative worth of different genres of material gave way to the salvage of shreds of culture: now the primary value of Yiddish songs became their perceived reflection of the lives of a people tragically destroyed. Immediately after liberation, and even during the war in some ghettos, folklorists began to collect songs from survivors.[9]

This re-evaluation of the boundaries of the Yiddish canon is clearly evident in the work of folklorist Shmerke Katsherginski, who devoted his activities to the Yiddish songs of the ghettos and camps.[10] A lithographer and songwriter who had himself been incarcerated in the Vilna ghetto before living with a partisan group in the woods in White Russia, he authored a number of songs that were widely sung in the ghetto, including 'Shtiler shtiler' (Quiet, quiet) and 'Yugnt himen' (Youth hymn). Katsherginski himself notes that the conditions of the ghetto led to an increased rate of circulation of songs: 'In ordinary times each song would probably travel a long road to popularity. But in the ghetto we observed a marvellous phenomenon: individual works transformed into folklore before our eyes'.[11]

From his research, Katsherginski prepared a collection of 236 song texts from the ghettos and camps, some accompanied by melodies, published by the New

---

[9]   Within this canon, among scholarly circles, debates about the authenticity of particular versions of folk songs continued: see, for example the exchange between Chemjo Vinaver, Harry Coopersmith and Beatrice and Uriel Weinreich in the letters section of the March 1951 issue of *Commentary* magazine.

[10]   For a biography of Katsherginski, see Werb (2008).

[11]   Katsherginski (1947), *Dos gezang fun vilner geto*, quoted by Werb (2008, 400).

York Congress for Jewish Culture in 1948.[12] His preface traces the emergence of salvage ethnography during the period preceding and during the war, during which he and others were active in attempts to preserve Jewish cultural artefacts:

> The work of a folklore-collector has always been very difficult. The writing-desk of such a collector has to find itself in every far-flung place: out in the sticks of a province-settlement, in the attics and cellars of the city, in the study-house, the children's school, and the union, and – wherever it is possible for people to be. If, before the war, some people looked at such a collector as a *crank*, in the more difficult conditions during occupation (in ghettos, camps, the woods and similar) even people who understood very well the worth of such collecting looked upon such collectors almost as maniacs. The public had reconciled itself to performing theatre in the ghetto, to sending children to school *for the time being*, in order to *distract* them a little, but to think what might happen *in a year's time*, and because of this to collect such trifles, *how, who, what* it expressed – for this few volunteers could be found. But … there were indeed such people. The wonder is even greater that nonconformist Jews were to be found at all, who were drawn into this work and believed it to be their holiest task (Katsherginski 1948, xviii–xix. Italics original. Translation mine).

That Katsherginski's attitude towards his material was not yet widespread even at the time of publication is clear from his substantial introduction to the volume, the majority of which constitutes a defence of his mission as a folklorist. Notably Katsherginski – along with his critic – recognises that he is not only collecting Holocaust material, but also laying the foundations of a new type of canon of Yiddish song:

> Whilst undertaking the collection-work, I also ran into doubters. The doubter said, 'I can understand the published texts which contain even a couple of poetic lines, but why immortalise graphomania, why canonise it? …' To this I answered, 'In the same way as every sacred page found among the ruins or on the ash of our homes is dear to us, just in this way we must preserve the *voices* of the dead as treasures, their simple, clear words which tell us about their life until they perished' (Katsherginski 1948, xxiv).

Katsherginski's comments suggest that he saw the role of the folkloric material he collected as twofold: to stand as a tangible memorial to its creators, and to convey their experiences, as expressed through song, to later generations. His interest in amassing all possible Yiddish cultural material was catalysed by the extreme destruction of the Holocaust. If early twentieth-century folklorists imagined authenticity in folksong to derive from its connection to a timeless past,

---

[12]   Katsherginski additionally published a smaller collection, *Dos gezang fun vilner geto* (The song of the Vilna ghetto), in Paris, 1947.

Katsherginski relocated this site of authenticity to encompass all pre-Holocaust Yiddish culture, making issues of 'contamination' by composed or commercial material irrelevant. He and his colleagues saw *all* ghetto songs as interesting, regardless of their authorship and musical quality, simply because they existed and therefore testified to the experiences of the lost millions. Katsherginski's published collection fully reflects this attitude: it includes not only complete songs, but also fragments of song texts, and a few pages of photographs to accompany the material. Folk songs, poetic songs and theatre songs are set side by side, leaving the texts and accompanying notes to speak for themselves both as musical and literary material and as a composite memorial to those who sang these songs, their lives and their cultural world. This all-encompassing approach to culture resonates with wider post-war developments in ethnomusicology, which shifted attention away from images of an anonymous 'folk' and towards a more all-encompassing engagement with culture. Nevertheless, it also diverges significantly from the methodological trends of mid-twentieth-century research on European folk music (for example, Bartók, Kodály, Wiora and others), who focused on analytical approaches to melody and classification.[13]

His doubters aside, Katsherginski was not alone in advocating the wholesale collection of Holocaust-era musical material. During the early years after the Holocaust, the gathering of this material was largely undertaken by survivors themselves. For some, this activity took on a quasi-religious significance. Katsherginski, in his account above, uses the '*sheymes*' to describe the documents he is collecting – a term traditionally used to refer to holy documents bearing the name of God whose destruction is forbidden by Jewish law – and the task of folklorists as their *heylikster avoyde* – literally, holiest work; similarly, the term *avoyde* is also used to describe divine service. The comparison of Holocaust-era material to *sheymes* has also been made by David Roskies:

> Whereas *bish'at hashemad* [during historical times of religious persecution] the Rabbis had enjoined the masses to perform *Kiddush Hashem*, to sanctify God's name in martyrdom, now, in a time of mass extermination, the latter-day rabbis enjoined the masses to preserve every scrap of evidence, to consider these documents as if they were *sheymes* – sacred fragments that bore the *shem* or Name of God (1999, 17).

Immediately following the Holocaust, Yiddish songs were collected in the DP (Displaced Persons) camps throughout Europe in which many survivors were gathered. The collection of folkloric material was organised in the DP camps by central historical agencies that sought to record testimonies concerning the atrocities of the Holocaust. The following advertisements appeared (some several times) in *Fun letstn khurbn: tsaytshrift far geshikhte fun yidishn lebn beysn natsi-rezhim* (From the latest destruction: journal of the history of Jewish life during

---

[13]   See Bohlman (1988) and (2001) for discussion.

the Nazi regime), a DP journal published in Munich between August 1946 and December 1948; they are reproduced by Margalioth (1997), in her survey of the cultural and literary life of the DP camps:

> Can you sing a song from the ghetto, camp, partisans etc? Come to the Historical Society where the song is immediately immortalised on a gramophone record.[14]

> Take down the songs, which were sung in the Nazi era in the ghettos, camps with the partisans etc. Take down the jokes, sayings, legends, anecdotes, predictions, which circulated in that time. When possible submit also the name of the author, place and date of creation. Send this all to the Historical Commission who preserves it and publishes it in print.[15]

> Sing Out and Immortalise Your Ghetto! Come to the CHC [Historical Commission] and submit onto gramophone records the ghetto and camp song, which you know. 7 minutes it lasts. Around the world these records will be demonstrated. The YIVO exhibition in New York waits for them. More than anything it is deserved by the honour and memory of your ghetto! Come, don't wait to be begged![16]

A further advertisement requests songs specifically for a publication of ghetto and camp songs by the Historical Commission; ghetto and camp songs themselves also appeared in every issue of *Fun letstn khurbn* (Margalioth 1997, 136).[17]

The new proximity of people from geographically disparate regions in the DP camps made it easier for Katsherginski and his contemporaries to collect Holocaust-era folkloric material from a wide range of sources. Writing in 1947, folklorist Y. Kaplan observed that 'folklore was enhanced by the encounter of various subgroups brought together in the camps, speaking with different accents or in different languages'.[18] This dissolution of previous spatial boundaries demarcating divisions within the Yiddish-speaking community also served to concretise the conception of Yiddish song as a single repertory. Not only were lives and Yiddish culture dissolved during the Holocaust, but so too was the landscape of the Yiddish cultural world. Just as the Nazi machine had not distinguished between town

---

[14]   *Fun letstn khurbn*, 1, 26. Translations of this and the two following advertisements from Margalioth (1997, 274–6).

[15]   *Fun letstn khurbn*, 1, 32.

[16]   *Fun letstn khurbn*, 3, 67.

[17]   Katsherginski and Leyvik themselves collected material from DP camps (Katsherginski 1948, preface); however, it is unclear from Katsherginski's account which camps these were.

[18]   Margalioth (1997, 136–7), quoting Y. Kaplan (1947), *In der tog-teglekher historisher arbet: fortrog gehaltn afn tsuzamenfor fun di historishe komisyes*. Munich, 12 May 1947, 18–19.

and country Jews, Litvak and Galitsyaner (Lithuanian and Galician), bringing disparate groups together in ghettos and concentration camps and leaving an uprooted population at the end of the war, so the songs of this mixed population now stood together as a single repertory.

Yiddish Song and the Historical Imaginary

While the attitude displayed towards folkloric material by Katsherginski and Kaplan, and echoed in the work of the Historical Commission in the Munich DP camp, relates specifically to the task of collecting Holocaust material, this change in approach has not been confined to Yiddish song originating during the war. Rather, if the first widespread change in attitude to Yiddish song catalysed by the devastation of the Holocaust was a tendency to collect all possible material and to group all Yiddish songs into a single category, all equally worthy of preservation, then the second, related change, was the closure of the Yiddish canon in 1945, an endpoint which came to symbolise the distinction between a 'living' and a 'historical' culture. The founding of the state of Israel shortly after the end of the war further emphasised this endpoint, concretising the rapid ascendance of an alternative normative Jewish culture, itself directly negating the Yiddish world through ongoing delegitimisation of Yiddish in favour of Hebrew, now codified as state policy.

In the light of the devastation of the Holocaust, ethnographic immersion in Eastern European Jewish life was no longer possible. Rather, the role of the folklorist was reconceptualised as a cultural mediator: courageously defying the grave, he could reach back to a different generation and haul songs back to the future. The creation of this end-point and ensuing historical imaginary is clearly evident in the foreword to *Di Goldene Pave* (The golden peacock), a song collection published by Moshe Gorali, Moshe Bick and Gideon Almagor in Haifa, Israel, in 1970:

> One of the most vivid manifestations of East European Jewry was the folksong … The terrible tragedy of the Holocaust, with the destruction of hundreds of communities and the death of millions of Jews, put an end to all singing.
>
> Graves do not sing.
>
> The dead praise not the Lord,
>
> Neither any that go down into silence (Psalm 115:17)
>
> What, then, is left for the collector of Yiddish folklore and music? The ethnomusicological 'field recording' method which records the songs and music

from the people at their source, i.e. at work, at the Synagogue, at a wedding etc., is in this case a fruitless pursuit. What is left? Where can one go?

The collector has, therefore, to resort to collecting the remnant and left-overs, to recording and writing down the as yet untapped tunes and melodies known to survivors of the Holocaust and random individuals ... (Gorali et al. 1970, 141).

The articulation of the end-point of the Yiddish canon is further evident in the structure of the contents of Yiddish songbooks published before and after the Second World War. Table 2.1 presents the tables of contents of five fairly large collections of Yiddish song published between 1923 and 1983. At first sight, their similarities are more striking than their differences. All five books present a broad spectrum of material; following the model of Ginzburg and Marek's pioneering 1901 collection and of other collections of European folksong, the editors of all these collections choose to categorise their songs by subject matter (apart from the inclusion in the last two collections of a separate section of songs by folk poet Mordechai Gebirtig), rather than, for example, by musical characteristics, by composition type (folk song, theatre song, art song and so on), by date of composition, or by authorship of music or text, a choice mirrored in the vast majority of general collections of Yiddish song.[19] Much else is common to these volumes too: each collection includes, among its categories, love songs, children's songs and workers' songs. Such subject matter is staple to European folksong, not specific to Yiddish song (although the content of individual songs reflects the Jewish experience in terms of religious and cultural references). The majority of such songs are ahistorical in reference, creating a sense of shared, timeless present in which the cycles of birth, childhood, love, work and death repeat endlessly.

The combination of categories in each of these volumes, nevertheless, reveals the compiler's stance regarding the historicity of Yiddish culture. In Bastomski's and the Arbeter Ring's collections, published during the 1920s, the 'timeless present' described above incorporates all the song categories included in the collections – an essentially ahistorical overview of Yiddish folk cultural life is given. Dobrushin's collection, on the other hand, which was published in Moscow during the turbulent 1940s, includes several categories of Soviet songs alongside the folk categories outlined above. In this way, the picture is bifurcated between 'ahistorical' material and material which refers to a specific time and place. Nevertheless, the complete image remains within the gamut of a present, rather than a historic, Yiddish culture: Soviet songs belong to Dobrushin's current time period, if not to an 'eternal' one.

The categories into which Bastomski, the Arbeter Ring and Dobrushin place the songs in their collections outline a continuous Yiddish culture based around an essentially repeating life-cycle, regardless of the changing circumstances – including revolution in Europe and emigration to America – against which this

---

[19]   See Bohlman (1988, 35) for comparative cases.

Table 2.1   Comparison of the categorisation of contents in five songbooks (figures in parentheses indicate the number of songs in each section)

Bastomski: Baym kval: material tzum yidishn folklor [By the spring: material from Yiddish folklore]. Vilna, 1923.	Arbeter ring: Tzvey hundert lider [Two hundred songs]. Chicago, 1929.	Dobrushin: Yidishe folks-lider [Yiddish folk songs]. Moscow, 1940.	Mlotek: Mir trogn a gezang: Favorite Yiddish Songs. New York, 1972.	Vinkovetzky, Kovner and Leichter: Anthology of Yiddish Folksongs. (4 vols.) Jerusalem, 1983.
Lullabies (5) Children's songs: play (22); counting rhymes (21) nickname, joke and mockery (45); Various children's songs (30) Songs from kheyder and the yeshivah [religious schools] (3) Love songs (14) Ballads (22) Wedding songs (12) Family songs (23) Conscription and soldiers' songs (6) Historical songs (4) Workers' songs (5) [Jewish] Holiday songs (6) Religious-national and Hasidic songs (12) Parodies and folk humoresques (12) Satirical songs (4) Jewish songs in other languages (7) Songs of war (34) Late additions (33)	Choir songs (53) Revolutionary songs (13) Folk songs (19) Workers' songs (15) Love songs (24) National songs (17) Theatre songs (19) Ensemble songs (25) Childrens' songs (25)	Children's songs: play, counting rhymes (37), lullabies (29) Love songs: love (63), parting (80), deception (39) Family and customs (52) Satire and humour: against religiosity (14), jokes and smiles (43) Historical, recruits, conscription and war: historical (14), recruits, conscription and war (23) Hardship, work and struggle: hardship (18), work (23), struggle (24) In prison and chains (18) Revolutionary lullabies (6) Soviet folk songs: Stalin (25), Soviet lullabies (8), Red Army (11), collective farm and village (24), Tshastushkes [a form of Russian poetry] (21), Soviet customs (11), Birobidzshan (6)	Songs of childhood (6) Songs of love and courtship (18) Songs for celebration and parties (10) Songs of work, poverty and struggle (15) Once upon a time (17) Songs of America (7) Songs for community singing (8) Songs in a quiet mood (6) Am yisroel khay! (Long life to the Jews!) (3) Songs by Mordecai Gebirtig (16)	Four volumes containing a total of 320 songs: Volume 1: Love songs, Cradle songs Volume 2: Children's songs, Family songs, Weddings and festivals. Volume 3: Humor and satire, Hassidic songs, Multi-lingual songs, Poverty, toil and deprivation, Jewish soldiers' songs. Volume 4: Struggle and resistance songs, Ghetto and partisan songs, Religious and national songs, Homeward to Zion! (A fifth volume of this collection was published in 2000, containing songs by Mordechai Gebirtig)

cycle of life may be played out. After the Holocaust, however, this image of continuity was no longer a viable reading of Yiddish culture, even in America. The categories used in the later collections by Mlotek and by Vinkovetzky et al. mark distinct epochs in the history of Yiddish culture, outlining a teleological progression rather than a continuous present. The inclusions of sections of Holocaust songs – both those by Gebirtig and the sections entitled 'Am yisroel khay!' (Mlotek) and 'Ghetto and partisan songs' (Vinkovetzky et al.) – and the reference to the founding of the state of Israel ('Homeward to Zion!', Vinkovetzky et al.), call the reader's attention to the two great events of the mid-twentieth century which, in their very different ways, essentially signalled the end of Yiddish culture as a normative Jewish way of life.[20] Underscoring this reading, these sections are placed at the end of their respective collections: the pagination of the books therefore also reinforces the message that creativity in Yiddish song ended at this historical point. Here the 'timeless present' of Yiddish folk culture – whilst continuing to be represented essentially by the same material as used in the 1920s collections – becomes historicised, presenting the reader with a three-stage timeline: (1) 'Folk time' (pre-Holocaust): ahistorical Yiddish culture; (2) the Holocaust and the founding of the State of Israel: end-point of Yiddish culture; (3) the present (time of publication): Yiddish culture consigned to the past, a pattern repeated in numerous songbooks from the post-war period. While, as discussed in the previous chapter, pockets of creative Yiddish activity continued in North America during the post-war years, outside the most optimistic Yiddishist circles, when there was no longer an East European Yiddish culture to look back to, the gradual decline of the number of Yiddish speakers in America – a process which had been happening for some years – became an unambiguous descent towards the eventual disappearance of Yiddish culture.

Yiddish Voices

Parallel to the collection of songs themselves, a similar commitment to the preservation of the voices of individual singers is evident in the post-war corpus of recorded Yiddish song. Documentary recordings focus upon individuals who are unusually talented, the individual personifying the collective, standing in for the whole realm of Yiddish folk culture. The liner notes to a cassette of field recordings of folksinger Mariam Nirenberg issued in 1986 note that 'in the post-Holocaust era, we can collect only fragments of a rich East European Jewish song world, now represented by individuals rather than communities' (Nirenberg 1986). Recognised as 'national treasures', the singers on whom such projects focus are frequently noted not only for their fine voices but for their knowledge of repertory and Yiddish folk ways. This fluency validates the recorded voices, serving yet

---

[20]   Notably, the reference to Israel only appears in the Israeli volume.

further to emphasise the distance between past and present: these figures represent a now virtually unattainable cultural fluency and authenticity.

One of the few collections of field recordings released on tape is *Az di furst avek*, an album of 21 songs sung by Lifshe Schaechter-Widman (1893–1974), recorded in the Bronx in 1954 by Leybl Kahn. Kahn's field recordings were not released until 1986, when Itzik Gottesman, Schaechter-Widman's grandson, produced the album for Global Village. Although known as an exceptional singer, Schaechter-Widman even in her own time represented an older, more traditional mode of Yiddish life, far from the commercial tradition of Yiddish song more often represented on recordings. When I asked whether she ever gave concerts, her daughter, Beyle Schaechter-Gottesman, highlighted the difference in outlook between her mother's world and the values of her New York Jewish contemporaries:

> No – never … In fact, she said that when she travelled by ship to America – she was still a young girl, and at that time she sang German songs, because [her hometown] belonged to Austria – the sailors and everyone brought her fruit and bananas so that she would sing. She didn't want to take anything – she didn't take any payment for singing. And here in New York, people wanted her to join the Yiddish theatre. But her brother, who was here – he really loved her – and he said 'Sis!' [laughs] 'If you go up there on the stage, I'll buy a revolver. First I'll shoot you, and then myself.' … Of course, she didn't sing [on the stage]. She really loved her brother, they were very close. He didn't want … it wasn't *moral* then, at that time, to be an actress or a singer. People had a different mentality then. She never once sang for money.[21]

The aesthetics of salvage ethnography are also reflected in musical sound and production. This is illustrated by two further recordings: Majer Bogdanski's *Yiddish Songs* (2000) and Arkady Gendler's *My Hometown Soroke* (2001). Both recordings feature elderly gentlemen singing Yiddish song: at the time of recording, Gendler was in his seventies and Bogdanski in his late eighties. In both cases, the musical focus is placed upon the voice of the singer: Bogdanski sings unaccompanied throughout; Gendler sings either alone or with an understated accordion accompaniment. The documentary-style close-up sound of the recordings minimises the perceived distance between singer and listener, authenticating the sound by reinforcing the perception that these are intimate, spontaneous recordings rather than highly polished performances. Indeed, according to the liner notes Gendler's recording was made 'in the very last hours before Arkady's plane left' during a recent visit by the Ukrainian to America; these words explicitly frame the recording as a last-minute attempt by folklorists to preserve Gendler's voice (Gendler 2001, liner notes).

---

[21]   Beyle Schaechter-Gottesman, interview with the author, New York, 30 March 2003. Translation from Yiddish mine.

The recordings are further authenticated by the authoritative discourse of the folklorist: both recordings contain substantial notes by respected academic figures. An interview with Bogdanski by ethnomusicologist Ruth Rosenfelder, several pages long, is reproduced in full in the liner notes, and Gendler's recording includes notes on song tradition and background by Mark Slobin and Michael Alpert. Greater emphasis is placed by all three writers upon the background of the singer himself as an exceptional representative of the tradition than upon the particular songs included on the recording: 'Arkady Gendler can stand in for a whole class of Yiddish folksingers' (Mark Slobin); 'This collection [Bogdanski's recording] of folk music is a unique opportunity to hear songs that illustrate the complex and vibrant life of Eastern European Jewry before the Second World War' (Ruth Rosenfelder).

The market for albums of unaccompanied song, a repertory better suited to intimate, domestic settings than to the concert stage, remains small; the release of a handful of collections of such material during the past two decades reflects the rise of interest in traditional Yiddish culture during this period. Much more recently, developments in internet-based digital media have enabled folklorists to explore new paradigms of publishing and dissemination. The An-sky Jewish Folklore Research Project's Yiddish Song of the Week website, established in 2010 and edited by Itzik Gottesman, uses an interactive blog to present folkloristic material, including field recordings, scholarly commentary, visual material and other resources, to a transnational audience in a format unprecedented in traditional formats of publishing (http://yiddishsong.wordpress.com/).

Mother to Child Becomes Folklorist to Public: A New Paradigm for the Transmission of Yiddish Song

The activity of salvage ethnography effected an important change in the persona of the folklorist. As the new custodians of a song repertory held to encapsulate the lives and voices of Yiddish-speaking Jewry, folklorists began themselves to be seen as authentic bearers of cultural memory, responsible not only for the documentation and preservation of the Yiddish song canon, but also for actively passing songs on to a new generation.[22] Barbara Kirshenblatt-Gimblett has described the rise of 'the popular arts of Jewish ethnography' (2001) during the post-war period, epitomised by the popular account of East European Jewish life, *Life Is with People*, first published in 1952, and by the musical *Fiddler on the Roof*, a fictional account of *shtetl* life based on literary and popular ethnographic sources. 'The popular arts of ethnography of the postwar period', she writes, 'exhibit not only an autoethnographic, but also an anti-ethnographic character. Such aesthetically mediated self-portraiture was intended to inspire, more than to inform, for its goal was cultural survival rather than museological preservation' (2001, 183). Just as

---

[22]   See Judith Cohen (1995, 196) for a parallel discussion of Judeo-Spanish song.

popular ethnography anthropomorphised the *shtetl* as encapsulating the essence of all East European Jewish life, recreating a world that had been destroyed (2001, 165), so post-war work on Yiddish song, affirmed of the ability of Yiddish song, as a repertory, to encapsulate the lives and history of East Ashkenazic Jewry. Indeed, folklorist-performer Ruth Rubin entitled her 1979 study of Yiddish folk song – still the only full-length English-language monograph on this topic – *Voices of a People*. She writes:

> Eastern European Yiddish folk song … reflects vividly the life of a community of many millions over a period of many generations. In the songs, we catch the manner of speech and phrase, the wit and humor, the dreams and aspirations, the nonsense, jollity, the pathos and struggle of an entire people (1979, 9).

Ruth Rubin herself, her life spanning almost the whole twentieth century (1906–99), became a symbol of the synthesis of performance and community work. Born in Bessarabia, she moved with her family to Canada at a young age, where she spoke Yiddish, English and French and attended the Yiddish supplementary school system. While she trained and worked as a stenographer, moving to New York in 1924, she studied music in evening classes. In her early twenties she published a volume of her own Yiddish poetry; following a wider interest in comparative folklore, her attention later turned to Yiddish folklore, with which she was occupied for the remainder of her life.[23] Rubin was a prolific collector and writer on Yiddish songs during the post-war decades, collecting over 2,000 songs, producing a substantial archival collection; she earned her doctorate in 1976 at the age of 70, and afterwards published a monograph on Yiddish song (*Voices of a People*, 1979).[24] Rubin's work consistently articulated her vision of Yiddish song as representative of the entire Yiddish nation. As Mlotek and Slobin note, this universalist conviction was reflected in her field methodology, which left little space for the acknowledgement of individualism among her singers, or to note the influence that their vastly different backgrounds might have had on their repertories (2007, xi, xiii).

Speaking during a documentary about her life and work produced by Cindy Marshall in 1986, she remarks:

> My focus from the beginning was – examining the songs as they reflect the life of the people. I found that in the Yiddish folk song, the people had poured out their feelings, which had no other place to go at that time. And this is what

---

[23]　For a full biography, see Mlotek and Slobin (2007).

[24]　An inventory of the Ruth Rubin Collection is held at YIVO in file ML 3776 R8. Copies of Rubin's collection are currently held by institutions including the Library of Congress, YIVO, the Rogers and Hammerstein Collection of Folkmusic at the New York Public Library, the Wayne State Archive of Eastern European Folksong in Detroit, and the Haifa Music Museum.

attracts me, what always amazes me, because the more I examine the material, [I find] the natural will to live, the natural wit, the wisdom.

Rubin's own position moved fluidly between performer and folklorist (Mlotek and Slobin 2007, introduction); indeed, she included herself as an unnamed informant on her collection of field recordings. This approach was propelled by her sense that Yiddish culture was in danger of loss. She gave lectures, formal and informal, all over the world, seeking to convince her audiences of the worth of the repertory. Rubin sang in Yiddish, unaccompanied, aligning herself with older performance traditions of folk materials; however, she lectured and wrote in English, attempting thus to bridge the gap between the generations. During Marshall's documentary she recalled:

> Some people call me a pioneer. I suppose I was the only one doing it, so that makes me a pioneer. But the pioneering part was, that I went with a Yiddish cultural baggage in English. And the Yiddish-speaking people were a little bit leery of that. I was looked upon askance because I was doing something that no-one else was doing and singing *a cappella*. No props, no lights, no costumes, no this, no that, and so it was very difficult, and I did it, really, alone.

Rubin's own flexible identity as folklorist and performer, coupled with her energy for the creation of an accessible yet 'authentic' performance experience enabled her performances to become intimate encounters, melding the products of folkloric study with nostalgic imagery. The vision of songs passed from mother or grandmother to child is frequently cited by those seeking to express a quintessential Yiddish cultural experience, as in the following two autobiographical accounts:

> She seldom indulged in attending any entertainments, but she delighted us by singing many old Yiddish songs of her girlhood, some of which I still remember … She was indeed the typical Yiddishe Mamma. (Bernard Homa [b. 1900] recalls his mother, B'racha Leah [Homa 1990, 24]).

> 'Dance!', call out my aunts with encouragement. 'You know how to dance!' And with this they all begin to clap their hands and sing. At first I just jump a little. But as the music grows louder and merrier, I dance with all my might. I dance for Sukkes, for sauerkraut, but mostly I just dance for pure joy [sings the melody of 'Der rebe elimelekh']. (Roslyn Bresnick-Perry [b. 1922] recalls her aunts and grandmother singing whilst making sauerkraut during the festival of Sukkes, in the *shtetl* in which she grew up in White Russia [Bresnick-Perry 1990, '*Sukkot* is for Sauerkraut']).

Compare the intimate, domestic imagery of the above accounts with the following extract from an autobiographical book by Brooklyn-based poet and translator Richard Fein, who recalls an experience not from his childhood, but from studying

Yiddish later in life. In the following extract, he describes an evening when, during his participation in the YIVO-Columbia summer programme, he and his fellow students gathered at Ruth Rubin's apartment for an evening of song:

> And so it was Ruth Rubin who first led me by the hand toward the Yiddish folk song, as if she sang for my ear alone. The clarity of her pronunciation of Yiddish words, at least to my grateful and unaccustomed ear, slowly made the songs more and more available to me. She is another *gilgul* of my grandmother (Fein 1986, 109).

The evening Fein describes was a more or less public event: a large group gathering as part of an academic programme. The imagery he uses, however, casts it as an intimate, nostalgic experience: he was 'led by hand', 'as if she sang for my ear alone'. Here, use of the word '*gilgul*' sheds light on his reading of the experience, referring to the mystical Jewish concept of the transmigration of a soul into a new body. With this word, he explicitly recasts his relationship with the folklorist, articulated by song, as a family experience, standing in for the close relationship he is unable to have with his Yiddish-speaking grandmother.

As his account continues, the distinction between Rubin as folklorist, Rubin as *folksmentsh* (representative of folk traditions) and Rubin as grandmother figure is further eroded:

> The packed room was plain, with little furniture. Most of us sprawled on the floor or sat on some chairs brought in from the kitchen. One window of the apartment faced south and west over the rooftops of Columbia University and framed a swatch of the steamy upper west side. The eyes then gazed toward the seemingly cool cliffs of the Palisades across the Hudson and lifted vaguely beyond toward the unseen space where America began.
>
> Grandmotherly, pedagogical and regal at the same time, and with an affection bestowed both on the listeners and the songs, Ruth Rubin carried no instrument but only a small, black loose-leaf book that she regularly consulted when choosing a song. She flipped the ringed pages seemingly not so much to look at a text as to help her decide which song she would next select, like a marriage broker of song detailing the attractions of her 'clients' for our consideration. She would introduce each of the songs with a few words: this song is one of many about women jilted by men; this children's nonsense song tells us something about the daily activities of Jews in Eastern Europe; this song marks a victory of fewer working hours won by the tailors. But the information was always less important than her rendition – unencumbered, keen. She sang as if she were sojourning among the tribe's photograph album – the images turning into jewels (Fein 1986, 108–9).

The nostalgic image painted by Fein of the 'grandmotherly' Rubin in the informal setting of her own apartment prolongs the picture of an intimate family relationship. Here, however, this family is expanded to encompass all of Yiddish-speaking Jewry. Fein uses the notion of a photograph album – the quintessential documentary record of family history and memory – to express the meaning that Rubin's songs hold for the whole 'tribe'. Rubin becomes the representative of the wider Old World: not only is she a grandmother figure, but also, in her action of choosing songs she is compared to another generic Old-World persona, the matchmaker. It is also telling that Fein describes Rubin's rendition as 'unencumbered'. Her seemingly direct, fluent contact with the Yiddish past stands in stark contrast to that of Fein and his fellow students, whose very presence on the YIVO/Columbia summer programme attests to a broken link in the transmission of Yiddish culture in their own families.

Just as the figure of the Yiddish folklorist could become invested with 'folk' qualities in the public imagination, conversely, the methodology of the folklorist – oral history and documentary recordings – could be domesticated by the wider Jewish public in its engagement with Yiddish repertoires and imagination of the Yiddish nation. The processes of recording and storage of Yiddish songs in archives – themselves yet another tangible representation of the Yiddish nation – has often been more visible than the recordings themselves, which have not often been released. The involvement of the public in the collection of folkloric material is nothing new: as discussed above, during the early years of the twentieth century, the St Petersburg Society for Jewish Folk Music and YIVO encouraged the general public to take part in the collection of Jewish folk song.[25] More recently, such collection projects have been sponsored by research institutions including YIVO, which established a Folksong Project during the 1970s, mobilising people to collect material from immigrants.[26] Aside from large organised projects, those involved professionally in Yiddish folklore have also frequently acted to encourage and facilitate individual song-collecting projects among the wider public.

A special 'music' issue (winter 1988) of *The Book Peddler/Der pakn-treger*, the newsletter of the National Yiddish Book Center, Amherst, MA, contains a substantial feature entitled 'Collecting Yiddish Folksongs: A Do-It-Yourself Guide'. Guest editor Henry Sapoznik writes:

> You don't need to be an 'expert' to launch an 'ethnographic expedition' and record Yiddish music on your own. All it takes is time, patience, a willingness to coax and to listen – and of course, a good quality portable tape recorder. You can start close to home: sit down with your own parents or grandparents, your aunts and uncles. Or perhaps make a visit to the local Jewish nursing home, gather in a circle with a group of older Jews, place a tape recorder (with a good microphone) on the table and ask them to take turns singing all the Jewish songs

---

[25]   See Soltes (1967) and Gottesman (2003) for discussion.

[26]   The aims of the YIVO folksong project are outlined by Kirshenblatt-Gimblett (1973).

they can remember. (Try to keep everyone from singing and talking at once – no small challenge in a roomful of older Jews but absolutely essential if you want your recordings to be comprehensible.) You'll provide the older folks with a wonderful afternoon, and you're likely to learn a lot and record many valuable songs in the process (1988a, 20).

The collection of folksongs is urged as a contribution to wider folksong scholarship; Sapoznik advises the budding folklorist that, 'in order to be of greatest value to future scholars, it is important that you document something about the background of each song: when, where, how and from whom it was recorded' (1988a, 20–21). To this end, a lengthy questionnaire by folklorist Barbara Kirshenblatt-Gimblett is reproduced as the final part of the feature.[27] Individuals choosing to collect songs are urged to send their tapes and completed questionnaires to the YIVO sound archive, and to share highlights of their work with other readers of *Der pakn-treger* via the Letters column, thus providing a forum for community recognition and celebration of contributions to the task of preservation.

Nevertheless, it is not only as a dispassionate contribution to folklore scholarship or as a community project that the wider public was drawn to collect folksong. Rather, at a time that those who remembered Eastern Europe were growing older, folksong collecting became a way to honour and preserve their voices; to re-frame the heritage of one individual as representative of an entire culture.

The *Pakn-treger* feature includes an article by one of these collectors, medical doctor Sheldon Benjamin, who recounts his collection of songs from his grandmother, Sarah Kaleh Benjamin. His language is emotional, seeing himself as individually responsible for the survival of a whole repertory, not just his grandmother's songs. Ironically, even in this case where the traditional paradigm of transmission – grandparent to grandchild – is in fact preserved, the metaphor of folklorism is such a persuasive agent of authenticity that the microphone necessarily mediates the transmission of songs between his grandmother and himself:

> I knew her life was finite. When she was gone, I thought, the Yiddish song, like Bubbe [Grandmother] and the shtetl she came from, would vanish forever. I was no longer just trying to learn the songs. I was trying to save them from extinction. For nearly fifteen years before her death, I never visited Bubbe without my tape recorder (Benjamin 1988, 21–2).

---

[27] This questionnaire was originally compiled in Yiddish for a YIVO project entitled *East European Folksong in Its Social Context: An Analysis of the Social Systematization of Folksong Performance* (Kirshenblatt-Gimblett 1988, 23).

The Yiddish Songbook: Building Collective Memories

Today, the large corpus of printed songbooks is one of the most publicly visible and widely circulated manifestations of professional engagement with Yiddish song during the post-war period. Despite the decline of Yiddish as a spoken language, during the period 1945 to 2008, over 150 new songbooks containing either exclusively Yiddish songs or a substantial amount of Yiddish material were published. This conservative figure is based upon books that appear in large archival collections in New York, Jerusalem and London, suggesting that a real estimate might be somewhat higher.[28] Nevertheless, the majority have not offered previously unavailable material to readers, nor have compilers particularly

Table 2.2   New Yiddish songbooks published between 1935 and 2005

Five-year period beginning	Number of songbooks found in library collections	Books whose principal language is:		
		Yiddish	Yiddish and other language(s)	Other language(s) only
1935	25	16	2	7
1940	13	11	1	1
1945	18	13	1	4
1950	17	6	3	8
1955	8	5	0	3
1960	16	6	4	6
1965	12	3	2	7
1970	20	6	3	11
1975	6	1	0	5
1980	12	3	1	8
1985	6	0	0	6
1990	11	0	1	10
1995	8	1	2	5
2000	11	1	5	5

Note: See note 28 below.

[28]   This survey is based upon extensive exploration of the collections of the following institutions: YIVO and other collections held at the Center for Jewish History, New York; the New York Public Library; the Jewish Theological Seminary, New York; Hebrew Union College, New York; the National Library of Israel; the British Library; the library of the Jewish Music Institute, London, and other smaller collections. For the purposes of this chapter, books containing at least five Yiddish songs (thus excluding sheet music), and of which songs in Yiddish constitute at least 20 per cent of the total contents, have been considered. Multiple editions or reprints of the same collection are not included, as these would skew the language data presented below. For full bibliographic details and contents of each songbook, see Wood (2004).

striven for textual authenticity in their material. Rather, they are collections offering an overview of 'typical' Yiddish songs, produced for use at home or in the community. In this corpus of songbooks, the role of folklorists in shaping Yiddish cultural memories is again clear. Here, rather than considering each song as a separate entity or as an exemplar of an abstract repertory, I will explore songbooks themselves as primary sources. Viewing songbooks as composite albums allows them to be seen principally as creative artefacts, situated within the milieu in which they were produced.

In their structure comprising 'frozen' cultural object and commentary, songbooks are reminiscent of other publications of similar structure, including photographic books. Jack Kugelmass comments:

> certain types of commercially created photo albums may play a role for large collectivities such as ethnic groups much like the role played by family albums for extended families. They celebrate group unity in the face of widespread dislocation, they provoke group memory, and they may even contribute to a collective dialogue on the nature of groups' patrimony and the perceived problem of cultural attenuation and social fragmentation (Kugelmass 1997, 31).

How is this collective dialogue instantiated? Through the act of selection and curation that they embody, songbooks play a role in constructing a core repertory of Yiddish songs which circulate within the wider Jewish community. While the generally conservative choice of songs included in printed collections may slow down the incorporation of new material into the mainstream, it also ensures the stability of a central Yiddish repertory and articulates a canon of cultural literacy. Nevertheless, it is not just the content of these books, but also the act of ownership that contributes to this dialogue of identity. Kugelmass continues, noting that 'for American Jews, a symbolic ecology of books constitutes not so much the individuality of the owner but a sense of membership in a collectivity, a vital link increasingly significant given the absence, or at least the fragmentation, of other communal institutions' (1997, 46).

Table 2.2, drawing on the survey of songbooks discussed above, shows new collections of Yiddish song published during each five-year period between 1935 and 2005, and details of the principal languages used for introductory material and commentaries:

Table 2.2 indicates that a steady stream of new songbooks was published throughout the pre- and post-war period, continuing into the twenty-first century. In contrast with the sudden destruction of Yiddish narrated by the organisation of the contents of these volumes, in this overall corpus slower processes of change in the Yiddish-speaking world are recorded. The decline in the proportion of books that are monolingual in Yiddish reflects the wider decline in fluency in the language during this period, paralleling the changing patterns of fluency in Yiddish schools discussed in the previous chapter. While the average number of publications per year has also declined over the seven decades covered in the survey, this does not necessarily represent such a steep decline in circulation of Yiddish songbooks, as only the first edition of each book is included in this table. Many older collections of Yiddish song have been reprinted during recent decades, both including the reissuing of pre-war material and new editions of more recent books. For example, Chana Mlotek's collection, *Mir trogn a gezang*, first published in 1972 and currently the most popular Yiddish songbook in Yiddishist circles, appeared in its fourth edition/seventh printing in 2000; the preface to this edition notes that to date almost 30,000 copies had been sold, a circulation unlikely to have been reached by pre-war songbooks (Mlotek 1972/2000, v). Further, new communication networks have facilitated the distribution of specialist publications to a wide, dispersed audience.

Songbooks and Their Narratives

Transforming songs into a printed text creates interpretative space: by means of forewords, notes to the songs and translations, a many-layered commentary upon the book's contents unfolds. Almost all post-war Yiddish songbooks supplement their song content with non-song material, mainly textual (forewords, introductions to individual songs, anecdotes and so on), and sometimes pictorial. Such material bridges Yiddish time past and present, forming a frame through which the songs are read. Songs tending to draw on disparate origins, and reflecting the gamut of Yiddish cultural pasthoods, are woven together into a coherent whole. The following discussion examines three popular songbooks, illustrating contrasting approaches to the use of narrative to frame collections of Yiddish songs.

Vinkovetzky, A., Kovner, A. and Leichter, S. (1983–1987) Anthology of Yiddish Folksongs. 4 vols. Jerusalem: Magnes Press

Vinkovetzky, Kovner and Leichter's collection, published by the Hebrew University in Jerusalem, represents the largest Yiddish song publication project undertaken in recent decades. The first four volumes contain 340 songs with melodies (see Table 2.1, above, for categories covered); three supplementary volumes edited by Sinai Leichter and published from 2000 to 2004, contain further collections of songs by Mordechai Gebirtig, Mark Warshavsky and Itzik Manger. The collection is trilingual, with prefatory material presented in English, Hebrew and Yiddish, and translations of songs into English and Hebrew included.

The roots of this publication lie in a folksong collection made by Aharon Vinkovetzky. Born in 1903 in the Ukraine, Vinkovetzky was brought up in a traditional Jewish environment, taking part in Yiddish cultural activities. He later moved to Leningrad where he studied and worked as a shipbuilder until 1963; at the same time he devoted himself to researching Yiddish folksongs and translating these into Russian. In Leningrad, 1969, he produced six volumes of songs, a collection totalling 244 songs, presented in the form of spiral-bound photocopied sheets. He moved to Israel in 1977, bringing his collections with him, and in 1979 approached the Hebrew University with a suggestion to publish an anthology based on his collection. A public committee was established to undertake this project, 'all of whom were inspired by the desire to preserve and to re-vitalize something of the cultural and folkloristic heritage of Eastern European Jewry that is no more' (Vinkovetzky, Leichter and Kovner 1983, vol. 1, vii).

The first volume of the collection contains a substantial written introduction by poet Abba Kovner (1918–87). Born in Sevastopol, Kovner was brought up in Vilna. During the war he was the leader of the left-wing Zionist youth movement in the Vilna ghetto, later becoming commander of the principal resistance group in the ghetto.[29] In 1945 he went to Palestine, but when he attempted to return to Europe he was caught and detained by the British in Egypt. Upon his release, he joined kibbutz Ein haHoresh; he was involved in an underground organisation which helped to bring hundreds of thousands of Jews illegally to Palestine before Israeli statehood was achieved, and fought in Israel's war of independence. He spent the rest of his life working as a writer, publishing several volumes of poetry; he also testified at the public trial of Adolf Eichmann in 1961.[30] Entitled 'Folksongs of a Vanished Era', Kovner's introduction moves between poetry and prose, outlining a picture of Jewish life in Eastern Europe by weaving together sources from Yiddish cultural life: song texts, Yiddish poetry and liturgical references. The history of Yiddish song is contextualised in relation to Kovner's own personal account of history and loss; the specificity of his experiences – memories timed to the hour and specific people and places recalled – testifies not only to the enduring importance and immediacy of these experiences but also, in their very uniqueness, to the existence of countless other individual accounts, each of which might also stand on its own for the lost Yiddish culture.

Kovner's account portrays his experiences of a living Yiddish culture in Eastern Europe from his present standpoint, '37 years, 21 days and 6 hours' (Vinkovetzky, Leichter and Kovner 1983, vol. 1, xiii) since his escape from the Vilna ghetto. The loss and distance of Yiddish culture is emphasised in physical terms: Vilna is not just 10,000 miles distant but '10,000 miles' walk' (1983, vol. 1, xiii) from Kovner's kibbutz. This physical distance mirrors the conceptual distance of Yiddish culture from the Israeli mainstream. While a significant proportion of those who settled in Israel came from Eastern Europe, and made a large contribution to Israeli culture, Yiddish culture, including song, did not thrive in modern Israel. Seroussi (1995, 116–19), Hirshberg (1995), Zerubavel (1995) and others note that cultural forms reflecting diaspora life were not considered appropriate by those aiming to create a new type of Jewish life. Instead, from the early years of the Zionist Yishuv, pioneers created a repertory of new Hebrew-language folksongs to provide a soundtrack for the new nation, aiming 'to extol the spirit of the pioneer settlers,

---

[29] The activities of partisans in the Vilna ghetto are outlined in the documentary film *Partisans of Vilna* (Kempner and Waletzky 1986), in which Kovner is the main speaker.

[30] Biographical details from the *Encylopedia Judaica* and from Kovner's biography in Vinkovetzky, Leichter and Kovner (1983, vol. 1).

whether rural or urban; to depict the romanticized scenery of the land; to enhance the revival of Hebrew through settings of both biblical texts and modern lyrics; and to unify people through communal singing' (Hirshberg 1995, 146).

By the end of the twentieth century, Yiddish song was not entirely absent from Israel: veteran Israeli singer Chava Alberstein, born in Poland to Yiddish-speaking parents, has recorded several albums of Yiddish songs since the early 1970s including a collaboration with the Klezmatics; Yiddish clubs including Jerusalem's 'Yung Yidish' host performances of Yiddish song; and more recently a modest Yiddish music revival has taken place among a younger Israeli generation, notably including Tel Aviv band Oy Division. Silber (1997) observes that a revival of Yiddish culture in Israel since the 1980s was aided by a law passed by the Knesset in 1996 encouraging public awareness of Yiddish culture. Nevertheless, as Flam (1997) observed, few Israeli singers perform in Yiddish, and none do so exclusively; further, few American Yiddish recordings are widely available in Israel. Illustrating a widespread Israeli view of Yiddish culture, Flam asserts:

> In Israel where Hebrew is the national language Yiddish symbolises the diaspora and the Holocaust. Therefore, Yiddish songs are symbolic and not an integral element of Israeli culture. Yiddish songs are sung mainly in commemoration ceremonies or in their Hebrew version. ... Israelis are not looking for an expression of their past, and do not need to distinguish themselves from the gentiles or remind the 'others' of their past. Therefore Israelis have no need for Yiddish singing except for its limited nostalgic meaning (1997, 1, 2, 6).

Kovner's introduction to this volume, however, challenges this limited relationship with the past. He closes:

> For the Eternity of Israel will not fail. And who knoweth the way of the spirit? In modern society, whether general or Jewish, and whether the Jewish society is dispersed among other nations or has its shape in the State of Israel, changes of spirit are producing people who will repeatedly ask about their origins and the root of their identity. A renewed acquaintance with folksong is capable not only of providing a nostalgic feeling, but – and I am sure of this – of restoring to modern man the voice of his forefathers, which will never become extinguished:

> *'Un mir haltn zikh in eynem,*
> *Oy-oy, zikh in eynem,*
> *S'iz azoyns nito bay keynem-*
> *Oy-oy, oy-oy!* '[31]

---

[31]   Text from 'Ale brider', a popular Yiddish song adapting a poem by folk poet Morris Winchevsky. Translation: 'And we stick together, oy, stick together, Nobody else does this like us, oy!'

> *Kibbutz Ein Hahoresh, Elul 5740*[32] (Vinkovetzky, Leichter and Kovner 1983, vol. 1, xlii)

Kovner's distinction between 'modern man' and his 'forefathers' here reflects the sharp sense of separation between pre- and post-Holocaust Jewish life seen also in the structure of the book (see discussion above). Nevertheless, giving a sense of historical continuity absent from Flam's commentary, he suggests that just as in the diaspora, there is an important place in modern Israel for Yiddish culture, here as elsewhere epitomised by folksong. This message is embodied in the very creation of this book under the auspices of Israel's oldest university, and is reinforced in the biographical sketch of Vinkovetsky provided in the book, in which Israel is portrayed as a utopia providing the resources to fulfil dreams, even those centred on Yiddish:

> In Israel, Vinkovetsky devoted his collection and research activity to the field of Yiddish folk songs. His searches in communal and private libraries enriched him with many songs that were not known in Soviet Russia. His untiring efforts and dreams of many years were now fulfilled in the publication of the four-volume 'Anthology of Yiddish folk songs'.[33]

Silverman, J. (1983/1999) The Yiddish Song Book. Lantham, NY: Scarborough House

The smallest in scale of the three song collections currently under discussion, Silverman's *Yiddish Song Book* is widely available: I picked up my copy of this American publication in a Jerusalem bookshop. Its re-issuing in a second edition testifies to its continuing popularity. The songbook includes 113 Yiddish songs with melody, transliterated Yiddish and English translation. If Kovner's introductory narrative emphasised his individual journey from Vilna to Israel, and from the Holocaust to freedom, the narrative introducing Silverman's volume is shaped around the experiences of an American Jewish family over three generations. Even the title 'Forshpayz' (Hors d'oeuvre) of the introduction to the first edition evokes the sound of *heymish*, down-home Yiddish:

> Yiddish has always been a family affair.

> In the Old Country you spoke Russian or Polish or Hungarian or Rumanian or Lithuanian or whatever on the 'outside' – but when you came home and closed the door, it was *mame loshn*, the mother tongue.

---

[32] August/September 1980.

[33] No English translation of the biographies in this volume is provided. Translation from Yiddish mine.

Then came the great exodus – greater than in biblical times, the Diaspora raised to the nth degree. As the thousands passed through Ellis Island they carried their *yiddishkayt* with them in their wicker baskets and battered valises. But slowly the *yiddishkayt* began slipping away. The children of the immigrants of the 1880s and 1890s were the doughboys in France in World War I. The children of the immigrants of the teens and twenties stood on the breadlines of the Depression and later were the GIs who liberated Buchenwald. *Yiddishkayt* stopped there. What sixty years of emigration was slowly eroding came to a terrible, nightmarish, inconceivable end in just six short years. The fountain was cut off at its source. And yet, and yet …

The wellspring of *yiddishkayt* runs deep. Maybe the mainstream was dried up, but the tributaries remain.

Consider this: my mother, Helen, who came to America from the *shtetl* of Dubrovno in Byelorussia as a teenager in 1913, and my son David, who was born in New York City fifty-six years later, both contributed directly to the writing of this book.

My mother's contribution consisted of her familiarity with much of the material itself and her knowledge of Yiddish as well as her willingness, her eagerness to find just the right word or shade of interpretation in the translations. My son's contribution was unique and, in a way, touching, for he, at the age of eleven, in his fourth year of studies at the Westchester Children's *Shul* [Yiddish secular school] in New York, was able to look up Yiddish words in the Yiddish-English dictionary – something that his father, who learned Yiddish by ear, was not able to do until recently.

The circle is unbroken. Yiddish has always been a family affair – an extended family affair as well … (Silverman 1999, xi).

Here, then, the Silverman family story is framed as a microcosm of the history of Yiddish. Unlike Kovner, Silverman emphasises the continuity of Yiddish culture. The mainstream may have 'dried up', but 'the circle is unbroken'. This image of a continuing tradition is heightened through the interspersion of 37 black-and-white photographs throughout the songbook. Silverman notes:

With two notable exceptions, the photographs in this book are a sort of family album. They show scenes from the lives of the maternal and paternal branches of my family and my wife's family, both in Europe and America, as well as the fruits of those branches: my children and their friends. They span five generations and about one hundred years – from beards to blue jeans, from Bessarabia to the Bronx, and from White Russia to Westchester (1999, xiii).

The 'family affair' of Yiddish is, then, continued through the book. The pictures themselves range from formal sepia portraits to postcards, to snapshots of children playing. (The 'two notable exceptions' of which Silverman speaks represent the period of the Holocaust: a group of pictures of Jewish life in and around Warsaw, 1938, and others taken in Vilna, 1943.) Many photographs are tied thematically to adjacent songs. An informal shot of Silverman's children grinning behind a set of Chanukah candles accompanies Morris Rosenfeld's 'O, ir kleyne likhtelekh' (O, you little candle lights); a group of women carrying banners on a 1930s May Day parade illustrates Dovid Edelshtat's 'Arbeter froyen' (Women workers); a picture of a train station beside a group of houses in Warsaw's suburbs, 1938 – a handful of people milling around the tracks which reach into the foreground of the picture – forms, with post-Holocaust hindsight, an ominous counterpart to 'Zay-zhe mir gezunt' (Farewell).

Through the mixing of family and Holocaust photographs and the juxtaposition of pictures and songs, Silverman's own 'family album' is both extended and bound to the wider history of Yiddish culture. As in Kovner's account, individual histories stand in for collective experience. If Kovner's story represents the personal pain and loss of the Holocaust survivor, then, in including the types of pictures which form the core of most family collections, Silverman's family becomes a prototype of the American Yiddish experience. Analogised by pictures, songs are no longer a cultural product 'out there' but are drawn into the intimate recesses of family identity and experience.

Mlotek, E.G. (Chana) (1972/2000) Mir trogn a gezang: Favorite Yiddish Songs (Fourth edition). New York, NY: Workmen's Circle
Mlotek, E.G. (Chana) and Mlotek, J. (Yosl) (1988) Pearls of Yiddish Song. New York, NY: Education Department of the Workmen's Circle
Mlotek, E.G. (Chana) and Mlotek, J. (Yosl) (1995) Songs of Generations: New Pearls of Yiddish Song. New York, NY: Workmen's Circle

In 1970, Yiddish folklorists Chana and Joseph Mlotek began a column in the Yiddish *Forverts* newspaper which provided a forum for enquiries and information about Yiddish poetry and songs. They were 'mobbed by interest' from readers.[34] Archived at YIVO, a large collection of correspondence between the Mloteks and their readers, largely in Yiddish, testifies to the importance of this column to their correspondents, who often write at length, citing personal family stories, or lamenting their own weak grasp of the Yiddish language, while requesting information about favourite or lost songs. Conversely, the correspondence also served as a tool for collecting new songs, or new versions of songs from readers.

Yiddish music continues to be a family activity for the Mloteks. Unlike Silverman's picture of Yiddish song as a private, domestic affair, however, this family's exceptional engagement with Yiddish cultural life, and in particular with

---

[34]   Chana Mlotek, interview with the author, New York, 9 August 2001.

music, places the Mloteks in a prominent position in today's American Yiddishist scene.[35] Chana Mlotek is music archivist at YIVO; before his death in 2000, her husband Yosl Mlotek was a long-time director of the Workmen's Circle Yiddish school system and an editor, poet, folklorist and author; his obituary in *Forverts* described him as 'one of the last lions and defenders of the Yiddish word'.[36] Among his many Yiddish musical activities, their son, Zalmen Mlotek, is currently co-artistic director of Folksbiene Yiddish Theater in New York City. Following in the family tradition, Zalmen's two sons have also appeared on the Yiddish stage in productions including the Folksbiene's popular show *Kids and Yiddish*.

Since the 1970s, the Mloteks have collected thousands of songs, and have published much material, including the three volumes listed above, which are currently used as standard sources of repertory by many musicians. Between them, these volumes contain some 354 songs, each presented with melody, chord symbols and capsule English translation. The process of selection of songs published in the books is strongly grounded in cultural practice. In the introduction to the fourth edition of the first volume, *Mir trogn a gezang!*, Chana Mlotek writes:

> The songs in this book represent a sampling of folk and popular songs, many of which are scattered in various song collections; some appear in very rare and inaccessible collections; and some were never before published. Folk songs comprise about one-third of this volume and were selected mainly on the basis of popularity and sometimes for their historical significance. Needless to say, they are only representative of the vast, rich treasure of Yiddish folk songs. The selection here was made not only on the basis of personal preference, but in the knowledge that they are favorites of many who sing these songs.

> Most of the songs represent the repertoire that we, second-generation American Jews, loved to sing in summer camps, at May 1st demonstrations, and at social gatherings. We learned many of these songs from friends who came here after the war, for whom these songs had been favorites in Poland and other East European communities destroyed by the Nazis. We came to love these songs, and made them part of our 'song-repertoire'. Now, we are passing them along to our children and friends (Mlotek 1972/2000, viii).

Like that of Silverman, then, Mlotek's introductory narrative describes a family involvement in Yiddish song. Here, however, this is contextualised within a wider milieu of Yiddish culture. By contrast with accounts such as Kovner's which emphasise the historical rupture caused by the Holocaust, in Mlotek's case this chasm is bridged via the continued involvement of her family and friends in an unbroken Yiddish culture; songs shared in the wake of destruction

---

[35]   See Jacobson (2004, 143) for discussion.

[36]   *Forverts*, 7 July 2000. Downloaded from http://www.forward.com/issues/2000/00.07.07/ed.html, 23 May 2002.

became reintegrated into family life. While very little material written after 1945 is included in the three volumes – reinforcing the reading of the Holocaust as an end-point of Yiddish creativity – the continuing Yiddish culture of which the Mloteks are part is nevertheless reflected in the contents of these volumes, in the influence of present popularity upon the inclusion of material. This includes both material favoured over the past decades by American Yiddish socialist groups and that popular within today's Yiddish culture, drawn from the Mloteks' *Forverts* column and from material popularised at new Yiddish cultural festivals such as KlezKamp.

Essentialising Yiddish Histories

In framing their collections of Yiddish songs within personal or family narratives, the compilers of all these song collections privilege memory over history as a paradigm for the communication of Yiddish song to a contemporary audience. Further, in assimilating a large number of songs into a single historical frame they write against the diversity of histories represented by the songs in their respective collections. Theatre, folk and art songs are presented side by side; sophisticated poetry is rarely distinguished from folk rhymes (or if it is, for example by the Mloteks, this is done in an understated way). This stylistic assimilation is also reflected in the music itself: in all of the books, songs are all presented in a standard format with melody, text and guitar chords. While this assimilation *is* representative of today's performance practice – solo singers, choirs and klezmer bands frequently adopt songs of diverse origins into their own performance repertory – it does not represent the original performance context of the songs. Rather, this style of presentation acts both to denude art and theatre songs of their original complex musical arrangements, and, conversely, to include accompaniments for songs which originally had none.

Mirroring processes seen in the work of the post-war folksong collectors discussed above, this stylistic assimilation reflects a general tendency in America for divisions within Yiddish culture to become smoothed over as Jews from diverse areas and backgrounds came together in immigrant communities. Feingold notes that the composite picture of a pan-Yiddish culture is an intrinsically American phenomenon:

> Forgotten by many students of the American Jewish experience is that only in America could the composite eastern European Jew be found by reading the Yiddish press or attending the Yiddish theater. Jews from Kiev, Riga, Warsaw, Krakow and everywhere in between sat together in that audience as they never did in their separate regional locales in Europe. It seemed like the absorbent new American society was determined finally to unify the Jews before totally dissolving their distinctive culture. The conflict between 'Bayer' and 'Pollack,'

'Litvak' and 'Galitzianer' first became subjects for Jewish humor and finally for memories (Feingold 1996, 58).

The primacy of collective memory over historiography as a paradigm for the representation of Yiddish cultural history in songbooks is even more evident where nostalgic imagery and historical detail come into conflict. For example, on occasion, the placing of songs in juxtaposition with extramusical material may override, intentionally or unintentionally, the literal meaning or documented history of a song. In Silverman's *Yiddish Song Book* (1983/1999, discussed above) at first glance, a photograph of an elderly gentleman relaxing on a rocking chair on a sunny wooden veranda, one leg crossed over the other, seems a suitable complement to the song 'Mayn rue plats' (My resting place). However, it is not until one reads Silverman's translation of Morris Rosenfeld's text that one realises that the poet's bitterly expressed resting place is not where flowers grow but 'where lives are wasted in the factory' (1999, 164), reflecting a harsh reality of immigrant Jewish life absent from the photograph.

A more extreme example may be seen in Sol Zim's *The Joy of Jewish Memories Songbook* (1984). Offering a book of 'nostalgic melodies in contemporary settings', the large majority of which are Yiddish songs, Zim writes, 'I have taken some liberties in altering some of the music to fit many of the new English texts. In many instances, I have kept the original YIDDISH LYRIC as part of the text so as not to lose the Jewish nostalgia. While I did not use literal translation of each word, I have retained the essence of each song' (Zim 1984, introduction)

What is this 'nostalgia' and 'essence' of which Zim speaks? The first song in this collection, 'Rozhinkes mit mandlen' (Raisins and almonds), is today one of the best known and most popular Yiddish songs, and is often cited as an archetypical Yiddish lullaby. In fact, 'Rozhinkes mit mandlen' was written by Yiddish theatre pioneer and composer Abraham Goldfaden in 1880 as part of his play *Shulamis*; the refrain is adapted from a Yiddish folk song. Although the authorship of the song is noted at its opening, at the end Zim glosses the song 'One of the sweetest lullabies of all time, passed on from parent to child as a blessing and prayer for future well being', a subtext barely consistent with either Goldfaden's text or the song's Yiddish theatre origin. While Zim presents the original Yiddish side by side with his English 'translation', his version has little to do with Goldfaden's original. The protagonist of the song is changed from a woman to a man; the aspiration of a mother for her son to learn a living by trading is changed to the aspiration of a father for his son to live a religious life. Zim's whole text adopts the language of nostalgia: 'sung by your *bobe* and *zede* [grandmother and grandfather]', 'a melody so sweet it has lived on for years', 'o how sweet to be a Jew'.

Nevertheless, Zim's interpretation of this song (which reflects his approach to this book as a whole) does not stem from ignorance or lack of immersion in the Yiddish world – according to his biography in this volume, he studied with Yiddish theatre composer Sholem Secunda and with cantor Moshe Koussevitzky. Rather, it points to an alternative set of values: instead of aiming for musical or historical accuracy, the value of these songbooks lies in the spaces they create for commentary and for risk-free interaction with material from the past, allowing elements of this material to be incorporated into contemporary Jewish culture, where authenticity lies in the recreation of community narratives, rather than in abstract textual, musical or historical accuracy.

Memory, Narrative and Creativity

'The power of collective memory', writes historian Yael Zerubavel, 'does not lie in its accurate, systematic, or sophisticated mapping of the past, but in establishing basic images that articulate and reinforce a particular ideological stance' (Zerubavel 1995, 8). In the case of Yiddish song, an ideological move towards salvage and memorialisation was quickly and pervasively instantiated during the post-war period, providing a robust rejoinder to the general decline of spoken Yiddish in America. Only three decades after Katsherginski's impassioned post-Holocaust defence of the collection of all available folklore, an exchange of letters in the Yiddish *Forward* newspaper in 1978 roundly – and publicly – dismissed the questions of a reader who – seeking publication of his own original Yiddish material in the newspaper – asked 'Who needs it? … Who is interested in the forgotten songs which we once sang?'[37]

A heterogeneous network of American Jews took upon themselves the responsibility of preserving the European Jewish Yiddish musical legacy: engaging with Yiddish culture in itself became a 'gesture of rebuilding or memorialization' (Shandler 2006, 18). The shape in which this legacy reappeared as a printed canon reflected the coalescence of a number of narrative strands. The parameters by which material was classified were inherited from late nineteenth- and early twentieth-century folklorists; the distribution of this material among a dispersed diasporic population was facilitated by industrial processes: since the mid-nineteenth century, the products of art and culture have been increasingly available for consumption in mass-produced, physical form, starting with the printed word and moving onto recorded sound, photography and, later, digital materials.

Nevertheless, while the formats in which cultural materials were produced show significant continuity with pre-war processes, the narratives that framed this material emphasised disjuncture and distance. With the ever-growing temporal distance between contemporary Jewish life and pre-Holocaust Europe, cultural heritage became reshaped into a text-mediated canon, and allowed space for commentaries that creatively bridged the gap between today's American Jewish life and pre-war Yiddish culture. Song collections and recordings were both shaped and re-read through post-war narrative lenses and the canonic imagery of popular fictive-ethnographic representations of Jewish Eastern Europe. These narratives further enable individual and family stories to be assimilated into

---

[37] Correspondence quoted anonymously by Hurvitz (1986, 2).

collective memories, leading to a cohesive sense of a historically and culturally grounded community.

This mediation might be read as a specific response to the lack of traditional channels for musical transmission in disrupted postwar Ashkenazi Jewish life. Nevertheless, processes in Yiddish culture also continue to reflect and build upon wider changes in the mediation of culture and history, both within and outside the Jewish world. In his influential 1994 essay 'Rupture and Reconstruction', historian Haym Soloveitchik observes that during the post-war decades, authenticity in Orthodox Judaism consensually became located in formal education and in texts rather than in mimetic traditions of practice. This resulted in the centralisation of authority in a canon of texts and selected interpreters, replacing a broad distribution of cultural authority among family members, mentors and institutions. By contrast, discussing the Reform movement, Mordecai Waxman discusses the professionalisation of the rabbinate: 'the rabbinic role is to be the representative of Judaism, the observer of Judaism, the propounder of Judaism' (1977, 182)

Both these processes are mirrored in the contemporary Yiddish world: the textualisation and canonisation of Yiddish culture, and the professionalisation of engagement with Yiddish song. Today's folklorists, academics, compilers and teachers play the roles of cultural representatives, standing in for a world lost to the observer, and providing an address to which questions about Yiddish culture could be addressed given the lack of surviving family members. Like the music camps discussed in Chapter 1, the representations of the Yiddish collective in these books are utopic, allowing the simultaneous expression of, in Soloveitchik's words, both rupture and reconstruction. Within this framework, nevertheless, lie the expressive spaces within which continuing creativity is shaped.

PART II
Yiddish Song and the
'Klezmer Revival'

Chapter 3

From Local to Global: A New Stage for Yiddish Song

The first part of this book focused on a cluster of practices involving Yiddish song embedded in a contemporary Yiddish cultural community.[1] This community articulates continuity with the Yiddish-speaking Jewish society of Ashkenazi Central and Eastern Europe and an ideological commitment to the preservation of its language and culture. The nature of this cultural heritage has repeatedly been re-imagined in the Yiddishist community in North America, encompassing both text and practice. New social and educational contexts allow the same material to be *lived* through embodied participation; new paradigms of recording and publication allow Yiddish culture to be packaged and handed down to new generations as heritage.

Nevertheless, during the past three decades, these spaces of participatory Yiddish culture have been joined by a parallel musical movement that has catapulted the contemporary performance of Yiddish song to international visibility. A revival, or revitalisation, of interest in East European Jewish music has created a public stage for Yiddish song as a *musical* phenomenon, performed by professional musicians participating in transnational and commercial musical networks alongside local protagonists addressing insider audiences. Consensually labelled the 'klezmer revival', this movement marked a new conception of the European Jewish musical heritage and a new coinage of the term 'klezmer'. In the Yiddish-speaking world, the term 'klezmer' was applied specifically to Jewish itinerant professional musicians playing an array of local and cosmopolitan instrumental repertories known collectively as *klezmorim* (the Hebrew '*kli zemer*' from which the Yiddish word derives literally means 'vessel of song'). These professional musicians played instrumental music primarily for weddings and other community events and celebrations. However, as Mark Slobin has noted, in the revival scene, 'klezmer' became an umbrella term for a reimagined genre, used by ensembles whose performances included diverse repertories, both instrumental and vocal, from the Yiddish-speaking Jewish world, often fused with elements from modern popular musics and joined by new compositions (Slobin 2002a, 1).

Indeed, early in the revival, some musicians were concerned about whether the music they were playing could accurately be termed klezmer: this material was certainly broader than the repertory of any single Old World musician (see

---

[1]   A previous version of this chapter appeared as: Abigail Wood (2007c) 'The Multiple Voices of American Klezmer'. *Journal of the Society for American Music* 1:3, 367–92. I am grateful to the Society for American Music for permission to reprint material from this article.

Kirshenblatt-Gimblett, 2002). The choice of the term klezmer, however, was not only convenient but also helped to locate the klezmer revival as something new, distinct from other contemporary approaches to the Yiddish cultural heritage. Indeed, many of the klezmer pioneers of the 1970s and 1980s initially arrived at klezmer via their involvement in the Balkan folk music scene or in American 'roots' musics, including bluegrass, rather than via the Yiddish cultural world. Mark Slobin has observed that 'as foundational klezmer figures have always admitted, the folk revival sensibility and professional background of performers was key to the emergence of klezmer on the American scene in the 1970s' (Slobin 2002a, 32).[2]

In seeking to define a general theory of music revivals, Tamara Livingston comments:

> Music revivals can be defined as social movements which strive to 'restore' a musical system believed to be disappearing or completely relegated to the past for the benefit of contemporary society. The common thread between these seemingly diverse phenomena is the overt cultural and political agenda expressed by the revivalists themselves. Through the re-creation of a past music 'system', … revivalists position themselves in *opposition* to aspects of the contemporary cultural mainstream, align themselves with a particular historical lineage, and offer a cultural alternative in which legitimacy is grounded in reference to authenticity and historical fidelity (1999, 66).

The klezmer revival is a close-to-paradigmatic illustration of the model of revival Livingston describes (indeed, Livingston illustrates her comments with, among others, klezmer pioneers Zev Feldman and Andy Statman). The revived klezmer music was not a Jewish musical mainstream but became a musical alternative to those dissatisfied with mainstream American and Israeli forms of Jewish musical expression (see, for example, London 2002).

In turn, this revivalist sentiment paved the way for the entrance of song into the klezmer canon. If stylistic authenticity was considered by many of the new klezmer musicians to be located in the Old World or Jewish America of the early twentieth century, the context for the performance of the revived klezmer music was modelled not specifically on Yiddish cultural traditions but on the wider 'roots' or, later, world music scene. Song entered the klezmer repertory as part of a wider pattern of change common to many modernised folk repertoires, which included the juxtaposition of material that was formerly geographically, temporally, functionally and stylistically diverse (see Bohlman 1988, ch. 8).

This gathering of diverse repertoires is one of the clearest markers of change between Old World and revived klezmer music, reflecting the changing contexts of klezmer from a culturally embedded, primarily functional music to the modern concert stage. By contrast with the purely instrumental ensembles of the Old World *klezmorim*, parallel vocal repertoires, mainly in Yiddish, are a core component of

---

[2]   See also Livingston (1999) for a theoretical discussion of revivalist ideology.

the repertory of many of today's klezmer ensembles. The majority of prominent klezmer bands include a singer, or at least have worked with one. This is not to detract from those bands that did focus – and continue to focus today – on purely instrumental music, but rather to acknowledge that many of the most prominent ensembles, both early in the revival (including the Klezmorim, Kapelye and the Klezmer Conservatory Band) and in later years (including the Klezmatics, Brave Old World, the Strauss-Warschauer Duo and the Flying Bulgar Klezmer Band) have featured vocalists from their inception, and have performed both vocal and instrumental numbers. Not only is the klezmer revival the most prominent context for the performance of Yiddish song today, but, vice versa, song has become integral to the klezmer scene, providing an important medium for musical and cultural creativity.

The history and trajectories of this revival/revitalist movement have been widely discussed by both scholars and practitioners (see, among others, Sapoznik 1999, Slobin 2000 and 2002a, and Rogovoy 2000).[3] The question of novelty versus historicity in the klezmer revival has been subject to particular debate. A number of musicians assert that they regarded their (re)discovery of klezmer music in the 1970s as something new – 'utterly contemporary', rather than a continuation of a historical genre. Others protest that klezmer music had never died. This newness is clearly echoed in the adoption or flowering of new or hybrid contexts for the transmission and performance of Yiddish music, such as the KlezKanada festival described above. Others objected to the term *revival*: as Barbara Kirshenblatt-Gimblett has observed, some argued that klezmer music had never fully disappeared, and that contemporary engagement with the repertory should be seen as a continuation of previous cultural practices, a reading consonant with the close relationship between core revivalist musicians and the established Yiddishist institutions described in the opening chapters of this book.

Positions taken in these debates illuminate ideological positions, anxieties and discourses of musical authenticity – themselves located as a late twentieth-century phenomenon by Taruskin, Butt and others – more than they define or delineate specific musical practices. Nevertheless, reading contemporary Yiddish cultural production through the lens of historicity tends to overemphasise the importance of internal debates about the enduring viability of Yiddish language and culture. In *Adventures in Yiddishland*, Jeffrey Shandler describes performance (festivals, concerts, theatre and more) as paradigmatic of the state of 'postvernacular' Yiddish culture:

> Singing, reciting, lecturing, or even conversing in Yiddish is no longer something one simply does (as presumably had once been the case). Rather, it is something one elects and arranges to do, one rehearses, studies, and appreciates; Yiddish

---

[3] Documentary films covering the early years of the klezmer revival include Michal Goldman, dir. *A Jumpin' Night in the Garden of Eden*, First Run Features, 1987 and Simon Broughton, dir. *Fiddlers on the Hoof*, BBC, 1989.

speech has been professionalized, aestheticized, academized and ritualized ... Implicit in every contemporary Yiddish performance, therefore, is a test of linguistic viability (2006, 153–4).

Viewed in linguistic terms, there is little to argue with here. Yet musical practice is more than just spoken language, and the klezmer revival participates in discourses of musical presenthood beyond the internal vista of the Yiddish language. The norms of the transnational music industry into which the klezmer revival has been drawn allow for alternative models of fluency and authenticity, propelled not only by 'insider' ideology, but also by a market-driven need for novelty and innovation.

Song occupies a position of tension between these two conceptions of the klezmer revival. As a musical form it is subject to the same processes of performance and arrangement as purely instrumental pieces. As a texted form, however, it also invokes debates about fluency and comprehension – and serves as a discursive space where these debates can creatively be addressed. Song texts play a particularly important role in helping to create and develop the ontological frame within which each ensemble presents its music. Together with other discursive material, including liner notes (in which song lyrics usually appear in translation), album iconography and onstage patter, songs offer a space for the explicit development of extramusical ideas surrounding each band and its music.

In the following four chapters, I explore this discursive space, suggesting that it offers a new perspective from which to consider changing regimes of fluency in Yiddish culture. In this chapter, following an introductory description of the entrance of song into the new klezmer canon, I focus on the musical practices and products of a constellation of vocalists who have occupied particularly prominent places in the 'klezmer revival' as performers and teachers. Michael Alpert, Lorin Sklamberg and Adrienne Cooper; all were involved in Yiddish music from the early years of the revival and have an extensive recorded legacy. I consider their work as members of prominent klezmer bands, illustrating a range of different approaches to the contemporary performance of Yiddish music. All three ensembles fall towards the innovative, experimental end of the klezmer spectrum, explicitly using song to express what Slobin has called an 'aesthetic, sometimes communal, vision' of a past-rooted contemporary Yiddish culture (Slobin 2000, 3). I suggest that song lyrics, melody, vocal style and packaging are key elements in a critical evaluation of the narratives and cultural politics employed by these musicians. The subsequent three chapters are thematic, exploring the boundaries of contemporary Yiddish musical space; the reappearances of Alpert, Sklamberg and Cooper and their colleagues in a variety of creative projects serves as a strand linking their personal musical journeys to the wider dynamics of the revival scene, and indicating the close network of connections among its most prominent protagonists.

Song Enters the Klezmer Revival

Like the contents of the songbooks described in Chapter 2, the vocal repertories brought under the klezmer rubric draw eclectically from different areas of Yiddish cultural life. Folk song and pseudo-folk song rub shoulders with *badkhones* (the improvised rhymes of a wedding jester), political and workers' songs by popular folk-poets, religious songs (including some from the Hasidic tradition), songs from the Yiddish theatre, which had flourished in both Europe and America since the late nineteenth century, and popular songs sold as sheet music in America, together with parallel East Ashkenazi religious vocal traditions including cantorial music, liturgical chant and Hasidic song (all primarily using Hebrew texts but musically related to other co-territorial Jewish musics).

Traditionally, most forms of Yiddish folk song were unaccompanied, domestic repertories; Yiddish theatre music represented commercial popular entertainment. Klezmer music, by contrast, was the music of communal Jewish celebrations: largely music for dancing, together with non-dance genres including music for listening and pieces associated with particular parts of the Jewish wedding ritual. This said, the combination of instrumental and vocal music within the Yiddish musical sphere was not entirely an innovation of the klezmer revival. At Old World weddings, klezmer musicians were joined by the *badkhn*, a wedding jester who acted as emcee and sang improvised rhymes in between musical numbers. The Yiddish theatre, itself dominated by musical numbers, and American popular Yiddish music offered models for songs with band accompaniment. Mickey Katz, a popular Jewish comedian who recorded Yiddish-accented parodies of American songs during the 1950s and '60s also included a klezmer-style instrumental 'break' in each of his songs (see Kun 1999, 350).

Musically, drawing upon vocal repertories in addition to instrumental material gave performers greater scope to create varied concert programmes, a prerequisite for success in a commercial music scene focused on stage performances and CD album sales. Some ensembles specialised in performing particular styles: the Klezmer Conservatory band, for example, re-created the sound of a prewar American klezmer orchestra. Singer Judy Bressler, herself from a family of Yiddish theatre performers, included a number of Yiddish theatre songs and popular Yiddish hits in the band's repertory. Others made more eclectic use of musical materials: recordings and concert repertories placed music from vastly different backgrounds side by side. The repertory of the New York-based band Metropolitan Klezmer, for example, includes Yiddish folk, workers' and popular songs placed alongside a diverse instrumental klezmer repertory.

As the 'voice' of a band, singers are invested with cultural authority: Deborah Karpel, singer with Metropolitan Klezmer, observed to me that audience members often automatically assumed that she was an expert on Yiddish culture simply because she sang in Yiddish.[4] Nevertheless, voluntarily or involuntarily, in

---

[4]   Deborah Karpel, interview with the author, New York, 14 August 2001.

providing the means to draw in audiences, or to reinscribe marginality, singers have played a prominent role in the identity politics of the klezmer revival. As a medium where discursive and musical practices coincide, and where different paradigms for bridging the gap between Old and New World have been modelled, song has been instrumental in connecting the klezmer scene to wider discourses of contemporary Jewish identity.

Since the vast majority of the North American audience for klezmer music does not fluently understand Yiddish, however, communication through Yiddish song is inevitably linked to a self-conscious awareness of difference on the part of both musicians and audience.[5] Negotiating this gap in understanding is an integral part of the establishment of a contemporary role for Yiddish music. Frank London of the Klezmatics describes using Yiddish 'as a distancing [device], like in a Brechtian sense ... because for most people, they blank out a little bit, they don't understand', and by contrast, 'using the vernacular to force them not to blank out ... and that can make people uncomfortable – they're often comfortable ... in that space'.[6]

This language gap also poses a problem for many singers: by no means all of those who perform with klezmer bands are fluent in Yiddish, and of those who are, still fewer have sufficient grasp of the language to write their own songs. The vernacular of the American klezmer revival is English, albeit seasoned with loan words drawn from Jewish, European, and Slavic languages (see Gold 1985). Yiddish has nevertheless remained the principal language of song within the klezmer revival. While some have chosen to write new Yiddish songs from scratch, then, other musicians have explored alternative techniques of creativity, including the use of arrangement to create new vocal material, or to infuse older material with new meaning. The following profiles focus particularly on the interaction of textual and musical creativity illustrating how each musician has approached the dual challenges of creativity and communication in Yiddish. I suggest that song lyrics, melody, vocal style and packaging are key elements in a critical evaluation of the narratives and cultural politics employed by these musicians as they negotiate the place of a local 'Yiddishland' amid a global music industry.

Michael Alpert and Brave Old World

Opening from Brave Old World, 'Welcome', *Blood* Orange*s* (1997)[7]

> Ay ay ay ay ay ay ay ay...
> A hartsikn gut helf aykh un a heymishn borekh-habo

---

[5]   Outside North America, particularly in Central and Eastern Europe, issues of communication are inflected by the closeness of German to Yiddish. See Chapter 4 for discussion.

[6]   Frank London, interview with author, New York, 3 April 2003.

[7]   Lyrics and melody by Michael Alpert and Alan Bern; translation from liner notes.

In di naye klangen fun Brave Old World af dem kompakt disk,
Un a gerus gants Idishland,
Fun San Francisco bizkl Brisk...

Ay ay ay ay ay ay ay ay...
Greetings to all and welcome
To the new sounds of Brave Old World on this CD,
And greetings to all Yiddishland,
From San Francisco to Brest-Litovsk...

A member of the early revival ensemble Kapelye, and a founding member of Brave Old World, Michael Alpert is a highly regarded veteran singer and teacher in the klezmer scene. As a native Yiddish speaker, he has also been the most prominent klezmer performer regularly to write and perform his own Yiddish songs.

Alpert models his approach to performance on elements of pre-Holocaust East European Yiddish vocal style, learned from extensive work with elderly informants, whom he frequently cites on recordings, performances and while teaching. His concert repertoire includes Old World folk songs, and his own compositions use musical elements drawn from this repertory. Nevertheless, the traditional and the contemporary are frequently juxtaposed or collide in his work, as in the song text cited above. Sung in the style of a traditional Old World *badkhn* (wedding jester), his text flits between Old and New World, counterpoising '*a heymishn borekh-habo*' (a home-style welcome), a phrase with a resonance of traditional Yiddish culture, with '*dem kompakt disk*' (this CD), clearly a term recently imported into the Yiddish language. It is perhaps no coincidence that Alpert chooses to mark the boundaries of 'Yiddishland' in San Francisco and Brest-Litovsk, locations representing his own native California and Lithuania, from where his father's family came. For Alpert, the constant negotiation between Old and New World is a personal narrative, reflected strongly in his creative work.

Michael Alpert attributes his involvement and standpoint in Yiddish music today to a combination of Old and New World cultural experiences: his experience of growing up among older East European Jews and his response to the American counterculture of the 1960s and 1970s. As a child, Alpert was also exposed to an unusually broad range of Yiddish cultural forms, growing up 'with one foot in the *frum* [religious] world and one foot in the lefty world': he spent time among religious cousins but also attended a Yiddish secular school where pupils learned Yiddish through songs. Further, the substantial age gap between him (b. 1954) and his father (b. 1906) gave him a stronger connection to an older Yiddish culture than was possible for most of his contemporaries – he labels himself a 'historical anomaly'.[8] For Alpert, this sense of difference and marginality fed into his identification with the American counterculture of the late 1960s and early 1970s, and eventually was to become central to his Yiddish performance persona.

---

[8]   Michael Alpert, interview with the author, Weimar, 31 July 2002.

Alpert's Yiddish musical career began when, having been involved in the Balkan music scene, including some time living in Yugoslavia as a teenager, he moved from Los Angeles to New York in 1979. There he found himself in a new Yiddish cultural milieu, from which sprang the ensemble Kapelye. Kapelye's choice of repertory was strongly influenced by the Yiddish-speaking backgrounds of band members: unlike many of those involved in the klezmer revival, three members of Kapelye had grown up speaking Yiddish at home. These band members brought knowledge of diverse repertories of Yiddish song to the band's repertory, which ranged from folk songs to Charles Cohan's 'Levine and His Flying Machine', a Yiddish popular song celebrating Charles Levine's 1927 transatlantic flight.

If Kapelye performed mainly precomposed material, it was with the formation of Brave Old World in 1989 that Alpert's voice as a singer-songwriter came to the fore. A quartet of musicians with considerable prior experience in Yiddish music and related genres, Brave Old World articulated 'the goal of developing a new Yiddish music, whose language and forms would be consciously created for the concert stage and a listening audience, but still deeply rooted in Yiddish folk materials' (Bern 1998). Although the Old World features in the band's name, they label their music 'New Jewish Music' rather than 'klezmer'. Rather than placing themselves within a continuing klezmer tradition, the disjunction between past and present is highlighted by placing their creations as 'new music', a global, non-situated term commonly used to describe contemporary high art music. That this is music primarily for the concert stage invokes a conscious remove from the East European folk tradition. Nevertheless, music 'deeply rooted' in folk materials suggests recourse to a cultural fluency difficult to achieve in a musical tradition whose roots were so comprehensively destroyed by Nazism.

Close reference both to the Yiddish cultural source and to the norms of 'serious' art music drives Brave Old World's musical creativity. In both instrumental and vocal material, the band juxtaposes precomposed material with compositions by each of the four musicians. Within the framework of the band, however, Alpert speaks in a personal voice. His lyrics are almost always in the first person and are frequently introspective. In keeping with his comments above, the sense of Jewishness he conveys is not one of mainstream Jewish-American affiliation. Rather, in locating his authorial voice firmly within a traditionally oriented Yiddish cultural setting disjointed from current reality, he reinforces the sense of marginality described earlier.

In 'Klaybt zikh tsunoyf' (Gather together), from Brave Old World's first album (*Klezmer Music*, 1990), Alpert celebrates companionship in a Yiddish cultural setting – the 'Yiddishland' of the song quoted earlier. Even within the intimate setting he portrays – a gathering of friends – Alpert, speaking in the first person, positions himself as an outsider ('I have come to you from far away'). Nevertheless, he stresses the strength of bonds formed via cultural companionship, addressing the song's audience as 'sisters and brothers … bound together like family'. This sense of companionship is reinforced by the melody: each phrase of text is answered by an untexted vocal phrase, the call-and-response pattern encouraging audience participation.

Brave Old World, 'Klaybt zikh tsunoyf' (Gather together), *Klezmer Music* (1990)[9]

> Klaybt zikh tsunoyf, mayne shvester un briderlekh,
> Un lomir zikh freyen vos mir zaynen yidelekh.
> Genug shoyn tsu veynen mit hertser farvundete.
> Vayl mir zaynen ale vi kroyvim farbundete.
> Khotsh ikh bin gekumen tsu aykh
> fun der vayter velt
> Ir zent mir alemen tayere nokh fun gelt
> To lomir zikh freyen biz in vaysn tog arayn
> Makhn a lekhayim un trinkn a glezl vayn.

> *Gather together, my sisters and brothers,*
> *And let's be glad that we're Jews.*
> *Enough crying already with wounded hearts*
> *Because we're all bound together like family.*
> *Although I have come to you from far away,*
> *All of you are dearer to me than money.*
> *So let's rejoice until the early hours*
> *Make a toast and drink a glass of wine.*

This articulation of shared conviviality builds a picture of Yiddish culture strongly based on ethnic and community ties; music becomes a place in which this community may, however briefly, be instantiated.

In other songs, however, Alpert makes different use of Yiddish cultural vocabulary. 'A shpay in yam' ('Spitting into the sea', *Bless the Fire*, 2003) is modelled as an East European Yiddish folk ballad (Brave Old World 2003).[10] This model is reflected in its subject matter – like many Old World ballads it is a song of unfulfilled love – and in its structure. The nine verses of the song form a narrative, and its melodic form is strophic; the verse melody forms an arch shape, and the last two lines of each stanza are frequently repeated (compare, for example, recordings of the repertory of Lifshe Schaechter-Widman, released in 1986 by Global Village).

Alpert's use of language again taps into an Old World Yiddish cultural vocabulary. He describes the beloved with the attributes 'charm, wisdom, and graciousness' (*kheyn, khokhme, edelkayt*), character traits highly valued in traditional Yiddish

---

[9] Lyrics and melody by Michael Alpert, translation mine.

[10] An excerpt from this song is posted at http://www.braveoldworld.com.

culture (Brave Old World 2003, translation from liner notes).[11] Further, Alpert sings the final verse of the song wholly in Ukrainian, alluding to the way Yiddish speakers in Eastern Europe were also speakers of other co-territorial languages and incorporated words from these languages into their Yiddish. This aspect of the Yiddish language was largely lost as its speakers moved to America and instead began to incorporate English words into their Yiddish – hence Alpert's use of Ukrainian is another marker of alterity, geographically locating him in Eastern Europe and identifying him with a past, rather than present, Yiddish-speaking community.

Alpert's own voice acts as an equally strong cultural marker. He sings in the regional accent of the Yiddish he learned from his European-born parents, again identifying himself with the sound of Old World, rather than New World, Yiddish. His vocal style, likewise, uses the metric flexibility and ornamentation typical of Old World Yiddish folk song. The traditional unaccompanied rendition of Yiddish folk song is also preserved in the musical arrangement: the song is accompanied by cimbalom and accordion, but the opening and the end of the song are left unaccompanied. Within the context of this arrangement, even the sound of unaccompanied folk song becomes a musical trope, a compositional device of contemporary music: the listener is reminded that this is a piece designed for the concert stage, not an Old World folk song.

'A shpay in yam' makes a strong statement of positionality. By alluding to elements typical of older Yiddish folk songs with a contemporary setting, Alpert resituates these elements as markers of his personal voice and worldview. Despite the gradual disappearance of the generation born in Yiddish-speaking Europe, Alpert continues to reach out to the Yiddish world that attracted him when he was younger. Rather than adapting his cultural voice to speak to a contemporary audience, by choosing this mode of expression Alpert maintains his self-conscious position of difference and marginality. The Yiddishland he describes, where folk creation continues, is attractive to those hungry for 'authenticity', yet today is an imagined landscape, its cultural references inaccessible to all but a small proportion of his audiences. Translation is not a substitute for comprehension: the illusion of a fully continuing Yiddish cultural tradition is broken by the need for liner notes, explanations and translations to convey this music to a modern audience.

Although the disjuncture between Old and New World is uneasily foregrounded in Brave Old World's work, the comments of one reviewer suggest that the appeal of the band's music also lies precisely in this expression of cultural tension and the creative reimagining of past Yiddish culture: 'The music and the words evoke a bucolic shtetl that never was, and in doing so, create a vision of Jewish life that transcends time and place to speak to us now'.[12] Alpert's songs embody a distinctive approach to bridging the gap between Old World Yiddish culture

---

[11]   See Rosmarin (2000, 170, 274). *Eydl*, lit. 'delicate, refined', is a common Yiddish girl's name.

[12]   Ari Davidow, review of Brave Old World, *Bless the Fire*, http://www.klezmershack. com/bands/bow/fire/bow.fire.html, last accessed 25 May 2012.

and contemporary America, grounded in his individual frame of reference and experiences of cultural community and marginality, which in turn resonate with Brave Old World's broader artistic approach.

Adrienne Cooper and Mikveh

The eponymous debut album (2001) of the all-female klezmer band Mikveh uses Yiddish song as a medium to evoke a multifaceted picture of women in Yiddish culture, reinterpreting Old World materials to resonate with a contemporary American Jewish women's sensibility.[13] Mikveh – named after the ritual bath in which observant Jewish women must immerse after menstruation before reuniting with their husbands – was founded in 1998 for a performance as part of a feminist campaign to stop violence against women and girls. The band, which brought together five of the most prominent female musicians of the klezmer scene, focused on repertory by and about women. The principal singer on the album, Adrienne Cooper, was, until her untimely death in 2011, a prominent and much loved performer and teacher in the Yiddish cultural scene. Her grandfather was a *bal-tfile* (lay synagogue cantor) and her mother a classically trained singer. Cooper's early background was in classical music, and as a young adult she studied singing, performing as a soloist and in ensembles. She began to perform Yiddish song as a graduate student in Chicago during the early 1970s and then moved to New York to study Yiddish in a summer language programme; she continued her study at YIVO, where she met many individuals involved in Yiddish song, including klezmer revivalists Michael Alpert and Henry Sapoznik, folklorist Barbara Kirshenblatt-Gimblett, the late Lazar Weiner, an important composer of Yiddish art song, and the late Wolf Younin, a Yiddish poet. In New York, she also met Zalmen Mlotek, a pianist and musical director prominently involved in Yiddish theatre and choral music, with whom she collaborated frequently.

Cooper continued to sing and perform in Yiddish. Her association with YIVO – where she studied for five years and worked for ten years, eventually becoming assistant director of the organisation – and other Yiddishist institutions gave her a broad exposure to Yiddish culture, language and song and had an impact on her subsequent choice of repertory.[14] Although it is not uncommon for singers involved in the klezmer scene to perform a variety of Yiddish repertories, Cooper has had a particularly diverse career, recording in both art and folk idioms and working in several music theatre productions. She was a member of Kapelye after Alpert's departure from the band, appeared as a guest artist on recordings by the Klezmatics and the Flying Bulgar Klezmer band, and also recorded solo material.

---

[13]   A grassroots Jewish feminist movement, particularly interrogating issues of identity and gender enactment, has existed for several decades; see, for example, the Jewish feminist journals *Lilith* and *Bridges*.

[14]   Cooper also worked for the Workmen's Circle, and co-founded KlezKamp.

Of *Mikveh*'s 14 tracks, 12 are songs; these songs draw upon traditional folk, literary and religious sources in addition to presenting newly composed material. Together, they present a range of different perspectives on women's lives and experiences within the Yiddish cultural sphere, including love, fertility, miscarriage and domestic violence. Images of womanhood associated with traditional Yiddish culture are set alongside the contemporary world of the band and of the wider creative circle of women of which they form part.

The album opens with a folk song of Hasidic origin, 'Royz royz' (Rose, rose), sung by Adrienne Cooper with solo clarinet accompaniment. The song juxtaposes the image of a rose lost far away in a large forest with the image of the divine presence distanced during the Jewish exile.[15]

Mikveh, 'Royz royz' (Rose, rose), *Mikveh* (2001)[16]

Royz royz vi vayt bistu	*Rose, how far away you are*
Vald vald vi groys bistu	*Forest, how vast you are*
Volt di royz nisht azoy vayt geven	*If the rose were not out of reach,*
Volt der vald nisht azoy groys geven	*The forest wouldn't seem so vast.*
Shkhine shkhine vi vayt bistu	*Divine spirit, how far away you are*
Goles goles vi lang bistu	*Exile, how long you last*
Volt di shkhine nisht azoy vayt geven	*If the divine spirit were not out of reach,*
Volt der goles nisht azoy lang geven	*Our exile would not endure so long.*

This text serves to situate *Mikveh* within a traditional Jewish historical-spatial framework. The exile – *goles* – refers to the period after the destruction of the Second Temple in Jerusalem in 70 CE and the subsequent dispersal of the Jewish population, a period of exile that led to today's Jewish diaspora. Despite the distance of two millennia, the destruction of the Temple continues to be commemorated in religious Judaism, both within the liturgy and by an annual fast day (the ninth of the Hebrew month Av). Here, however, this lamenting of the exilic condition also, ironically, stands as a salute to diasporic Jewish culture: Yiddish is quintessentially a language of the exile, and this song is by no means alone in reflecting the contribution made to Jewish music by the diverse cultures with which the Jewish population has come into contact during the exilic period.

'Royz royz' also emphasises the theme of the feminine in Yiddish culture. The divine spirit – *shkhine* – to which the song refers is commonly held to represent the feminine aspect of God. This notion appears in the Zohar, the principal text of mystical Judaism (kabbalah), but has also been taken up by contemporary Jews seeking to address perceived gender imbalances in traditional Judaism. Mikveh's rendition of

---

[15]   The song, adapted by a Hasidic rabbi, is said to have originated in the song of a Hungarian shepherd boy calling out for his beloved Rose.

[16]   Traditional lyrics and melody; translation from liner notes.

Royz Royz presents this feminine topos via a woman's voice. Whereas Yiddish folk songs are sung by both women and men, in the popular imagination women are more strongly associated with the performance and the transmission of Yiddish songs.[17] As discussed at length in the preceding chapter, many stories and personal reminiscences place Yiddish songs in the mouths of a beloved mother, aunt or grandmother.

Cooper situates her own voice alongside the voices of generations of Yiddish-speaking women. The minimal accompaniment and the free rhythm of the song suggest a folk idiom and focus the listener's attention on the voice, yet the unusual pairing with solo clarinet immediately places the song in a contemporary performance context – like Alpert's 'A shpay in yam', 'Royz royz' is explicitly arranged for concert performance. Cooper sings softly in a low register, producing a warm tone more reminiscent of a popular American 'folk' sound than an 'authentic' East European Jewish vocal style, again making her performance accessible to a contemporary American listener.

This performance style resonates with Cooper's own approach to Yiddish repertory; in interview, she contrasted her style with that of Alpert. For Cooper, approaching song material from a contemporary perspective formed a vital element of communication with her audiences. Rather than trying to re-create a historically 'authentic' performance style rooted in the past, she wanted her audience to 'encounter this material where we are, which to me is not at a remove, it's not at a distance from the material'.[18] Like Alpert's, her performance persona was self-consciously created, though unlike his projected marginality, Cooper actively bridged the distance between her repertory and her audience.

The use of recently composed material reinforces Cooper's contemporary encounter with Yiddish song. The album's third song, 'Soreles bas mitsveh' (Sorele's bat mitzvah) is an adaptation of a song by the contemporary New York Yiddish poet Beyle Schaechter-Gottesman. It was originally written for the bar mitzvah of Schaechter-Gottesman's nephew; here, Cooper adapts the song to celebrate the coming of age of her daughter Sarah.

In contrast with the enduring pictures of femininity painted by 'Royz royz', 'Soreles bat mitzvah' invokes a specific contemporary community of creative Jewish women who pass culture down to a new generation. This community includes the band members and other people: Cooper's daughter reappears later on the album

---

[17]   Perhaps the most familiar example of this association can be found in the text of the Yiddish theatre song 'Rozhinkes mit mandeln'. Written by Abraham Goldfaden in 1880, the song entered the folk tradition and remains one of the best-known Yiddish songs today. The verse describes a widow singing to her only son; the refrain is the song she is pictured singing. Other Yiddish songs referring to this topos include Aaron Litvin's satiric 'Zhamele' – for an English summary, see Mlotek and Mlotek (1988, 88).

[18]   Adrienne Cooper, interview with the author, Lantier, Quebec, 25 August 2001. This contrast in approach is clearly audible when comparing Cooper's recording of 'Royz royz' to the version of this song recently recorded by Michael Alpert as 'Gules gules' (Brave Old World 2003).

as co-author of a song, and the liner notes of *Mikveh* credit, alongside Schaechter-Gottesman, the late Yiddish folksinger Bronya Sakina as a source of musical material. The latter women represent an older generation of Yiddish culturalists, thus enhancing the impression that this band forms part of an ongoing, evolving Yiddish culture. The vocal arrangements on *Mikveh* additionally contribute to this sense of community. Cooper is the principal singer, but hers is not the only voice featured. Accordionist Lauren Brody sings a substantial amount of solo material, and frequently Cooper and Brody sing in duet or in close harmony with other members of the band. This simultaneous sounding of a number of voices again tends to locate the individual musicians within a communal view of Yiddish culture, and highlights the roles of women in the process of cultural transmission and change.[19]

The remainder of the songs on the album engage some of the varied experiences of women during the encounter between Yiddish culture and modernity, expressed in traditional and contemporary Yiddish song, from tales of romance and a celebration of sexuality and fertility to a folk song about domestic violence and a newly composed song about miscarriage. These songs mediate the experiences of the band as contemporary American women and the wider experiences of women within Yiddish culture. Additionally, they draw attention to subjects that have customarily been marginalised within contemporary American discourse. The women Mikveh portrays resist essentialisation, moving beyond the female roles canonised in the Yiddish musical tradition.

Mikveh still leaves open questions pertaining to women's roles in contemporary Yiddish music and culture, however. One is illustrated in track 10, 'Eyshes khayil' (A woman of substance). This Hebrew text, an alphabetic acrostic from the Book of Proverbs, is 'traditionally recited [by religious Jews] in the home on Friday night, the eve of the Sabbath in honour of women's work and worth' (Mikveh 2001, liner notes). The end of the text is particularly well known, and seems to reflect a contemporary feminist sensibility:

> Sheker hakheyn vehevel hayofi, isho yiras hashem, hi sishalol
> T'nu lo mipri yodeyho, Viyhaleluho bash'orim maseho.
>
> *Grace is false and beauty is vain; a woman who fears God, she shall be praised.*
> *Give her the fruit of her hands, and let her own deeds praise her in the gates.*[20]

When considered in its entirety, however, the text of 'Eyshes khayil' (Proverbs 31:10–31) is deemed problematic by many Jewish feminists today. Kolot, the Center for Jewish Women's and Gender Studies, notes that it 'presents an old-

---

[19] For discussion of similar processes of cultural transmission in the parallel case of Judeo-Spanish repertory, see Judith Cohen (1995).

[20] Proverbs 31:30–31 (my translation).

fashioned and restrictive idealization of women'.[21] The portrait it paints of a 'woman of substance' centers on her domestic achievements, and it is her husband who 'sits among the elders of the land'. The translation given by Mikveh in the liner notes attempts to circumvent some problematic elements by abridging and paraphrasing the text. Cooper's choice to sing this Hebrew text using an Ashkenazic accent (which was used in the Yiddish-speaking world, but today has been largely abandoned outside the strictly Orthodox community in favour of Israeli pronunciation) immediately calls to mind today's strictly Orthodox communities where contemporary feminist values hold little sway and where women are not permitted, by Jewish law, to sing in front of men other than their husbands and close relatives, yet where Yiddish is still spoken on a daily basis and where many musical traditions of the Yiddish world are preserved.

Mikveh's rendition of this song casts it as a celebration. At the opening, Cooper's voice is joined by the other musicians singing close harmonies that create a sound evoking a Bulgarian women's choir. Later, instrumental interludes are added; the song gradually speeds up to a climax on the final two lines cited above. In recasting 'Eyshes khayil' as a concert piece, the members of Mikveh attempt to reclaim a problematic element of traditional Jewish liturgy for women's voices but at the same time distance themselves from the model of contemporary Jewish liturgical music associated with popular progressive female cantor-songwriters such as Debbie Friedman, whose musical roots are closer to American light pop than to the Yiddish musical tradition. In Mikveh's arrangement, nevertheless, the song loses its religious or spiritual context: this is music for listening, not a Friday night ritual. This is further underscored by Cooper's occasionally inaccurate rendition of Ashkenazi pronunciation – if singing Eyshet Chayil in an Ashkenazi accent immediately references the strictly Orthodox world, in this rendition it's also clear from these mistakes that *Mikveh* is not embedded in this context. Likewise, the remainder of the album avoids making a strong statement – feminist or otherwise – about women's roles in Yiddish culture. Even the title, *Mikveh*, adopted here as a positive symbol of Jewish femininity, is linked to a religious requirement that many Jewish women, even Orthodox feminists, find particularly challenging.[22] Further, the experiences of contemporary women musicians in what largely continues (with a few notable exceptions) to be a male-dominated music scene remain to be addressed.

Mikveh does, however, bring to the fore the active role played by women as cultural transmitters within the Yiddish song tradition, echoing Judith Cohen's comments on the Judeo-Spanish song tradition: 'Women express themselves not only through song but also by developing new strategies and contexts for transmitting traditional materials' (1995, 182). In helping to define a present-day North American Yiddishist women's sensibility and presenting a variety of

---

[21]   See http://www.rrc.edu/kolot/ritual/resources-new-traditions, last accessed 25 May 2012. This site suggests an alternative formulation of the text for use by contemporary women.

[22]   See, for example, Miriam Udel-Lambert, 'Immersion in Reality', *Forward*, 23 June 2006, http://forward.com/articles/832/immersion-in-reality/, last accessed 23 November 2012.

perspectives on women's experiences in Yiddish culture past and present, the band enables its audiences to engage with traditional material while remaining firmly within a contemporary musical and cultural aesthetic.

Lorin Sklamberg and the Klezmatics

The Klezmatics present a third approach to klezmer's interpretation of contemporary Jewish culture. One of the longest-established and most prolific of today's klezmer bands, the Klezmatics are part of a second wave of revival bands that formed in the late 1980s. Known for their characteristic countercultural aesthetic and rock style, and also for their direct engagement with queer identity, the Klezmatics recorded nine albums over the ensuing 20-year period; these recordings illustrate multiple approaches to the arrangement and creation of new Yiddish vocal material.

In contrast to Mikveh, who combine songs from a wide range of sources in a single album in order to build up a many-layered Yiddish women's voice, the Klezmatics combine multiple strands of musical and textual material in individual songs. Their distinctive approach to repertory and arrangement allow contemporary musicians to comment on preexisting material, producing songs with a fully integrated musical texture. This juxtaposition of materials, reflecting the gamut of the musical experiences of band members, moves back towards the kind of expression of individual musical personalities exemplified earlier by Alpert and Brave Old World; nevertheless, here, rather than reflecting a sense of marginality, this individuality is strongly rooted within a contemporary Jewish identity, which resonates with other present-day trends within the American Jewish community.

Vocalist Lorin Sklamberg recalls that songs became part of the band's repertory from the very beginning. Although he had experience in other Jewish vocal styles, including some working as cantor of the gay synagogue Beth Chayim in Los Angeles, Sklamberg came to klezmer with little experience of Yiddish song. Sklamberg's work with elderly informants and historical research formed, like Cooper's, an inroad to Yiddish repertories. When the Klezmatics formed, Sklamberg was working for the design department of YIVO, through which he could access an important collection of both commercial and field recordings.[23] The band began to draw this material into its repertory. Sklamberg used a similar combination of research and listening experience to develop his vocal style and was especially influenced by Yiddish theatre singer Aaron Lebedeff and by Hasidic recordings.[24]

Released in 1988, the Klezmatics' first album, *Shvaygn=Toyt*, includes five vocal numbers among its 12 tracks. The opening number, 'Ershter vals' (First waltz) is a sentimental Russian waltz tune with Yiddish text and is perhaps atypical

---

[23]   Sklamberg is currently YIVO's sound archivist.

[24]   Sklamberg, interview with author, New York, 9 August 2001. With Uri Caine and others, Sklamberg and London explore the Hasidic musical tradition in more depth; see Chapter 5 for discussion.

of the band's later choice of repertory; 'Dzankoye' and 'Ale brider' (All brothers), among the most popular songs of the klezmer revival, share two features that have undoubtedly contributed to their popularity. First, each has a sing-along refrain with little or no text. In enabling audience participation, such songs help to create an illusion of familiarity and shared cultural fluency and to bridge the gap between the performance of revived music and contemporary cultural expression. Second, the subject matter of these songs, both of which derive from the Jewish socialist tradition, resonates with the very nature of the klezmer revival. From the revival's earliest years, several klezmer bands identifying with leftist 'progressive' secular politics have included songs of socialist origin in their repertories. 'Dzankoye' – the name of a town in the Crimea – hails from 'the short period in the 1920s when the Soviet Socialist revolution allowed Jews to own land for the first time' (Klezmatics 1988, liner notes). The lyrics brim with confidence in the Jewish socialist future mirrored half a century later in the klezmer revival, which explicitly promoted in its lyrics a proud, contemporary Jewish identity based on European roots rather than Israeli or assimilated American culture: 'Jews, answer my question: where's Abrasha? He drives that tractor like a train! ... Who says Jews can only be traders who eat greasy soup with mandlen [croutons] and can't be workers? Only our enemies would say that' (Klezmatics 1988, translation from liner notes).

Like 'Dzankoye', 'Ale brider' is a socialist song conveying a universal message of community. Here, though, the Klezmatics expand the text to include material reflecting their gender politics, an important facet of the band's identity. Written by Yiddish poet Morris Winchevsky in 1890, the original song begins: 'We are all brothers and sing happy songs. We stick together like nobody else' (Klezmatics 1988, translation from liner notes). Popular among Jewish socialists, the song became widely known, incorporating numerous new stanzas. The Klezmatics continued in this pattern, adding stanzas reflecting contemporary progressive politics. Their liner notes explain: '[The] original poem included the lines: "We are all brothers. ... Religious and leftists united, like bride and groom, like kugl and kashe [potato pudding and buckwheat]...." In true Klezmatics tradition, we all sing, "We're all sisters, like Rachel, Ruth and Esther," and "We're all gay, like Jonathan and King David"' (Klezmatics 1988, liner notes).[25]

This recording marks only the beginning of the development of the Klezmatics' musical persona. The real impetus for this development came not only from the band itself, but also from market forces. In describing klezmer as a 'sub-commodified' genre, Slobin acknowledges the importance of the 'heritage music infrastructure' to klezmer music (2000, 32). Within this wider commercial sphere, klezmer bands must compete with other ensembles championed by the world music industry. Sklamberg recalls that early in the band's career they took part in a Berlin music festival where the presenter wanted 'a hip klezmer band that somehow was going to go take the music somewhere else', an Ashkenazi equivalent of popular Israeli-Yemenite singer

---

[25]   The use of gay markers by the Klezmatics, including this song text, is discussed in detail by Kaminsky (2001).

Ofra Haza, then a major artist on the 'world music' scene.[26] The Klezmatics rose to this challenge, grounding their approach within an aesthetic based on the fusion of traditional Yiddish musical materials with other strands of the musical identities of band members, all of whom also perform in genres outside klezmer.

In pursuing this goal of musical innovation, the Klezmatics began to incorporate new compositions, both vocal and instrumental, into their repertory. Whereas their original instrumental numbers may be written from scratch, their new songs are often formed via a process of bricolage, using existing texts and combining them with 'found' musical materials derived from instrumental music as well as with newly composed materials. Trumpeter Frank London, credited with many of the band's original arrangements and compositions, identifies this reciprocal, creative relationship between vocal and instrumental genres as typical of Yiddish music: 'The vocal songs become instrumental tunes, and instrumental melodies get words put on them'.[27]

Some new songs are simply new melodies to older Yiddish texts: 'Hevl iz havolim' (Vanity is vanities) on *Rise Up!* (2003) uses a combination of two folk song texts, 'Hevl iz havolim', originally published, according to London, by Soviet Jewish folklorist Moshe Beregovski, and 'A redl iz di gore velt', published by Ruth Rubin in her collection *Voices of a People*, setting them to a new melody. Other compositions take texts from a wider range of sources, several of which are particularly provocative, from 'Honiksaft' (Honeyjuice) from *rhythm + jews* (1992), which transforms a Yiddish translation of the biblical Song of Songs into a homoerotic love song, to Yiddish eroticist poet Celia Dropkin's 'Es vilt zikh mir zen' (I want to see you) from *Jews with Horns* (1994). The latter contains the lines 'Es vilt zikh mir zen vi du shlofst, ven du farlirst dayn makht iber zikh, iber mir … Es vilt zikh mir zen dikh a toytn' (I'd like to see you sleeping, when you lose your hold on yourself and on me … I'd like to see you dead).[28]

Other original songs set new texts: among them is 'Mizmor shir lehanef' (Reefer song, subtitled 'A psalm, a song of hemp'), a tongue-in-cheek song about marijuana intended to expand the more 'traditional' repertory of Yiddish drinking songs. The text, by Canadian Yiddishist Michael Wex, is written in idiomatic English, using traditional religious Jewish imagery to compare smoking cannabis to Sabbath rest and religious enlightenment. The title of the song is itself a parody: 'Mizmor shir' is the Hebrew appellation with which many biblical psalms begin. The liner notes to the Klezmatics' recording not only translate the Yiddish text into English but also gloss the idiomatic language used by Wex, shedding light on the in-jokes otherwise liable to be understood only by that segment of the audience with a traditional religious upbringing, and by outlining an appropriate Yiddish translation for 'good shit'.

---

26   Sklamberg, interview with the author, 2001.
27   London, interview with the author, 2003.
28   Text and translation from liner notes.

Klezmatics, 'Mizmor shir lehanef' (Reefer Song), *Possessed* (1997)[29]

Dem yidn brengt der shabes ri	*Shabbos brings Jews rest,*
Menukhe, glaykh-gevikht.	*Repose, equilibrium.*
S'i'mir shabes yedn in der fri –	*Every morning is Shabbos for me –*
Aza frumyak bin ikh?	*Am I really so religious?*
Aza frumyak bin ikh,	*I'm really so religious,*
Aza frumyak bin ikh.	*Really so religious.*
Az ikh tsind mir on a splifele	*When I light up a spliff*
Un ver mikh oyfgerikht.	*And start to do all right, feel real good.*

Although only the textual in-jokes are explained in the notes, London's music uses a combination of elements to reflect the references of the text. The opening of the verse melody refers to a shape commonly found in East European Jewish liturgical music: an upward leap of a fifth, repeated notes on the fifth scale degree, and a return to this scale degree at the end of the phrase, as shown in Example 3.1.[30]

Example 3.1 'Reefer song' verse melody

This is connected to the chorus by a linking passage that creates an exotic, 'oriental' atmosphere by the use of slow-moving melodic lines overlaid with improvisatory bouzouki motives shown in Example 3.2.

Example 3.2 'Reefer song' linking passage

The three verses are punctuated first by a polytonal instrumental improvisation, and then by a chorus, which is set to part of the well-known klezmer melody 'Ot azoy' (Like this), shown in Example 3.3. At a point in the 'Ot azoy' melody where

---

29   Lyrics and translation by Michael Wex, melody by Frank London.

30   For examples of this phrase structure in liturgical music, see Idelsohn (1932, excerpts 29, 41, 55, 93 etc.).

the audience would usually call out 'Ot azoy! Gut azoy!' (Do it like this! It's good this way!), Wex's text instead calls out 'Reykht a splif – kanabis' (Smoke a spliff – cannabis). This musical in-joke forms a counterpart to the many textual references of the lyrics.

Reykht a splif   Ka na bis

Example 3.3 'Ot azoy' melody

If the Klezmatics' musical creativity focuses on the fusion of eclectic Old World and contemporary musical elements to create a hip, up-to-date sound, the band is equally interested in exploring the contribution of Yiddish to contemporary alternative forms of Jewish cultural expression. In addressing the challenge of communicating with a contemporary audience through Yiddish music, the Klezmatics have explored the visual and textual expressive space of the CD as a means to link their work with wider social issues. First, assuming that the majority of their American audiences are not fluent in Yiddish, commentaries attached to translated lyrics allow listeners access to verbal references made within song texts, such as the queer references and social issues explored above. Further, the band's engagement with these issues is reinforced by their inclusion in the CD notes of writings by authors outside the band, which frequently expand on the social and political sensibilities expressed in the album.[31] For example, Ellen Kushner's reflections on the post-9/11 world in *Rise Up!* (2003) mirror those of the band, who translated and recorded singer-songwriter Holly Near's 'I Ain't Afraid' in Yiddish and English in the wake of the terrorist attacks: 'I ain't afraid of your Yahweh / I ain't afraid of your Allah / I ain't afraid of your Jesus / I'm afraid of what you do in the name of your God'.[32]

To explain the presence of these essays, Sklamberg notes: 'I think it's about connecting what we do to a larger world or a worldview. So we've asked people to write material who somehow are connected to us, either culturally or politically … I guess that we want people to see what the band does in a larger context'.[33] This appeal to a 'larger worldview' is embedded in a wider trend in contemporary American Jewish life. From the 1970s onward, a number of sites for 'alternative' Jewish expression have emerged, many of which seek to reclaim and find new

---

[31]   These essays were written by fictitious character Allolo Trehorn for *Shvaygn=Toyt*; Michael Wex and Irena Klepfisz for *rhythm + jews* (1992); Michael Wex for *Jews with Horns* (1994); Tony Kushner for *Possessed* (1997); and Ellen Kushner with Delia Sherman for *Rise Up!* (2003).

[32]   Holly Near, translated to Yiddish in liner notes for Klezmatics (2003).

[33]   Sklamberg, interview with the author, 2001.

meaning in elements of traditional Jewish ritual and culture with a contemporary sensibility (see Wertheimer 1998, ch. 4). These include the political magazine *Tikkun* and, more recently, countercultural *Heeb* magazine, not to mention many internet-based discussion venues such as Jewschool and Jewlicious.[34] These magazines and websites frequently promote and review 'progressive' klezmer recordings, helping to draw voices like the Klezmatics into Jewish-American discourse well beyond the klezmer scene.

Conclusion

In reaching beyond the internal discourses of the Yiddishist community, the klezmer revival has enabled new paradigms for the performance and arrangement of Yiddish songs. These are influenced not only by past performance practices, but also by the economics and aesthetics of a contemporary revival: renewal is not only an ideology, but also a requirement in a competitive commercial music scene where professional bands need to be differentiated and stand out. These three case studies foreground the role of song as a medium that allows the exploration of both communal and individual positionality within the klezmer scene.

The songs explored here challenge any construction of a normative 'voice' of the klezmer scene, but rather invoke a range of alternative reconfigurations of the Yiddish musical heritage. This in turn points to a new politics of Yiddish culture. In focusing on language, Shandler's model of postvernacularity posits the end of fluency and the move towards a highly valued but atomised Yiddish. Such a Yiddish necessarily focuses on performance rather than creativity: the Yiddish language becomes an end rather than a means. Here, however, musicians point towards a new kind of vernacular use of Yiddish: aesthetic rather than ethnic or linguistic; embedded among rather than separated from other cultural forms.

The following three chapters explore the boundaries of this creative space, focusing on moments of transcommunalism and transnationalism in Yiddish music. Chapters 4 and 5 consider points of encounter between Yiddish musicians and the klezmer scene's most prominent Others: post-Holocaust Europe, and the strictly Orthodox Hasidic world. Finally, Chapter 6 turns to the limits of revival discourse: Solomon and So-called's album *HipHopKhasene* sets the juxtaposition of a core 'local' group of musicians and the global media mainstream in sharp relief. The techniques of hip hop allow the musicians to set past and present Yiddish voices side by side yet also point to the boundaries of this new musical vernacular, a question to which I return in a brief epilogue.

---

[34]   See, for example, http://www.jewschool.com and http://www.jewlicious.com.

Chapter 4
A Space for Reflection: Creative Encounters with Europe

While new spaces for Yiddish music are created and celebrated in north America, the historical geographies of Yiddish remain. In Central and Eastern Europe, Yiddish language and culture was shaped by a thousand years of close contact with co-territorial peoples; in the same places its future was cut short and its speakers murdered by the Nazi regime. For the generation of American Jews born after the Holocaust, the European connections of Yiddish were already displaced, embodied for some in the accents and foodways of parents, grandparents and other members of an older generation, in memorials, in literature and memorial books. For their European contemporaries, Jewish culture was no longer part of the everyday cultural language of urban Europe and local Jewish communities had been reduced to tiny shreds of their former size.[1] Of an estimated nine million Jews who lived in Europe before the Second World War, six million had been murdered, most others had left, and much of the physical heritage of Jewish life – synagogues, shops, businesses, homes and graveyards – had been destroyed or reappropriated.

A revival of public interest in Yiddish music occurred in both north America – primarily among Jews – and Europe – primarily among non-Jews – at a similar time. While the internal discourses and cultural dynamics of each 'revival' were very different, commentators consensually ascribe both to a post-war second generation seeking to engage with elements of their own history that had become dormant or suppressed during the post-war years. For those who came of age in the 1960s, later joined by a postcommunist Eastern European generation, this played out in the wider context of 'a broader general revival of interest in lost traditions and veiled history that also, for example, produced folk music, genealogy, and "alternative" lifestyle movements as well as Vietnam-era antiestablishment protests and political groupings' (Gruber 2002, 16)

The internal processes of the revival of klezmer music in north America in the 1980s have been discussed above and elsewhere. While this revival was largely couched as a countercultural, rootsy, music-centred phenomenon, in Europe public interest in Yiddish music was embedded in a broader pattern of folk revival, and became interlaced with wider public processes of memorialisation, often undertaken with institutional and official backing, including by an emergent

---

[1]   While significant klezmer scenes also exist in England and France, in this chapter 'European' primarily refers to Germany, Poland and other Central European countries.

European Union keen to promote harmonious multiculturalism. In her 2002 monograph *Virtually Jewish: Reinventing Jewish Culture in Europe* Ruth Ellen Gruber has comprehensively documented these processes, discussing the creation and performance of 'virtual' Jewish spaces in Europe, which seek to memorialise European Jews, to reinsert a Jewish presence into public space and to enable Europeans to confront their past, yet have at times overwhelmed local Jewish communities.[2]

Music has played a prominent role in this European revival of Jewish culture. Yiddish music was not entirely absent from the German soundscape during the post-war decades, and its prominence increased in Germany and Austria during the 1970s and 1980s. Contrary to the American focus on instrumental klezmer music, most European performers focused on Yiddish song, which was readily comprehensible by German speakers. A handful of performers sang Yiddish song in East Germany, including Lin Jaldati, a Communist Jew from Amsterdam who had given illegal concerts of Yiddish song during the war before being deported to a series of camps. In 1952 she moved to East Germany, dedicated to building the socialist state, and continued to sing in Yiddish, later joined by other family members (see Ostow 1989, ch. 7 and Mummert 1988). From the 1960s onwards several Yiddish songbooks were published in Germany, their contents dominated by Holocaust-era material.[3] During the 1970s and 1980s performance of Yiddish song grew among German and Austrian folk musicians, including the prominent West German group Zupfgeigenhansel. By the mid-1980s, a thriving local Yiddish music scene included chart-hitting songs and Yiddish music festivals (see Gruber 2002, 204–7).

Nevertheless, beginning in the mid-1980s, the arrival of professional American klezmer musicians in Europe heralded both musical interchange and a wave of questions and conversations concerning identity and authenticity in Yiddish music. Invited for concert tours and festivals, and later running workshops, these musicians were feted as 'genuine' Jews, performing ethnic identity, and representing the authentic continuation of pre-Holocaust musical traditions.[4] Reflecting on these encounters, German klezmer musician Heiko Lehmann wrote:

> In 1984 Yiddish and klezmer changed in West Germany. For the first time an
> American klezmer band, one of the bands who pioneered the klezmer revival in

---

[2]   For wider contextual discussion, see Fulbrook (1999), Lehmann (2000), Markovits and Noveck (1996) and others.

[3]   The earliest of these concentrate upon Holocaust songs (see Janda and Sprecher 1962, Jaldati and Rebling 1966 and Behrend 1967). Later songbooks include a wider range of songs (for example Frankl and Frankl 1981, a general songbook, republished in 1996, and Gradenwitz 1988, love songs). Holocaust songbooks, though, still dominate Yiddish song publication in Germany (for example Ortmeyer 1996, and the collection published by Lemm 1992, of songs by Mordechai Gebirtig).

[4]   See Cohen (2009a, 222) for discussion of similar cases.

America, came to tour Germany: New York's *Kapelye* … German performers had the chance to see Yiddish songs and klezmer music performed by 'authentic' musicians i.e. Jewish musicians. 1984 was also the year when director Peter Zadek invited Israeli clarinetist Giora Feidman to participate in his production of Joshua Sobol's *Ghetto*. *Kapelye* and Feidman paved the way to Germany for American-Jewish performers. They were to come back (2000, 2.4.2).

Lehmann's account exemplifies the pervasive, mutual sense of alterity that shaped such encounters. A primary notion of difference, between American Yiddish musicians, most of whom were Jews, and European, mainly non-Jewish, audiences, informed the attitudes of both parties, dominating questions of authenticity and musical ownership.

Substantial European audiences newly hungry for 'things Jewish' coupled with generous public funding programmes meant that work in Europe made an important contribution to the financial livelihood of professional American Yiddish musicians. With some irony, singer Michael Alpert noted that 'in 1993, Germany is one of a very few countries where you can make a living playing Jewish music' (Brave Old World 1994, liner notes). This tide of interest has proved durable. By the close of the twentieth century, such tours, later expanded to encompass practical workshops, and expanding geographically from Germany to Central Europe and later the former Soviet Union, had come to play a significant part in the working schedules of many American klezmer musicians. Ethnomusicologist Mark Slobin observed that 'rippling out in concentric circles from early festival activity in a number of countries, the effect of American recordings and touring groups intensified during the 1990s, showing no signs of peaking by the end of the decade' (2000, 82). A number of American bands worked with German agents and began to release their recordings in both North America and in Germany; the Klezmatics' schedule for 2001 included at least five trips to Europe.[5] In 2010, the Yiddish summer festival in Weimar and the Krakow Jewish Culture festival, both focusing primarily on Yiddish music, incorporating workshops, concerts and other public events, and including many American musicians on their performance and teaching roster, celebrated their tenth and twentieth anniversaries respectively, each having grown from a modest programme to a major international event.[6]

Discussing the performance of Yiddish music in contemporary Europe, Ruth Ellen Gruber suggests that music's participatory, interpretative and expressive nature provokes particularly 'vexing' questions of positionality (2002, 184). The importance of American musicians as central figures and role models in emerging European klezmer scenes – be it as performers, representatives, teachers or 'authentic Jews' – has repeatedly been asserted. Meanwhile, questions of identity, authenticity and musical ownership have catalysed intense debate among both American and European scholars discussing the German and Polish klezmer

---

[5] Lorin Sklamberg, interview with the author, New York, 9 August 2001.

[6] See http://www.yiddishsummer.eu/ and http://www.jewishfestival.pl/.

scenes of the 1990s and 2000s. A number of scholars have explored the approaches and motivations of (mainly) non-Jewish European musicians seeking to (re-) engage with an absent Jewish past, and to (re-)create a Jewish cultural space in contemporary Europe.[7] Questions of identity politics, power and representation are particularly complex and scholarly standpoints remain unresolved.

Nevertheless, notwithstanding the intense scholarly scrutiny accorded to these European musicians, there has been relatively little scholarly discussion of the experiences and motivations of the American Yiddish musicians who travelled to teach and perform to them.[8] These visits to former centres of European Jewry have taken place against a complex and changing background of post-Holocaust European–Jewish–American relations. That such experiences have been emotionally laden and potentially transformative is readily evident in written accounts. Travelling to Krakow, Poland, to take part in the city's third Jewish Culture Festival in 1992, American Yiddish singer Adrienne Cooper writes:

> The twenty-foot festival billboard towers over the concert hall and smaller posters are all over town – they show a vivid photograph in full color – a challah [Sabbath loaf] with a scorched Jewish star woven into its crust. When I first see the poster, I hate it. It seems crude, embarrassing. After a couple of days, the very things which were the source of my discomfort, the association of Jews with food, with appetite, have become what moves me about the poster: Jewish music as nurture, sustenance (1993, 13).

In this chapter, I consider how experiences of performing and teaching in Europe fit into, enrich and challenge the wider American Jewish narratives in which the contemporary Yiddish music scene discussed in this book is grounded. Via a series of case studies, I probe a small yet interesting body of creative work by American Yiddish musicians that arose directly from encounters with contemporary Europe from the mid-1980s to the mid-1990s. This time period is significant: for these musicians, as for the wider American Jewish community, these years marked an early period in the development of such post-war encounters: European borders were beginning to ease, against a context of increasing public engagement both sides of the Atlantic with the legacy of the Holocaust. Nevertheless, at this time American Jewish travel to Europe was still an exception; unlike later years when such travel became widely institutionalised, and thus familiarised, whether through Holocaust commemorative travel programmes such as the March of the

---

[7]   See, for example, Lehmann (2000), Slobin (2000), Gruber (2002), Ottens and Rubin (2002), Saxonberg and Waligórska (2006) and Ray (2010); a number of discussions in languages other than English are also referenced by these authors. See also reactions to German klezmer in the American press, including Kettmann (1998) and Brown (2001).

[8]   Judah Cohen's account (2009a) of three American Jewish musicians and bands touring Europe is a notable exception, however the visits he discusses took place reflect a rather later period of engagement (mid-1990s–2000s) than those discussed in this chapter.

Living, or through the growth and proliferation of European klezmer festivals, now long part of the 'everyday life' of many American Yiddish musicians.[9] In a real sense, musicians travelling to Europe in these early years were pioneers, and sought public expressive spaces in which to process their experiences and to convey them to a wider audience.

Here, I discuss two published diary accounts and two new Yiddish songs in which musicians reflect upon these early experiences of visiting contemporary Germany and Poland (in person in three cases, virtually in the other). The songs and texts discussed here reflect and refract a particular time and place, arising from a haphazard intersection of three principal currents which collectively afforded the conditions for these interchanges to take place: the continuing landscape of Yiddishism, fostered by American identity politics, provided the supportive environment for creative artists to give their East Ashkenazic heritage a central place in their work; the falling Iron Curtain put Central and Eastern Europe back on the travel map for Americans; meanwhile, the rising tide of Holocaust awareness on both sides of the Atlantic provided wide public support for this work. Situated within the wider discursive world of the contemporary Yiddishist scene, these accounts illustrate a wider interrelationship of textual and musical expression, pinpointing the interstice between personal experience and musical experience.

Brief Encounters: American Yiddish Musicians Report on European Travel

While leafing through Jewish journals in a New York City library, two articles caught my eye. Both were by prominent American Yiddish musicians; each gave an account of the musicians' experiences of performing in Europe. These also represent two of the earliest of the encounters discussed above: the first account, by Henry Sapoznik, discusses the visit of Kapelye to Berlin in 1984 (Sapoznik 1988b), and the second, by singer Adrienne Cooper, chronicles her visit to the 1992 Jewish music festival in Krakow, Poland (Cooper 1993). Sapoznik and Cooper's professional engagements as musicians frame their texts; nevertheless, unlike the posters which discomforted Cooper, and unlike the musical performances they document, which addressed Polish and German audiences, both the articles discussed here are aimed at an insider, 'back-home' American Jewish audience, evoking wider American Jewish discourses of post-Holocaust cultural encounter.

Both short articles are constructed as a series of diary entries, a literary form that enables the writer to perform a vulnerable counter to their confident, public persona on the music stage. Each account opens with the writer's journey itself,

---

9   The 'March of the Living', a programme focused on Holocaust commemoration and contemporary Jewish identity, in which American Jewish high-school students travel to the death camps in Poland and to Israel, began in 1988, the same year as the Krakow klezmer festival; the development of both reflects increased ease of travel especially following the fall of Communism. See Sheramy (2007) for discussion.

setting into relief the sense of a palpable distance between two opposing cultures. Dramatising their experiences to the reader, both Sapoznik and Cooper offer primarily experiential accounts, with close attention to detail. Both accounts are written in the first person and in the present tense, which lends further immediacy and intimacy to the writing. Sapoznik begins from a point of exceptionally heightened disjuncture: a picture of Kapelye playing at the Passion Kirche in West Berlin, the musicians standing in the sanctuary of the church in front of a huge cross. The diary mode further heightens the immediacy of the account, presenting the reader with a stream of thoughts and experiences, without the structural need for full interpretation. He writes:

Brussels, 26 July.

Today's the day: 'Return to Ashkenaz: Part I' (title for a new movie …) We have to get up early to make the 6 hour drive; Leon [our agent] has scheduled a press conference for us at 2:00 – and we all know how punctual the Germans are … All through the trip Ken [our clarinetist] and I were trying to ease our discomfort by making 'jokes' ('Boy, it's good we're doing this tour now; it wouldn't have been anywhere near as lucrative 40 years ago'. 'Ach, I love the Jews: some of my best friends were Jews …') We even managed a 4-part harmony on 'Springtime for Hitler'.

Uncomfortable? Who, me?

You bet.

Trepidation being in Germany and doing what we're doing. Kapelye as professional Jews: ('Hi! I'm a child of some of those who got away …') I'm sure that when I walk down the street and look at any German over 60 I'll ask myself 'What did he/she do during the war?' ('We were in the Resistance'. Was everybody?) Now I think about folks back home registering surprise about us playing in Germany. 'You're going to play *where*?' … Later I go out for a walk and see my first honest-to-goodness real German swastika spray painted on a wall. Oh boy! Now this is a swastika! Not like those wimpy, half-baked attempts I see back home in the subways. These people know from swastikas here. Welcome back … (1988b, 34–5).

Both the diary mode and the theme of the journey are common devices in American Jewish writing expressing the encounter between Old and New World.[10] The frame of the journey creates a sense of instability, suggesting that the experiences to be discussed lie in a liminal space, outside the framework of 'normal' life. In Europe, the ordinary becomes exotic: reports of the concerts both Cooper and Sapoznik are

---

[10]   For examples, see Shandler (1989).

there to give are placed side by side with anecdotes of chance encounters, airport formalities, visual scenes and so on. Rather than concentrating solely upon their experiences as musicians, every part of their trip – including those parts of travel usually considered mundane – is described and assumes equal significance. This exoticism is here cemented by Sapoznik's suggestion of a film title, a re-reading of this journey through the eyes of fiction. This instability mirrors the uncertainty Sapoznik expresses concerning his and the band's role in Germany.

The physical distance of travel also serves as a metaphor for cultural or historical distance. Both Cooper and Sapoznik encounter and make sense of their experiences through the spectacles of Jewish history; even Cooper's description of bucolic scenes seen from the Krakow–Warsaw train is punctuated by a signpost for a former Hasidic site. In his catalogue to an exhibition entitled *Going Home*, Jeffrey Shandler observes that the sense of traversing history has long characterised American Jews' travel encounters with Europe. 'Typically', he notes, 'the physical discontinuities of the "Old" World and "New" World are joined through the temporal logic of *past* and *present*. More than a journey across space, going home is travel through time' (1989, 4).

Memorial activities frame this encounter between past and present, and provide an outlet for feelings of discomfort. Following a substantial account of her plane trip, the first impression reported by Cooper upon leaving the airport in Warsaw is that 'signs of Jewish life are not apparent in Poland. One's first impulse is to head for the places of mourning – they're identifiable' (1993, 12). On her way to Krakow, Cooper did just this: along with several other American musicians travelling with her, she stopped at the park in Warsaw marking where the Jewish ghetto had been during the Second World War:

> Our little group engages in a spectrum of memorial behaviours, our tools – the camera, a book of psalms, silence, compulsive talking. The religious men in our contingent walk purposefully to each monument and read a psalm or recite *kaddish* (the memorial prayer for the dead). I lift the camera to my eye and snap repeatedly – the monuments, a willow tree, the bed of freshly planted begonias, the Poles reading on the park benches, the psalm-sayers, the ones who need to talk, the ones who need to stand alone … (1993, 12).

As Cooper describes, there is no homogeneity in her group's responses: each chooses to conceptualise and to deal with their experiences in a different way, to take on a different role: religious, photographer, tourist. Such behaviours, like the self-conscious joking of Sapoznik and his colleagues, serve as distancing strategies, embedding the encounter within a ritual behaviour or behind the lens of a camera. As Susan Sontag has observed, the camera helps its holder to feel secure in an unfamiliar space, suppressing anxiety and providing an opportunity for action instead of exposing oneself to disorientating experiences (1973, 8–10).

The liminal experience of both journey-diaries is compounded by a sense of insecurity relating to contemporary anti-Semitism, both imagined and experienced.

Encounters such as Sapoznik's sighting of a swastika, above, serve to reinforce the image of Europe as a liminal, potentially dangerous space, forestalling any sense of comfort and familiarity. Real and perceived dangers are rolled together into a pervasive sense of discomfort. Cooper observes:

> From the moment I arrive in Poland, I have the distinct sensation that I am passing – I am safe because I am not recognisable as a Jew. Two members of our travelling group are Hasidim. My sense of safety coexists with a feeling, later confirmed by experience, that I pass, where these two men do not. They are dressed like targets – beards, *peyes* (unshaven sidelocks), hats, black suits and exposed *tsitsis* (the fringes of a ritual undergarment worn by religious men). And indeed they do not pass. One of them, Andy Statman, had been chased in the streets of Kiev, where he had concertized before coming to Poland, and was detained, on one excuse or another, at every East European border he attempted to cross … I feel vulnerable – we have all become visible with the Hasidim in our midst (1993, 12).

Such encounters form a stark contrast to the secure, mainstream normality of Jewish existence in North America. They reinforce a heightened awareness of Jewishness, and tend to confirm rather than challenge central American Jewish narratives about Europe. Such narratives pre-date the Holocaust: Jeffrey Shandler notes that even for early American Jewish travellers to the Old World, the journey reinforced negative perceptions of Jewish Europe, 'thereby confirming the wisdom of migration' (1989, 4). In his study of today's American Jewish tourism to Poland, Jack Kugelmass also suggests that the repositioning of the self from an American privileged position to a European position of victimhood acts as a ritual performance that helps participants 'to bridge fundamental discontinuities in life: those between American and East European Jewry, between postwar and prewar Jewry, between the living and the dead, and between power and powerlessness' (1994, 179).

Here, however, Cooper and Sapoznik's positionality is further complicated by their status as invited performers. As visiting Yiddish musicians, they are not only cultural tourists, seeking shards of the past, but are a tourist site in themselves, their identity publicly highlighted. Unlike the 'internal tourism' of their regular performances, in which Yiddish heritage is presented to a primarily insider, American Jewish audience, here their performance is a dual one, both musical and ethnic. Just as Europe is exoticised by these Jewish travellers, they are also presented as an exotic Other, an exoticism that extends to their whole journey, on stage or not. The Jewishness of the musicians provides legitimation for their work, but this is tempered by the cost of adding considerable stereotyped baggage. As musicians, their role is clear-cut, expressed in concert contracts, festival brochures and pay cheques. As Jews, their performance is much less clear-cut, and they have little control over their self-image, slotted into a convenient ethnic category based more upon images of the Jews of the past than upon living, contemporary Jewish culture.

Within this strongly constructed cultural binary, the Yiddish language serves as a mediator. While the use of Yiddish indexes a past-focused Jewish identity, it also serves as a means of communication, particularly in Germany: while few of the audience may be Jewish, listeners will understand much of what is said in Yiddish, owing to the closeness of the languages. The experience of mutual comprehension initially came as a shock to Yiddishists used to being one of only a handful of their generation conversant in Yiddish, confounding established constructions of fluency. Michael Alpert, another member of Kapelye travelling on their 1984 tour, notes that it was 'strange to find we could do our show in Yiddish and it would be understood better here than back home' (quoted in Sapoznik 1999, 225). Meanwhile, Sapoznik frames the linguistic encounter as yet another ambiguous layer of the travel experience:

> 27 July. I just can't get used to it. Walking down the street today I thought I heard someone behind me speaking Yiddish. I turned and quickly realized that he was speaking German. Brrrr. It really upset me but I found myself enjoying the sensation of hearing 'Yiddish' spoken on the street. I walked down the street kind of half listening to the babble going on about me, making believe it was Yiddish … Michael [Alpert] (our lead singer) made a fabulous quip: he told the crowd the reason we do the show in Yiddish is we were told in America that they speak a dialect of it here. That went over real big (especially with the band) (1988b, 35).

A few years later, as part of a new ensemble, Brave Old World, Alpert made use of this mutual comprehension directly to address a German audience via a Yiddish song (the song, 'Sing, My Fiddle', is discussed at length below). However, the choice to perform in Yiddish was not only made for reasons of comprehension. Kapelye also framed their use of Yiddish as an opportunity to take on an educational role, a direct illustration of what was lost in the Holocaust. This educational role also reasserts Kapelye's agency in the encounter, projecting their own choice of agenda rather than one imposed from outside:

> We have decided to do intros mostly in Yiddish with limited English because … because we're in Germany. We want our audiences to hear the language that their parents, grandparents, grandparents' neighbours, and friends nearly destroyed (Sapoznik 1999, 224).

Sapoznik and Cooper's accounts document the intense feelings and experiences, the wariness and strong reactions associated with an initial encounter with a historically charged landscape. During the years that followed, such visits became a more regular part of the diary of American Yiddish musicians, and the very fact of the visit no longer became in itself newsworthy. Nevertheless, discomfort remained prominent in American Yiddish musicians' discussion of experiences concertising in Europe, now often displaced from immediate experiences of anti-Semitism to a more general perceived stereotyping of Jews and Jewish culture. In 1994, Michael Alpert suggested that, in Germany, two images – Hasidim and the Holocaust – are all-pervasive, and obliterate recognition of the real breadth of Yiddish culture:

> Too often [in Germany], our Yiddish tongue conjures up only the sainted rebbe of the 'vanished' shtetl, the wandering *luftmentsh* and stumbling *shlimazl* chasing dreams, those idealized, dancing Hasidim whose images bedeck the walls of so many suburban Jewish homes. *Ein so fröliches Volk* … such a happy people. Or else a faceless black-and-white stream en route to Auschwitz … Where are the modernist poets of Vilna and New York, the avant-garde artists of Moscow and Vitebsk, the proletarian intelligentsia of Warsaw? (Brave Old World 1994, liner notes)

A number of music workshop programmes, including the Hasidic music workshops discussed in the next chapter, have explicitly sought to undo such romantic visions of the Yiddish past. It is not only the perception of past Yiddish culture, however, that is constrained by such stereotypes. Such images also jar with the arrival of today's musicians from a climate of modern progressive American Jewish culture, a cultural space very different from the spectrum of contemporary European Jewishness. Lorin Sklamberg, lead singer of the Klezmatics, a band whose rock band image, downtown sound and queer politics particularly highlights this difference, muses:

> The thing is that, like everything else with the Jewish world, you're kind of strapped with what people perceive as a responsibility. Once, a concert that we did in Luxembourg, it was in the summer, it was, like, a million degrees, and you know, in the summer, if you're playing in a rock concert, you dress like a rock musician – wear shorts and a T-shirt or whatever. We came off stage, and there was this man with his wife, he was wearing a suit and a tie, and he said – this wasn't an old person, either – it was like, 'How can you dress this way? You represent the Jewish people'. You know … someone in East Germany once said, 'Why don't you dress more like Jews?'[11]

For others, discomfort is often related to powerlessness and lack of control over one's own image or lack of ability to project one's own narrative. Remembering an incident that had occurred a few nights previously during a jam session at a café in central Weimar during the summer of 2002, Michael Alpert recalled:

---

[11]   Lorin Sklamberg, interview with the author, New York, 9 August 2001.

A couple of people came up to me – I don't know, maybe they heard me speaking German or something – but they came up and said, you know, '*Wir wollten fragen Sie, woher kommt die Musik*', '*was für Musik ist das?*' [We wanted to ask you where this music comes from – what sort of music is this?], and I said, this is '*jiddische muzik*' [Yiddish music], or '*osteuropäische jüdische muzik, also wir kommen meistens aus den Staaten, also nicht alle*' [East European Jewish music; most of us come from the States, but not all of us] … I talked about the workshops and, you know, East European Jewish music but we're not from Eastern Europe … I had said, you know, I'm part of a group with those three people, we're from the United States, and lot of this is East European Jewish music, but through the lens and filter of us being Americans – and I sort of went into all of it. And then after a few minutes … he said, '*Dann kommen Sie dann alle aus Israel?*' [Then do you all come from Israel?] Which is classic – I mean, this is not the sort of person I would say is a raving anti-Semite, it's just sort of a classic … attitude, I think, in a lot of Europe – I know it very well in Germany.[12]

These final comments evince great cautiousness, belying the 'easy' comprehension experienced by Kapelye, and reinforcing a strong binary distinction between Yiddish cultural experts and European audiences. Similarly, in 2001, Barbara Kirshenblatt-Gimblett still characterised the encounter as a one-way process, with cultural capital still firmly in American hands: 'in recent years American Jews have also been exporting Europe back to itself, as the success of klezmer music and young American klezmer musicians in Europe attest' (2001, 183).

In Cooper's and Sapoznik's accounts of performing in Europe, music primarily played a functional role. Concerts provided a reason for invitations to Europe, catalysing encounters with the landscapes of the Holocaust and with complex issues of positionality; the performance of the Yiddish language via song served as a medium of encounter between performers and audiences. Nevertheless, in turning to song, other American Yiddish musicians have created a further role for music in this discursive space, recasting song as an arena for explicit discussion of the emotional encounter with contemporary Europe. Two such songs will be considered here: 'Ikh heyb mayn fus' (I lift my foot) by Josh Waletzky, and 'Sing, My Fiddle' by Michael Alpert. Both singer/songwriters set their own original Yiddish texts, inspired by and addressing specific personal experiences, and both songs appear in a focal position on CD albums released by the artists. Waletzky and Alpert share some similarities in their background: both were born in America after the war and grew up in Yiddish-speaking families, and both have been involved professionally in many areas of Yiddish creativity. The two songs, however, differ substantially, reflecting the individual backgrounds of the two artists, the musical traditions they situate themselves within, and their intended audiences, and also reflecting the contrasting ways in which the European Jewish legacy fits into their individual views of Yiddish culture and creativity.

---

[12]   Michael Alpert, interview with the author, Weimar, 31 July 2002.

From Writing to Music: Europe in New Yiddish Songs

Josh Waletzky: 'Ikh heyb mayn fus' (I lift my foot). Ariber di shotns (Crossing the Shadows), 2001

> The immediate impetus for writing *Crossing the Shadows* came in an editing room in 1995, where I was working on a PBS special, *Itzhak Perlman: In the Fiddler's House*. The sight of Jewish music inhabiting a large square in Krakow was strangely thrilling and disturbing at the same time. I began writing: '*Ikh heyb mayn fus, nor zi vil nit tantsn* – I lift my foot, but it doesn't want to dance …' (Waletzky 2001, liner notes)

'Ikh heyb mayn fus' (I lift my foot) is the first number on *Crossing the Shadows*, an album of 14 original Yiddish songs with words and music by Josh Waletzky. '*Crossing the Shadows*', writes Waletzky, 'is written in the musical language of Yiddish-speaking Jews, which is for me, the most direct language of my self and my community' (2001, liner notes). Like the written accounts discussed above, Waletzky's song records a moment of emotional response to his experience of Jewish music being played in today's Europe. Further, like Sapoznik's and Cooper's diaries, his comments reflect an American Jewish experience, and are aimed – like his album itself – at an American audience. Unlike the other musicians discussed in this chapter, however, for whom an actual journey to Central Europe was the catalyst for an outpouring of material, in Waletzky's case the trip was 'virtual'. The image which inspired this song came while he was editing the documentary *Itzhak Perlman: In the Fiddler's House*, released in 1995, an hour-long film which features Perlman jamming with members of American klezmer bands (including Brave Old World, the Klezmatics and the Klezmer Conservatory Band) both in New York City and in Krakow. This film itself played an important role in the American klezmer scene, substantially increasing the visibility of the klezmer revival via national broadcasting and two popular CD releases.

Notwithstanding the wide audience of *In the Fiddler's House*, Josh Waletzky's songs reflect a much more intimate American Yiddish culture. I attended the launch of the album in May 2001, at the Tonic club in New York. Situated in a former kosher winery on Manhattan's Lower East Side, during the early 2000s Tonic hosted 'avant garde, creative & experimental music', including a two-set 'Klezmer Brunch' every Sunday, a series featuring Jewish vocal and instrumental music.[13] The club's basement formed an intimate performance space with a small stage, a bar, a few tables and chairs; a few large old wooden wine casks had been carved out to make additional seating areas. A couple of dozen people, a good number of whom knew each other personally from the New York Yiddishist scene, gathered for the launch of *Crossing the Shadows*. The performance was informal;

---

[13]   http://www.tonic107.com/, accessed 6 January 2002. See Barzel (2010) for further discussion of the music scene at Tonic; the venue closed in 2007.

each song was introduced by the musicians: as on the album itself, Josh Waletzky (lead voice and piano) was joined by Deborah Strauss (violin and voice) and Jeff Warschauer (mandolin, guitar, voice and percussion).

Crossing the Shadows was Waletzky's first album of original material in Yiddish, released six years after the initial inspiration described above. The 14 items on the album span a wide range of subject material: Waletzky's reaction to Jewish music in Poland, as described above, inspired the initial song of the collection; however, the following numbers treat subject matter ranging from the large news events of the Irish and Middle East peace processes to traditional Yiddish motifs of nature, marriage and the Sabbath. Most of the texts are in the first person, crystallising Waletzky's individual voice as a singer-songwriter, and lending the collection an air of intimacy. This is enhanced by the chamber sonorities of the music – this is music for a private gathering rather than a large stage – and by the dedication of individual songs to members of Waletzky's family.

Involved throughout his life in Yiddish culture and music, Waletzky situates his musical background in a Yiddish-American framework, shaped by the network of Yiddishist institutions discussed in Chapter 1. If his album grew from the moment of inspiration he describes, it also represents a wider coalescence of artistic and practical impulses. Born in 1948 to American-born Yiddish-speaking parents, he grew up in the Bronx, and whilst Yiddish was not the main language of the household, he recalls that the language played a symbolic role in his home life:

> We spoke Yiddish at home in a kind of a programmed way. We studied Yiddish in the *folkshul* [Yiddish secular school] we went to; Friday night, at the dinner table, we spoke Yiddish. So that was a deliberate attempt to get us to be Yiddish speakers, to increase our fluency. I think certain years of my growing up we spoke twice a week, on Tuesday and Friday, something like that. So there was a real, conscious attempt, so *zalts* [salt] and *fefer* [pepper] and all these things, kind of terms and attempting to convey one's experience of the day in Yiddish, this was all part of our growing up. But English was the primary language of the household, the primary language of communication. So Yiddish was reserved for kind of a special spot in the family life. I guess there were three things: that we studied, that it was spoken at certain times, at the table, and we sang a lot.[14]

Waletzky's musical development represented a similar fusion of English and Yiddish expression. He had a formal Western musical education, attending the Julliard preparatory division whilst at high school, studying piano, music theory and composition. At the same time, in addition to singing in the family home, he attended a secular Yiddish school three times a week at which the composer Vladimir Heifetz taught music, introducing Waletzky to his style of choral writing – and he regularly attended Boiberik, a Yiddishist summer camp. For Waletzky, the

---

[14]   Unless otherwise indicated, the following quotations are taken from Josh Waletzky, interview with the author, New York, 30 May 2001.

camp integrated family and community: both of his parents had attended the camp in their younger years, and his mother, Tsirl Waletzky – a paper-cut artist whose work appears on the cover of *Crossing the Shadows* – was an art teacher there. Nevertheless, the camp, as a semi-permanent Yiddishist heterotopia, provided a wider, ongoing musical environment and a form of apprenticeship:

> Yiddish music also pervaded my summer home of 22 years, Camp Boiberik. Boiberik (the name was taken from a story by Sholem Aleichem) was a vibrant community of children's camp and adult resort built around a Yiddish cultural program. I learned songs voraciously from my family, Yiddish schools, recordings and printed sources; but Boiberik was my musical hometown. During my own eight-year turn as Music Director, I compiled or composed dozens of songs each summer for programs and pageants. By my last summer in Boiberik, at age 27, I was a full-fledged Yiddish composer, writing in a living musical language (Waletzky 2001, liner notes).

Based on these experiences, Waletzky situates his Yiddish identity firmly in an American framework, grounded in a continuing expressive tradition:

> This was all to me an unbroken tradition. I never grew up with a sense of a broken tradition. I mean, not to minimise the fact of the Holocaust, the feeling that the whole world that this ultimately derived from, had been destroyed. But for me it was important, my sense of the fact that my parents, after all, had been born here … So I was American, you know, completely, not any sense of being an immigrant, and the music that my father sang, to me, was American music. I was aware, of course, that it was not English, but I didn't perceive of it as something, you know, from old 78s or something pastiche, or anything like that. I like to say that it's not … for me it's not in quotation marks, any of this stuff – this is my music! [laughs].

This immersion in Yiddish musical culture formed a foundation for Waletzky's later activities, as his involvement with Yiddish music continued into adulthood. His song 'Wissotzky's Tea' (based on a Sholem Aleichem story and originally written for a Boiberik production) was first recorded as part of a collection of new Yiddish songs by Yiddishist organisation Yugntruf (*Vaserl*, 1977). The song later entered the repertory of various klezmer bands, and was recorded by other ensembles including the Klezmer Conservatory Band (*A Touch of Klez!*, 1985) and the Maxwell St Klezmer Band (*Maxwell Street Wedding*, 1991). Like Sapoznik and Alpert, Waletzky was a member of Kapelye – one of the bands at the forefront of the beginning of the klezmer revival – during its early years, and was also part of a group of younger Yiddish speakers in New York who frequently got together for Friday night dinners, speaking Yiddish and singing songs.[15]

---

15   Michael Alpert, interview, 2002.

By profession a documentary filmmaker, Waletzky's film work has intersected with his interest in Yiddish music on several occasions. He directed and edited *Image before My Eyes* (1980), a film about Jewish life in Poland during the 1930s, and *Partisans of Vilna* (1986), a documentary about Jewish resistance during the Second World War. The soundtracks of these films include both new and archival recordings of Yiddish song and instrumental music; the soundtrack album of the latter was nominated for a Grammy. The former included material collected by the YIVO folksong project (discussed in Chapter 2), in which Waletzky was informally involved. Material collected by this project also formed part of the soundtrack of *Image before My Eyes*, alongside other vocal and instrumental recordings from the YIVO archives.

As Waletzky notes in the interview segment opening this section, the song 'Ikh heyb mayn fus' – which marked the beginning of the creative process that led to *Crossing the Shadows* – arose from a specific intersection of film-making and Yiddish music. He described seeing a specific scene from *In the Fiddler's House*, showing shots of a huge Jewish culture festival in Krakow. His response evinced a sense of ambiguity and discomfort:

> So I was watching the [film of the] performance in the square in Krakow, and I had a very strong reaction of these two directions: it was thrilling to see such a large number of people responding to the music, but at the same time, there was something completely wrong, you know [laughs]. So, I began to write the song. You know, sometimes a melody comes first and then words come, and then sometimes vice versa, in that case they both actually came together, it was a single idea – 'ikh heyb mayn fus nor zi vil nit tantsn' [I lift my foot, but it doesn't want to dance].

While the discomfort Waletzky felt while editing this scene provided the immediate inspiration for this song, at the same time this film project also served to link him to a far more local scene: a new core of New York-based musicians competent in Yiddish music:

> I was working on *Itzhak Perlman: In the Fiddler's House* and I was stimulated to think about writing something. I saw a number of performers that I had not seen before, like Deborah Strauss. I had seen performances by Brave Old World and perhaps the Klezmatics; I was familiar with the Klezmer Conservatory Band, seen them perform a few times when they were in New York, but by that time there were so many bands – I just wasn't familiar with a lot of these performers. So there was kind of a feeling of – wow – and the better musicians among this group were very impressive and wow, you know, there's people to sit at the table with, and among them were Deborah Strauss and Jeff Warschauer [the two artists with whom he collaborates on this album]. Also I reconnected with Meyshke, Michael Alpert [the musical director of the film], who I had known in Kapelye, and we were quite friendly and quite close, but I hadn't seen much of

over the years. And these things just brought out a feeling of there being a *svive* – a context, a surrounding, an environment in which to write.

In the text of 'Ikh heyb mayn fus', Waletzky freezes his moment of inspiration and elaborates upon it:

Ikh heyb mayn fus,	*I lift my foot,*
nor zi vil nit tantsn	*but it doesn't want to dance*
iber di farbrente beyner;	*over the incinerated bones.*
ikh her nokh dayn geshrey,	*I still hear your screaming,*
bruder-lebn, shvester-lebn,	*dear brother, dear sister,*
iber di tsetrotene shteyner.	*over the trampled stones.*
Ikh heyb mayn kol,	*I lift my voice,*
nor es vil nit zingen	*but it doesn't want to sing*
unter di farshemte beymer;	*under the disgraced trees;*
ikh her nokh dayn geshrey,	*I still hear your screaming,*
bruder-lebn, shvester-lebn,	*dear brother, dear sister,*
vu vestu gefinen itst dayn keyver?	*Where, now, will you find your grave?*[16]

The two verses are related through parallelism, balanced both in structure and content. In using this device, Waletzky alludes to a tradition of the use of parallel structures to impart internal equilibrium in Jewish poetry, dating back to Biblical poetry including the Psalms.[17] Reading the Krakow scene through the historical frame of the Holocaust, painful meaning is projected onto everyday scenes, which bear echoes of that history, becoming 'trampled stones' and 'disgraced trees'. The actions of the dancers seem to disrupt the rest of the dead: 'where, now, will you find your grave?' Responding to this scene, Waletzky's protagonist expresses visceral inability to take part in the joyful acts of dancing and singing; his voice is silenced by screams from the past.

While the poetic form of 'Ikh heyb mayn fus' is clear and unambiguous, the musical setting mediates and complicates this expression. Waletzky articulates the 'contradictory emotions' he describes through the use of devices operating within many dimensions of musical structure. Characteristically, he situates his compositional process within the established tradition of Yiddish song:

Now, I love the simpler forms of folksong, but I guess I have to say that there are any number of Yiddish folksongs that have three or four, some cases five or six,

---

[16]   Text and translation Josh Waletzky, reproduced with permission. The CD, as well as printed versions of the music and text of the songs, may be obtained from the publisher: josh.waletzky@yahoo.com.

[17]   For further discussion of parallelism as a poetic device in classic Jewish texts, see Lichtenstein (1984).

sections to them, and I'm particularly attracted to them musically, and that's the direction that I wanted to feel free to have the song expand into. The connection between the sections is the thing that interested me greatly, compositionally, in working on this. So, 'Ikh heyb mayn fus' has a slower section and then a faster section, and how do they connect? Because I was exploring emotions that were contradictory, and the interesting part of the thing musically was to explore that feeling musically. So how do you go from 4 [beats in a bar] to 3? That's very interesting. My whole style here is very understated – harmonically, in every way – because to me for this composition I was interested in, I guess I would say, the deepest roots of this are unaccompanied vocal singing, and that's kind of the whole musical language of it.

The verses of the text correspond to 'verse' sections of music, which alternate with a contrasting, wordless *nign* (dance melody).[18] The opening of the *nign* melody and the second phrase of the verse melody are transcribed as Examples 4.1 and 4.2.

Example 4.1 'Ikh heyb mayn fus' *nign* melody (opening)

Example 4.2 'Ikh heyb mayn fus' verse melody (second phrase)

The musical features of the *nign* and verse contrast across several musical dimensions. The *nign* is untexted, in duple metre with a regular pulse; its C major melody has a range of an octave, and percussion is used exclusively in this section. By contrast, the verse is texted, in triple metre with rubato; the melody moves to C minor, extending in the second phrase to a range of an octave and a fourth (see Example 4.2). The mandolin is used exclusively in the verse sections. These

---

[18] While the terms '*nign*' (Yiddish) and '*nigun*' (Hebrew) are often used interchangeably, Waletzky points out, citing Feldman (1994, 7), that the Yiddish word *nign* refers specifically to a vocal dance tune. This usage is distinct from more general reference to *nigun*, a Hebrew word meaning 'melody', commonly used to indicate religious vocal melodies of Hasidic origin (Josh Waletzky, email communication, 31 August 2012).

differences serve to differentiate the sections, giving each a distinctive character. The music of the verse mirrors the expressive sphere of the text: its minor key, use of rubato, wide vocal range and long phrases convey a sense of introspection and melancholy. Waletzky, as narrator, speaks to the dead, situating them within the close family bonds he describes above: *bruder lebn, shvester lebn* (dear brother, dear sister). Their resounding cry is echoed in the melody of the song, which arches to a peak at this point, further collapsing the distance between the historical and the contemporary present.

By contrast, the major key, regular pulse and short phrases of the *nign* suggest a joyful mood. Here, the use of percussion hints at the footsteps of the dancers on Waletzky's screen; his voice sings along with the scene in front of him, this time collapsing spatial, rather than historical, distance. This musical reference to dancing further sets into relief the inability of the protagonist of the verses to join in with these usually effortless and cheerful activities. In this context, the absence of the voice in a third, instrumental verse acquires further programmatic significance.

Other aspects of the two sections provide cohesion to the song, drawing together these two emotions. The pulse, while regular in the *nign* and irregular in the verse, is roughly equal throughout; a four-bar link section following the *nign* effects the move to 3/4 while preserving the pulse exactly, smoothing the transition between sections. In their instrumentation, both sections make use of the staggered entry of voices and of countermelodies. Structurally, elision is present in both sections. In the verse, this reflects the construction of the text: each three-line half of each verse represents a single thought; an eight-bar phrase is allocated for each of these segments. Whereas the listener might expect the opening phrase of the verse to rest following a modulation to the relative major at bar 5, the phrase continues onwards. In the *nign*, all four phrases move from tonic to dominant, thus depending upon the opening of the next phrase for tonal resolution. The verse and the *nign* also share aspects of their motivic construction. Both make use of repeated bars containing a falling pattern, outlining the interval of a fourth (*nign*) or fifth (verse). This figure (marked 'x' in Examples 4.1 and 4.2) is musically static, serving to delay the further progression of the melody, and recalling the hesitance of the text.

Functioning as an integrated whole, the song serves as an expression of feelings that are not only contradictory, but also interdependent. Ultimately, both musical and textual resolution is found wanting: the song ends on an open harmony and the discomfort of the text is left unresolved. This is a stop-frame glimpse by a distant narrator, an emotional image frozen in time, which does not feel the need to answer to the questions it raises.

Michael Alpert and Brave Old World: 'Sing, My Fiddle', Beyond the Pale, 1994

If Josh Waletzky's album *Crossing the Shadows* is aimed at an intimate audience of Yiddish insiders, by contrast, Brave Old World's *Beyond the Pale* was released on an international label, addressed to both American and European audiences. *Beyond the Pale* was BOW's second album, released in 1994; the album's title, explained in the liner notes, refers both to 'the expression meaning "beyond established borders", "outside the norm", "provocative"' (Brave Old World 1994, liner notes), adjectives with which the band characterises their approach to Yiddish music, and to the Pale of Settlement, the Russian-controlled area in which Jews were permitted to live and travel, established by Catherine the Great in 1772 during the partitioning of Poland.[19] The visual material of the CD explores the theme of distance between the USA and Europe, here expressed in spatial terms: the cover shows a stylised old-fashioned map with the borders of America and Europe at either side and a large expanse of ocean in the middle.

Musically, the 14 tracks of the album span a variety of klezmer melodies and Yiddish songs, from traditional songs learnt by singer Michael Alpert from Ukrainian-born folksinger Bronya Sakina, to material composed by members of the band themselves. Most of the origins of pieces, at least where alluded to in the notes, are European rather than American, and the band's own compositions recall European settings. These references are not a response to a fleeting encounter, but rather reflect prolonged engagement with contemporary Europe: the band in its present form grew out of ad hoc concert dates in Berlin in 1988, and its members continue to spend a significant proportion of their time working in Germany, performing, recording and teaching.

Directly addressing the subject of performing Jewish music in Germany 'Sing, My Fiddle' comprises two tracks which frame the other material on the CD: 'Berlin Overture' and 'Berlin 1990'.[20] Together the two tracks form one extended song, creating and maintaining an extramusical standpoint that implicitly undergirds the rest of the album. Liner notes continuing the themes of the song text reinforce the role of 'Sing, My Fiddle' as interpretative frame: not only do the two parts of the song flank the other songs in programming terms, but the printed, prose format adds a physical dimension to this narrative, literally enveloping the CD in discourse. The first part of the song, 'Berlin Overture (Sing, My Fiddle, Pt. I)', is glossed:

> An original Yiddish song written in 1990, inspired by the feeling in the air – and on the ground – in Berlin following the fall of The Wall. After ten years of playing Jewish music in Germany, the irony has not abated (Brave Old World 1994, liner notes).

---

[19]   This area was a swathe of land incorporating today's Lithuania, Belarus, Ukraine and parts of Poland. These restrictions lasted until 1917, although they were lifted for certain professions during the 1850s.

[20]   For ease of reference during the following discussion, the title 'Sing, My Fiddle' will be used to refer to the song as a whole, and 'Berlin Overture' and 'Berlin 1990' to refer to its first and second parts respectively.

and the second part, 'Berlin 1990 (Sing, My Fiddle, Pt. II):

> *'And the walls came tumbling down ...'* Or did they? The main body of the song
> that begins this recording (Brave Old World 1994, liner notes).

Introducing 'Sing, My Fiddle' to a primarily German audience at Klezmer Wochen
Weimar 2003, Alpert explained the background to his song:

> It's a song I started writing in 1990, just after the fall of the Berlin Wall ... I
> finished it between 1990 and 1993 – we recorded it with Brave Old World in
> 1993. ... [I] wanted to express a lot of feelings that I had about this at the time
> – this very complicated, complex mass of feelings I had about making Yiddish
> music in Germany. By this point, by 1993, or let's say, when I started, 1990,
> I had already been doing that for about six years ... and I was thinking a lot
> about, you know, what does this mean, to be an American Jew in Berlin, this city
> that was undergoing these enormous changes, that was on the border of many
> different worlds ... People were pouring into Berlin from all over the world,
> especially from Eastern Europe: from Poland, from Romania, from Turkey,
> everywhere, because it was clearly this city that a lot was going on in, and that
> the world was meeting in. Suddenly Berlin was becoming a world city again, as
> it was, to some extent, prior to the Second World War.[21]

Unusually among Alpert's song output, rather than a pastiche based on historical
Yiddish song forms, here he adopts a contemporary singer-songwriter voice.
'Berlin 1990' opens with a single voice accompanied by finger-picking guitar
in a minor key in triple metre. The sound world is reminiscent of 1960s folk
ballads, a musical genre associated with social protest, casting the singer as a lone
protestor in a difficult world – associations which reinforce the imagery of his text.
In conversation with me, Alpert particularly credited his use of song for social
and political comment to German *Liedermacher* including Heinz Rudolf Kunze,
whose music had been prominent in Germany during the period of BOW's work
there. This reinforces fellow band member Alan Bern's statement that BOW's
immersion in contemporary German culture strongly influenced the group's artistic
development, enabling them to see music as a platform for serious commentary:

> By [1989] Brave Old World was performing regularly in Germany. The
> audiences we encountered in Germany approached our concerts as serious
> events of both cultural and political consequence, not as light entertainment. It's
> a deep historical irony that just these conditions helped us to view ourselves as
> artists and supported our full development into that role (Bern 1998).

---

[21]   Michael Alpert, 'Meet the Artists' session, Klezmer Wochen Weimar, 8 August
2003.

Like Waletzky's 'Ikh heyb mayn fus', and, indeed, like the diarists whose accounts of working in Central Europe opened this chapter, Alpert writes in the first person, using the singer-songwriter mode to voice his own personal experiences, and anchors his voice resolutely in the here-and-now. Unlike the other authors, though, who address their accounts to unspecified (assumed American) audiences, Alpert's song explicitly addresses German youth. While such audiences play a significant part in allowing BOW to earn their livelihood through Yiddish music, Alpert nevertheless addresses his audience from a bitter and critical standpoint, announcing that not 'keyn mol' (never) but 'keyn eyn mol' (not even once) 'has it been easy for me to be here' (verse 2).

Alpert expresses this discomfort through a kaleidoscope of experiences, as if the adoption of the singer-songwriter voice opens the floodgates for the expression of pent-up thoughts. One of the most prominent of these is his sense that the immediate shadow of the Holocaust always hangs over his presence as a Jew in Germany: '... Dem nekhtns a viderkol tomid faran / "Zikhroyne levrokhe" bay itlekhn shpan' (Yesterday's echo forever at hand, 'Of Blessed Memory' at every turn) (verse 3). Rather than dwelling on commemoration, however, Alpert turns to the wider impact of the Nazi period upon the here and now: if not for the Holocaust, 'volt ikh ekhet gevezn eyropes a kind' (I too would have been Europe's progeny) (verse 4). This sense of a loss and distance clarifies the envy expressed in verse 2: 'nor kh'bin aykh mekane / Ir, hayntike kinder fun nekhtikn faynt / Vayl aykh iz di tsukunft / Eyn land un a shprakh / Bes mir haltn shtumerheyt do ... (Yet I envy you / Today's children of yesterday's enemy / Because yours is the future / One land and a language / While we are left here, speechless). He explained to me:

> 'Un a shprakh' [and a language], I mean, there's a *world* that lives in Germany, whereas we have to sort of invent these words for, you know, travel agency and boarding pass, because we don't *have* this kind of modern, totally functional Yiddish culture, in the same way as ... a *land* and *universities* and, you know, television stations ... And 'mir blaybn shtumerheit do' [we are left here speechless], we're left to *shtumer reyd* [talk silently], because we don't have that ... whole language to speak.[22]

Faced with this impenetrable barrier of communication, the protagonist ultimately turns from verbal to musical expression: 'To zing mayn fidele ...' (So, sing my fiddle ...). Here, in contrast to the encumbered voice, the violin is conceived as capable of 'pure' musical expression – sing me a sweet diaspora song with a longing that's pure – unencumbered by textual baggage.

Alpert's text later becomes accusatory – anger about past German crimes is deflected into criticism of today's xenophobia. As the song begins, his protagonist is wandering around a Polish market in Berlin, an uneasy allusion to images of the Wandering Jew. Watching immigrant traders, Alpert suggests that new

---

22   Michael Alpert, interview, 2002.

populations have now moved into the cultural spaces once occupied by Jews, but that once again their lives are subject to racial discrimination. Acknowledging the complexities of the relationship between different peoples, Alpert nevertheless recalls, '[I] was spending between three and seven months a year here. And when I heard that Germany was deporting Roma, East European Roma, I just really sort of saw red – it was like, you know, this incredible chutzpah to do this'.[23] In his choice of Yiddish words, Alpert draws direct parallels with the Nazi past, starkly invoking a comparison with *Kristallnacht*, the night of Nazi terror against Jews in 1938, a symbolic moment of anti-Semitism: 'Me yogt zey sheyn vider durkh nekht fun krishtal' (They chase them again through nights of broken glass). Past and present merge still further as Alpert predicts that the destruction of European Jewish culture is about to be relived.

The direct manner in which Alpert addresses his audience is, however, complicated by the use of the Yiddish language. While the song operates upon the assumption that a German audience can understand basic Yiddish, this understanding is undermined by Alpert's frequent use of words with non-Germanic linguistic origins: in the first verse of 'Sing, My Fiddle', the words *malokhim* – angels, *pleytim* – refugees, *soykhrim* – vendors, and *koynim* – customers, among others, are all words of Hebraic origin, unfamiliar to most German speakers. Once or twice Alpert uses longer Hebrew quotations in his Yiddish: the phrase at the beginning of verse 2, 'hamavdil beyn koydesh lekhol' (he who divides the sacred from the worldly) is part of the final blessing of the Havdalah ceremony which ends the Sabbath, a point in the Jewish weekly cycle of disjuncture and new beginning. In using this linguistic register, Alpert chooses directly to undermine the mutual comprehensibility of German and Yiddish, reflecting his own experiences: linguistic comprehension is not the same as really understanding the Other. As he writes in the liner notes:

> Around us, [in Berlin], the population speaks a corrupted Yiddish, which they write in the alphabet of the Christians. We understand each other's words – mostly – but it often stops there (Brave Old World 1994, liner notes).

The sentiments expressed in the song also play out through its expanded strophic structure. The text of 'Sing, My Fiddle' has four verses – one in 'Berlin Overture' and three in the more substantial 'Berlin 1990' – which alternate with a repeated refrain. While each of its two parts forms a self-contained musical number, the slow progress of the strophic structure acts to unify the song into a clearly coherent whole. Further, the long introduction and short coda of 'Berlin Overture' is juxtaposed by a short introduction and lengthy coda in 'Berlin 1990', serving to give the overall form balance whilst rendering its individual components less structurally satisfying in themselves. Variation also occurs within this strophic structure itself: no two verses use exactly the same combination of musical

---

[23]   Michael Alpert, interview, 2002.

material, and an instrumental verse following verse 2, and a contrasting section following verse 4 serve to break up the simple repeated verse-refrain pattern.

Like in Waletzky's song, the music adds further commentary to the text. While the guitar-based singer-songwriter idiom comes from outside Yiddish music, the melody itself uses shapes derived from Yiddish folk or liturgical music, though constructed in a way that is compatible with a Western tonal harmony. While the verse ends with a strong dominant-tonic cadence, the refrain ends with a melodic, rather than harmonic, cadential figure, the flattened second referencing a typical cadential figure in the *Mogen Ovos* mode.[24] Here, the cadence consists of a double voice-leading pattern, the top 'part' of which falls 3-2*b*-1 while the lower 'part' rises 7*b*-1. A version of this figure in linear form, as outlined in Example 4.3, is commonly found in Yiddish folk song (the folk song 'Borsht', track 5 of the same album, uses this figure prominently).

Example 4.3   *Mogen Ovos* voice leading progression

Another figure drawing on an identifiably Yiddish melodic form is the contrasting section following verse 4: it is unmetred, and based upon the *Mi Sheberakh* mode rather than the C minor/*Mogen Ovos* of the rest of the song. This mode features a prominent augmented second between flattened scale degree 3 and raised 4, an interval which Mark Slobin (1980) identifies as a symbolic marker of Yiddish music.[25] Nevertheless, this section is linked to the verse material via an ascending minor triad, which opens both this section and the verse melody, and is first introduced in the piano improvisation opening 'Berlin Overture'.

Contrasting musical styles also add depth to the narrative of the song. The harmonic accompaniment to the verse melody forms a neutral textural background to the song. In terms of instrumentation, this 'neutral style' is characterised principally by the use of the piano, in an improvisatory idiom, using elements derived from jazz, such as added-note harmonies and wide-ranging patterns of block chords. This piano style is used throughout 'Berlin Overture', as both solo and accompaniment, and reappears in the refrain and coda of 'Berlin 1990', thus framing the musical expression of the song. Outside this accompaniment, however, the contrast between Yiddish culture and today's Berlin is played out by the superimposition of explicit references to other musical styles.[26] Each brings a

---

[24]   This mode is related to the natural minor; see Horowitz (1993) for discussion.

[25]   See Idelsohn (1929, 185) and Horowitz (1993) for discussion of the use of the *Mi Sheberakh* mode (which takes its name from a prayer) by East European cantors.

[26]   The process of explicit reference to other musical styles during the course of a piece has been described by theorists in the context of other musics. Leonard Ratner uses the

set of associations from an external sound-world to 'Sing, My Fiddle', enabling the creation of a broad expressive territory by the juxtaposition of stylistically heterogeneous elements.

If the use of the piano is stylistically neutral throughout the song, the voice represents a consistently Yiddish element, identified with the Jewish protagonist of the text. In performing the song, Michael Alpert interprets the melody in a Yiddish folk style, using ornaments such as the *krekhts*, a quick upward move after a note is established, and sliding approaches and continuations of individual notes. He also uses rhythm to refer to a specifically Yiddish idiom: most bars of the melody contain three notes; rather than singing these as three crotchet beats within a 3/4 metre, Alpert tends towards a xx--x- rhythm, often anticipating downbeats. This rhythmic configuration is typical of a Yiddish dance style, the slow *hora* (heard elsewhere on this CD in Yiddish folksong 'Di Sapozhkelekh', track 8). Further, during untexted sections, Alpert vocalises the melody to syllables such as 'oh-no-no-no', a characteristic feature of the singing of untexted Yiddish dance and religious melodies (also used at the opening of Josh Waletzky's 'Ikh heyb mayn fus'), and adds a raised-tonic cadential figure echoing that of the Bobover Wedding march also heard on this album. These features of Alpert's style, typical specifically of European Yiddish vocal music, set the sound of his voice apart from the accompanying instruments.

During the instrumental section following verse 2, the conflict between 'German' and 'Yiddish' understanding of the same material – a concept previously explored in textual terms – is couched in musical terms: the voice is placed in a duet with the double bass, which here alludes to the style of German art music. This style is articulated in several ways: the bass is bowed, and phrases the 3/4 bars in a waltz-like pattern, using typical European classical 3/4 rhythms such as x--x-x or x-x-x- rather than the xx--x- *hora* pattern preferred by the voice. Harmonically, the voices frequently move in parallel sixths, again typical of a Western classical sound-sphere. Further, while this section is the same length as a double refrain, the use of the verse melody rather than that of the refrain means that the *Mogen Ovos* cadence figure illustrated in Example 4.3 is not present in this section. The situation of the Jewish musician working in Germany is, then, expressed here in purely musical terms: while the voice continues to sing with a recognisably Yiddish sound, for this section it is subservient to the 'German' musical idiom.

---

term 'topic' to describe 'subjects for musical discourse', characteristic figures associated with various feelings, affections or situations, which would be alluded to in pieces written within the Classical style (1980, 9). In a Classical symphony, allusions might be made to dance forms, to military music, to the 'singing style' or the 'brilliant style'; by the use of characteristic figures, such as the imitation of hunting horn calls, these allusions would be recognised by contemporary audiences. Here, the 'neutral style' of 'Sing, My Fiddle' is analogous to the mainstream Classical style in Ratner's model, and the superimposed styles here act in a similar way to musical topics.

The final section of the song consists of eight repetitions of the refrain, during which different musicians fade in and out, improvising in a variety of styles over its chord structure. The styles in which they play are not arbitrary: Alpert comments that, 'what we tried to do at the end was to put many of the different sounds of the musical ambiences that you could hear in Berlin in the early 1990s into it'.[27] A series of urban musics come into and out of focus as if the listener was moving around the streets of Berlin. This changing focus is created for the listener by the artificial fading of each sample: we never hear the opening or the ending of each improvisation; further, outside the constraints of purely acoustic music, the band's membership is multiplied – some members are heard simultaneously playing two instruments. Set against a 'neutral' piano and guitar accompaniment we hear a café-style accordion, clarinet jazz, tilinca and saz. These are street musics, representing the 'refugees of a new kind' of 1990s Berlin, described in the first verse of the song. It is not only, however, what is present in this mixture which illustrates the Berlin of the song. The 'Yiddish' cadential figure is again absent from the refrain in this coda – instead, the refrain closes here with a perfect cadence; the voice with its Yiddish text and Jewish associations has stopped singing. There is nothing Jewish to be found here in Brave Old World's Berlin.

'Sing, My Fiddle' has been subject to extended discussion both by Alpert and other commentators during the ten years since it was composed (see, for example, Jacobson 2002).[28] That the song struck a chord with its audience is certain: according to Mark Slobin it even reached the German hit charts (2000, 31). Talking about the song in 2003, over a decade after it was written, Alpert reflected on the emotions expressed in the song and how his standpoint had since changed:

> It's a pretty bitter song in some ways. Because, you know, there's an enormous amount of bitterness I could feel, and have, at times, felt – although I didn't start coming to Germany feeling bitter. I came feeling very idealistic, about doing all that which was so important, and that we were having this kind of contact with each other. Then I became very cynical about it … But it's not a cynical song exactly. … Sometimes I feel, was it too much taking the moral high ground? I think, in a way, there's every reason to do it and it was important to write it. I would like to write a similar song about America – because my intent was not only just to take Germany to task for all of that. I don't lose a lot of sleep over it these days, but [quiet voice] I have, at times gotten quite worked up at the fact that Yiddish civilisation doesn't exist any more, largely because of what came out of this country. There were other factors at work too, and others have gotten into the act since then [ironic laugh] – the Soviet Union, Israel in its way, America in its way, too – but in a very different way than Nazism.[29]

---

27   Michael Alpert, 'Meet the Artists' session, Klezmer Wochen Weimar, 8 August 2003.

28   This song is also mentioned by Ray (2010, 15).

29   Michael Alpert, interview, 2002.

Alpert's developing standpoint is also evident in the reprise of 'Sing, My Fiddle' on Brave Old World's later album *Songs of the Lodz Ghetto* (2005). Both parts of the song appear on this album, embedded into a narrative recalling the Lodz ghetto; here, however, the song is truncated, consisting now only of the refrain and second verse. Alpert's angry words are gone, as are the sounds of contemporary Berlin; his emotions are now channelled into the untexted vocal version of the refrain with which this version closes. He sings with a raw, open vocal sound reminiscent of a cry. Following the original text of the refrain, which longs for an imaginary 'pure' expression of longing, this sound reiterates the inadequacy of a texted medium to express the intended emotional content of the song.

Ongoing Encounters

That Sapoznik and Cooper both chose to publish their diary accounts, and that Alpert and Waletzky chose to frame their albums with the songs discussed above, indicates that the materials discussed here occupy a discursive space of some importance in the eyes of their authors. While their personal standpoints reflect the different patterns of experience of each musician, all affirm that the experience of their encounter as American Jewish musicians with the European lands bearing the stain of the Holocaust demands expression.

The themes raised by these songs and accounts mirror wider trends in American Jewish writing. While the travels to Germany and Poland discussed here are not fictional, it is revealing that during the same time period, 40 years distant from the events of the Holocaust, fictional visits to Germany became a prominent theme in American Jewish literature. These accounts echo the hallmarks of the texts discussed here: Suzanne Klingenstein notes that even casual encounters during visits to Germany acquire significance as reflected interactions with a still enduring past, and questions about Jewish–German relations are read through a 'principle of simultaneity' (1993, 568), by which the historical encounter is imprinted into the here and now, implicitly addressing difficult questions about how Jews should relate to Germany and the Germans, and ultimately, about how one should approach the legacy of the Holocaust itself.

Further, difficult encounters are widely acknowledged to function as a source of creative energy. In her perceptive study of the encounter with 'traumascapes', Maria Tumarkin suggests that encounters with landscapes that bear the imprint of traumatic historical events are characterised by a dual response: the reaction of feeling overwhelmed by incomprehensible experiences is coupled with an urge to express one's experiences (2005, 11, 242). Writing becomes a way to access experience, bridging between past and present resonances of a place. Creative writing of this type should not only be read as a static product expressing a distanced reflection on complex experiences. Rather, these texts are dynamic creations; writing offers a flexible space for reworking experience. Exploring texts that embody witnessing and testimony, literary scholar Shoshana Felman and psychoanalyst Dori Laub suggest that 'issues of biography and history are neither simply represented nor simply reflected, but are reinscribed, translated, radically rethought and fundamentally worked over by the text' (1992, xiv–xv).

In the examples discussed above, this reworking takes place on both personal and communal levels. Alpert and Waletzky work over their experience by using a combination of song, instrumental music and untexted vocal expression to explore the boundaries of emotional discourse. Both songs are rooted in the here-and-now of their times, freezing an interpretative moment; both respond at least partly with ambiguous textual and musical gestures, reflecting a complex and changing emotional landscape. Likewise, Sapoznik and Cooper's use of the diary mode draws the reader to interpret the text as process, not product.

Outside their immediate surroundings, however, such texts also contribute to an ongoing, yet largely unspoken re-evaluation of the discourses and boundaries of the wider American Yiddish music scene. As Judah Cohen illustrates, discourses of cultural authenticity, post-Holocaust 'return' and personal catharsis continue to dominate 'first encounter' accounts of American Jewish musical travel to Europe. Such discourses tend to reinforce static notions of authenticity and cultural capital. Discussing a trip to Poland by student klezmer band the Klezmaniacs, Cohen observes without irony that their 'appearance in Eastern Europe mark[ed] another opportunity for east European populations to acknowledge American Jewish artists as "guardians" of an absent European Jewish culture, and therefore recognize them as particularly qualified to bring that culture back' (2009a, 238). While he credits such performances with effecting cultural bridging and 'a local rethinking of European Jewish history' (2009a, 244), there is little evidence in Cohen's discussion that local European audiences played a role in this 'rethinking'; rather, the musicians he describes served as ambassadors for American Jewish cultural life, and their narratives, documented in CD releases, documentary films and press reports, tended to be played out to an American Jewish audience against a rather passive European landscape, and uncritically to reiterate ingrained discourses.

Nevertheless, despite the endurance of such imagery, and despite the persistence of misinformed and damaging stereotypes about Jews among some quarters in Europe, as American Yiddish musicians have come to perform more regularly in Europe, a reconfiguration of roles begins to challenge the binary constructions of identity and authenticity that underlay the earlier accounts documented in this chapter. Increased crossovers in language use and joint European–American performance projects index increasing trust and a more nuanced understanding between performers and audiences of different backgrounds. When I attended the 'Klezmer Wochen Weimar' workshops in 2002 and 2003, the language of instruction and conversation frequently moved between English, German and Yiddish: there was no one language in common among those present, and language choice at any one point was made via a combination of convenience, competence and ideology; during the same period, the young German band Tickle in the Heart toured Germany with native Yiddish speaker Peysekh Fiszman, Fiszman telling traditional stories in Yiddish in between the band's Yiddish songs and klezmer numbers.

Further, increased conversation has led to a new role of such visits in the American Yiddish music scene: contemporary Central and Eastern Europe as a site of Yiddish authenticity. While earlier accounts suggested that musicians saw Europe primarily in terms of employment, education and personal encounter, more recently musicians have been keen to explore contemporary Europe as reflecting shared cultural space. Discussing a workshop with Polish musicians, Michael Alpert mused, 'I feel like they know that we have one part of the picture they don't have so much – but they also know that they have another part of the picture that we don't ... when I say we, I mean that most north American Jews don't have'.[30]

In terms of Yiddish song, such sites of cultural interchange can be located in both expressive and sonic terms. After the official oppression of Soviet Jews for decades by Communist governments, during the 1990s contact began to be established between American and Soviet Jewish musicians. New music festivals have allowed American musicians to meet Russian and Ukrainian Jewish musicians on their own territory. During an interview in August 2001, Adrienne Cooper remarked, 'Teaching in Russia has really changed me, I just found out after four years of doing it'. She continued, explaining:

> I just figured out that I was really affected by watching the women that are in that community. Because on the one hand they're very feminine in a way that we in the West aren't so much any more – not so much in Europe, but in North America. And at the same time they were very clear and tough. But there is a sort of femininity that ... that we don't do here any more, it's just not done [laughs]. And seeing that in the context of Yiddish music sort of shifted something in me, and I think, being in the area where this music developed, and where it's indigenous, or *was* indigenous, brought me around to much more of a feeling of ... the sensuality of the music, and the innocence in it, and the folklore, almost fairytale quality that's in it, how it functioned to tell stories, you know, about the environment. And I think being in the environment and being with these people who live a little more overtly passionately than we do, was very helpful – emotionally. Very emotional. And so it's kind of re-framed a vocabulary of music that I'm interested in, simpler older songs.[31]

Cooper's nostalgia for a perceived lost 'European' expressive palette begins to realign the structures of power and authenticity implicit in the earlier texts discussed above. For Cooper and for other musicians who have begun to teach regularly in Europe, discomfort in the American–European encounter has been displaced by nostalgic, spatial views of cultural transmission that permit European musicians, potentially both Jewish and non-Jewish, to partake in Yiddish musical authenticity; musical encounters become a space of exchange rather than export. This tendency is borne out by wider practices: at the 2010 Krakow festival,

---

[30]   Michael Alpert, interview, 2002.
[31]   Adrienne Cooper, interview, 2001.

while the stars continued to be North American Jewish musicians, they appeared and taught alongside a younger generation of Europeans; conversely, European musicians have joined the staff of American Yiddish music camps. If the 'edge' of raw emotional encounters is dulled as such encounters develop and become everyday, it is clear that the European–American–Yiddish encounter continues to trigger productive creative landscapes.

Chapter 5

Encountering the Yiddish Other: Hasidic Music in Today's Yiddish Canon

If the voyages to Europe discussed in Chapter 4 represented a long physical journey leading to an internal, personal encounter with the Yiddish past, here I turn to a contrasting journey undertaken by a number of Yiddish vocalists, this time leading to a no less intense encounter with an alternative Yiddish present.[1] Only half an hour or so from central Manhattan, the strictly Orthodox Hasidic neighbourhoods of Brooklyn seem both near and infinitely far away from the buzzing Yiddish music scene described here. It is perhaps ironic that today the two American Jewish groups most committed to the preservation of the Yiddish language stand at opposite poles of the modern Jewish spectrum: leftist, secularist, Yiddishism versus strict ultra-Orthodoxy. The physical distance between the Yiddish cultural scene discussed in this volume and the Hasidic neighbourhoods of Boro Park or Williamsburg may be very small, but the cultural distance is nonetheless great.[2]

Hasidic Jews (literally, 'pious') follow a mystical strand of Judaism founded in Poland by Rabbi Israel ben Eliezor (c. 1698–1760), known as the Ba'al Shem Tov. Hasidism began as a popular movement, which spread quickly through Central and Eastern Europe. The Hasidic world was structured in groups, each led by a *rebbe*, a spiritual leader, and maintaining its own customs and institutions. Now, however, the majority of Hasidim live in cities in America, Israel and Europe, including large communities in Brooklyn, New York, where many arrived during the 1950s after the Holocaust. Today's transplanted Hasidic groups still bear the names of the places in which they were founded, reading like a map of Eastern Europe: Bobov, Ger, Lubavitch, Munkacs, Satmar, Skver. Notwithstanding some internal diversity in outlook and practice, Hasidim are among the most religiously stringent of today's Orthodox Jews, self-consciously performing difference from both mainstream North American culture and from other, less observant Jews. Among their North American compatriots, Hasidic Jews are recognised by their

---

[1]   A previous version of this chapter appeared as: Abigail Wood (2007b) 'Stepping Across the Divide: Hasidic Music in Today's Yiddish Canon'. *Ethnomusicology* 51:2, 205–37. I am grateful to the Society for Ethnomusicology for permission to reprint material from this article.

[2]   As in the remainder of this book, I use 'Yiddish music scene/community' to describe the wider community of those engaged with producing contemporary Yiddish music. In the context of this chapter, this more specifically refers to music produced outside the strictly Orthodox community.

characteristic style of dress: men wear black and white, their *peyes* (unshaven earlocks) hanging from their black hats; women dress modestly, married women covering all their hair with a scarf or wig.

The use of Yiddish as a spoken language is another marker of difference. Unlike the majority of those discussed in this book, most Hasidim use Yiddish on a daily basis as a vernacular. As an everyday language, Hasidic Yiddish is used alongside other local vernaculars (American English or Israeli Hebrew) and contains frequent code-switching. In an important study of Hasidic girls in Brooklyn, anthropologist Ayala Fader suggests that for Hasidic Jews, Yiddish is a vehicle of nostalgia for an idealised lost past, indexing a pious and less materialistic Old World Judaism (2009, 129–30).

While the high value accorded to Yiddish and reference to Old World cultural forms is shared by Hasidic Jews and cultural Yiddishists, this does not generally translate into close contact and communication between the two groups. The strictly Orthodox lifestyle of the Hasidim is maintained within close, closed communities, deliberately separated from the outside world which they perceive to be full of values alien to their own and potentially detrimental to a religious lifestyle.[3] This extends not only to American culture as represented in the media, but even to secular Yiddish culture. It is rare to see strictly Orthodox Jews, including Hasidim, at events in the cultural community discussed above. Those who choose to cross the divide stand out against the normal backdrop of either community: a lone black-and-white clad Hasid attending a Lower East Side Yiddish poetry reading stood just outside the performance space, the physical border of the space perhaps also representing a harder-to-cross border of values and expectations.

This social distance is largely echoed by non-Hasidic Yiddish musicians. Those with whom I discussed contemporary Hasidic culture used the term 'world' to distinguish the '*frum* [religious] world' or the '*hasidish* [Hasidic] world' from the 'normal world', 'our world', 'the klezmer world'. This choice of word was almost certainly unconscious, an everyday colloquial English expression; however, its use nonetheless underscores the conceptual distance between communities, for which reason this usage is retained here. In wider American Jewish discourse, Hasidim are often viewed as exotic symbols of 'authentic', timeless Judaism. A documentary film by Menachem Daum, advertised as the first in-depth documentary about the Hasidic community, captures this social separation in its title: *A Life Apart: Hasidism in America* (Daum 1997). Aiming 'to convey the Hasidim's sense of purpose and meaning, their sense of humor, and their often quite foreign ways', the sense of exoticism portrayed by the film places it into the kind of documentary style usually associated with distant tribes or intriguing wild animals, rather than with today's culturally diverse New York.

Notwithstanding the cultural chasm between this Yiddish cultural scene and the strictly Orthodox Hasidic community, however, recently a handful of contemporary Yiddish musicians have begun to undertake a musical exploration

---

[3]   See Fader (2009) and Vaysman (2010) for discussion.

of Hasidic musical material and performance practices, part of a wave of creative projects focusing on religious Ashkenazi repertoires. New ways are being found for material originally intended to function in particular religious contexts to be performed in a non-Orthodox environment, with emphasis moved from religious to musical, experiential and spiritual aspects of the repertory. This chapter explores this transcommunal musical appropriation and its wider cultural context. If from a purely musical standpoint these new projects might represent an unremarkable instance of borrowing between cognate repertoires, within their wider context they are another important locus of contemporary creativity in Yiddish song, and also represent a notable move to evoke spaces of experiential spirituality within the largely secular, mixed Jewish and non-Jewish Yiddish music scene.

From its inception, music assumed a special significance in Hasidism: music, song and dance are seen as a form of communication with God. Song and instrumental music are widely referenced in Hasidic spiritual and philosophical texts. The Hasidic text *Sefer Mekor Mayim Chayim* (Book of the Source of Living Waters, Yaakov Meir Pado, 1836), recounts:

> It is told of the Ba'al Shem Tov (may his memory be for a blessing) that he used to hear utterances within the sound of the violin … The book *Or Hameir* recounts: … [The Ba'al Shem Tov] once heard a wicked person playing the violin, and understood [from its sound] all of the sins that [the wicked person] had committed from the day of his birth. And if he was able to interpret these sins from the voice of an instrument, how much more so from singing with the mouth? From the melody which someone sings, a learned person blessed with interpretation can know all of that person's sinful actions, because he brings all of his strength to the melody which comes out of his mouth.[4]

Vocal music underpins Hasidic musical life. Prayer and religious events frequently involve extensive singing. The principal Hasidic musical form is the nigun – literally melody, but used to refer to religious songs which are either wordless or set to short religious texts.[5] Nigunim are sung at a variety of occasions, ranging from formal prayer to *farbrengens* and *tishes*, religious Hasidic gatherings incorporating singing and homiletic discussion.[6] Melodies range from the slow and introspective

---

[4] *Sefer Mekor Mayim Chayim, parshat Vayakhel*, beginning 'u'vasefer likutei maharan', translation mine. I thank Rabbi Harvey Belovski for helping me to locate this and many other sources. Other teachings by Rebbe Nachman on the subject of music can be found in many places in the *Likutei Maharan*. See also, for example, *Kedushas Levi* (Rebbe Levi Yitzhak of Berdichev), *Shabbat Nachamu*, beginning 'vezehu haremez umeholot becramim', and *Niflaos Yehudi*, 74 beginning 'od shamati'. All texts are readily available in electronic form via the Otsar haHochma software.

[5] Plural: nigun*im*. The alternative transliteration '*nign*' is also commonly used.

[6] See Koskoff (2001, chapter 1), for detailed discussion of a contemporary Lubavitcher *farbrengen*.

(*tish* or *dveykus* nigunim) to fast dance melodies; untexted melodies may be adapted for *zmires* (singular: *zemer*), Hebrew and Aramaic paraliturgical songs sung around the Shabbes table (see Vinaver and Schleifer 1985, 191–2, Koskoff 1978 and Beregovski 1982, 299–301). While traditional Jewish law dictates that no instruments or recorded music may be played on the Sabbath or holidays, on other occasions the singing of nigunim may be reinforced by instrumentalists.[7]

Although core repertories of nigunim associated with individual sects and the performance practices associated with singing nigunim in large-group settings are specifically associated with Hasidism, in the wider context of Ashkenazi Jewish musics, boundaries between Hasidic and non-Hasidic, vocal and instrumental, secular and sacred music are porous and flexible. Musically, Yiddish folk song, klezmer and Hasidic vocal music represent overlapping streams in the musical-aesthetic heritage of Jewish Eastern Europe.[8] Melodies of Hasidic origin, were adopted into instrumental repertories. Walter Zev Feldman identifies the *khosidl*, a name referencing Hasidism, as part of the 'core' repertory of East European *klezmorim*, some resembling vocal nigunim (Feldman 1994). Slow or unmetered Hasidic *tish* or *dveykus* nigunim also served as introspective instrumental pieces.[9]

Until recently, American Yiddish musicians, largely secular in outlook, have had little reason to differentiate Hasidic material from other parts of the repertory. The performance projects discussed here, however, explicitly focus on vocal performance of nigunim and *zmires*, and represent a more substantial engagement with Hasidic sources, and a greater emphasis on religious song – often using Hebrew and Aramaic texts – than was previously found in the klezmer revival. The motivation to explore these repertories is not only musical: these musicians assert that the experiential spirituality associated with this repertory can be accessed through music, in particular through the voice, without necessarily subscribing to the uncompromising, nonliberal religious practices of the Hasidic community.

The first section of this chapter explores these performance projects via the work of two individuals, Sruli Dresdner and Frank London, who are among recent pioneers in both performing and teaching traditional Hasidic song within the mainstream Yiddish musical scene, yet whose approaches to this material both as musicians and in their own relationships to the Hasidic world contrast markedly. Second, I turn to performance practice. Drawing primarily from teaching sessions

---

[7]   This is readily audible in a swathe of YouTube video clips documenting contemporary Hasidic gatherings. Accompanying instruments range from synthesisers to the more traditional violin band maintained by the Bobov sect.

[8]   See Wohlberg (2010) for a wider discussion of the relationship between secular and synagogue song in Jewish Eastern Europe; in the same volume, Janet Leuchter questions such categories as 'secular', 'religious', 'Hasidic' and 'Yiddish' in labelling East European Jewish song (2010, 123–6). I thank Naomi Cohn-Zentner for bringing this volume to my attention as I was preparing this manuscript for publication.

[9]   Examples of different genres of Hasidic melodies being played as instrumental klezmer music can be heard on Leon Schwartz, *Like in a Different World*, 1993.

during a Yiddish music workshop, I explore the discourse used by musicians to present Hasidic vocal material to their students and to construct and teach a 'Hasidic' performance aesthetic. These musicians seek to reframe aspects of Hasidic religious practice as musical features and aesthetic preferences, in turn using musical performance as a vehicle to access spiritual experience.

Finally, I explore the wider cultural dynamics of this more or less one-sided musical dialogue with the Hasidic world from outside. Approaching Hasidic vocal music first and foremost as performers engaged in the contemporary performance of cognate musical traditions, yet also seeking to produce a marketable musical product, the underlying assumption of all these musicians is that a meaningful, stylistically grounded performance of Hasidic musical material can be achieved outside the cultural confines of the Hasidic community, and outside the strictly religious contexts of traditional Hasidic performance. Religious Hasidim are neither among the producers nor likely consumers of the music discussed here, which is not marketed to the religious community, and does not adhere to Orthodox religious values such as not pronouncing or spelling the name of God outside prayer, or restricting the voices to men alone. Rather, the musicians discussed here reconfigure musical symbols to reflect their own search for a meaningful balance between East European Jewish and modern American culture. They place themselves neither as insiders nor outsiders: none are practising Hasidim, but all approach Hasidic music as part of their own heritage, whether through direct family connections or as insider performers of cognate Ashkenazi musics. Further, in challenging the premise that authentic spiritual and musical expression within this repertory must necessarily lie within the strictly Orthodox Hasidic community, these musicians also question the bifurcation of secular and religious culture implicit in popular and scholarly literature, also challenging the frequently aggressively secular voice of the ethnographic outsider. Instead, they lay the path for a broader conception of the interrelationship between sound and culture, in which creative borrowing and transcommunal imagination become means for the ongoing construction of musical meaning.

Bringing Old World Hasidic Material into the Yiddish Music Scene: Two Musicians Discuss Their Work

Sruli Dresdner

> I like to say that I had a very, very strict religious, Hasidic childhood, which was miserable torture to live through, but the music was really good.[10]

---

[10]   All quotations in this section, unless otherwise noted, from Sruli Dresdner, interview with the author, Scarsborough, NY, 3 April 2003.

Unlike the majority of musicians active in the Yiddish music scene, clarinettist and singer Sruli Dresdner grew up within the Hasidic community. If his unhappy childhood led him to reject the observant way of life within which he grew up, he nevertheless remained attached to the music of his community. Today he works as a musician with duo partner Lisa Mayer, playing for Jewish celebrations and concerts, principally outside the Orthodox community, and teaching the Hasidic repertory of his youth alongside standard klezmer numbers. Within the klezmer scene, this degree of traditional religious background is rare, making Dresdner a valuable authority on questions of style and text as well as the source of a huge repertory of nigunim.

Even among those who grew up religious, Dresdner's musical repertory is unusual. His distinctive vocal style and knowledge of nigunim reflect not only a Hasidic childhood, but one among a community which, as he explains, was strongly affected by external pressures of post-war American Jewish life, which led to groups who might otherwise have remained separate joining together in their desire to preserve their Hasidic lifestyle. He explains:

> When I was growing up, my parents attended a *shtibl* [small prayer-house] in Queens, New York. And at least at that time, Queens, New York didn't have so many of what we would now call 'Haredi' or 'Hasidic' Jews, say, the category of people who like to wear a hat when they *daven* [pray], and women who wear wigs, and so on … So in this small neighbourhood of Kew Gardens … the people who were Hasidic, wanted to wear the hat, you know, who felt closer to that kind of thing and wanted a much more traditional kind of European-style, very religious environment – they all gathered together in this one shtibl.
>
> And from a musical standpoint, I heard, therefore, music from all over the Eastern European world – certainly all over the East European Hasidic world. We even had a few token *Litvaks* [non-Hasidic Lithuanian Jews], because they would come here even though this *davening* [prayer] was what they called *nusach sfard* [version of liturgy adopted by Hasidim], but because they also wanted to wear a hat and it was the only place they felt comfortable … So I heard a lot of music from all over the place, and there was a sense of seriousness about it, because there was the sense that they were keeping alive a dead or dying – or murdered – culture, so there was a fervency to the whole experience.

Dresdner described three contexts in which he learned and sang (or played) nigunim: formal prayer, in the home, and special events, including Jewish holidays. In each case melodies were transmitted orally; the dynamics of each musical situation, including the choice of nigunim and performance practice, varied according to the requirements of the particular context. During prayer, nigunim primarily had a liturgical function. Typically, in traditional Jewish worship each liturgical text was not exclusively associated with one or two melodies; rather, the prayer leader was responsible for selecting melodies for the service he led, and was hence able to introduce new material, which would soon become part of the community's repertory. As Dresdner describes:

> In the *shtibl* environment, the music is very informal ... nigunim were very much a part of *davening*, and the idea was that everyone would sing along, and the person leading the prayers, he would pick the melody, but the idea was if everybody didn't know it, then the third time, or fourth time he picked the same melody, people did know it and they would sing along.

Dresdner also learned nigunim in the home. Singing around the table is a common activity in religious Jewish homes, the only option for music making on Shabbes and Jewish holidays when playing instruments or recorded music is prohibited. Dresdner came from a family which was particularly interested in preserving an older repertory of nigunim. He recalls:

> My father was particularly traditional, and very much liked to sing the songs that his father sang, which is a very nice repertoire of Old World stuff. My mother's father considered himself a collector of nigunim. So that was one of the things he liked to do, so he would have, you know, a library in his house of thousands of nigunim, and he liked to always look for new ones and find new ones, or ones that were new to him, and incorporate them into what he did.
>
> AW: A library how – written?
>
> SD: No, no, not written. Just in his head.
>
> AW: Wow!
>
> SD: But my father, he spent a fair amount of time at his father-in-law's house, so he learned a lot of melodies there as well.

Hearing nigunim on Jewish holidays also contributed to Dresdner's musical background. While he describes as a young person having had a 'love-hate' relationship with the music of his religious upbringing owing to his discomfort in the religious world, the serious atmosphere of Jewish holidays also made a profound impact on him:

> [The nigunim] burrowed deep into my head, because they were good – a combination of the fact that the melodies were really powerful, but also the fact that they were taken so seriously. So the context was also powerful. I mean, these are people who on Yom Kippur really felt they were *davening* for their lives, and generally their lives hadn't been so good, and in some cases they weren't so

good, and so prayer was very important, and it was taken very seriously.[11] So in that sense it was very important, and in my home, with my relatives, the idea of tradition was taken very seriously.

During his youth, Dresdner recalls:

> I guess I was musical, and, you know, my musical milieu was religious music. So in addition to the traditional stuff, it was also, [at] that time, [a] sort of nascent, or developing world of contemporary religious, contemporary Orthodox Jewish music, and what I mean by that is music that was designed for the Orthodox Jewish market. And I was, you know, somewhat a fan of that as well. That's really what we had in the house.

Some of these albums 'had a little bit of a klezmer feel to them'. Enjoying this sound and wanting to emulate the recordings he heard, Dresdner took lessons with klezmer clarinettist Paul Pincus. Playing the clarinet at special events – including Purim, a Jewish holiday on which instrumental music is permitted – he also included his older Hasidic repertoire alongside newer, popular religious repertory:

> It's funny, because even in the *yeshiva* [religious school] days I would play this older music, and I *knew* – and on *Simchas Torah* for example, we didn't play music but we would sing music and choose tunes – and I had a sense of the power of the older melodies, and I knew if people were dancing but they were flagging, they were getting tired, that if I would pull out one of these older melodies, it would rejuvenate the dancing.[12] And people didn't understand it themselves, they thought they wanted newer stuff, but the better music … helped them dance better.

Some time after having left the strictly Orthodox community, as an adult Dresdner encountered the klezmer revival, attending a number of klezmer camps and later becoming a staff member. He observes:

> It was very interesting to me, on the one hand, to be introduced to a whole repertoire of music that I had no idea was Jewish music. That was very eye-opening for me, as a much wider repertoire, not just in terms of tunes, but in terms of style … But at the same time, it also made me feel like the nigunim, on the other hand, were really also great. And I like both, you know – the klezmer music was great, but the music, the nigunim had a seriousness that I didn't

---

[11]   On Yom Kippur, the Day of Atonement, the fate of individuals during the coming year is said to be sealed.

[12]   Simchas Torah (Rejoicing in the Torah) is a Jewish holiday on which instrumental music is not permitted, but on which services and celebrations traditionally include much singing and dancing.

always feel [in] the klezmer music, not that there isn't some seriousness in the klezmer repertoire. So it made sort of this connection in me, it made me pull out the nigunim that I had absorbed as a child, and connect them, and examine them, in relation to this repertoire … So I started to play this stuff, and sing this stuff a little bit, and people liked it, and I liked it, and so we started to do more of it! But it's nice for me, it's nice to get these melodies out, because they *are* powerful, and they *are* really great – I think many of them are.

At KlezKanada, Dresdner met Michael Alpert, with whom he began to perform and teach Hasidic material:

> We formed a group called the Singing Table – we talked about it for years, and we had some great informal moments, like on a street corner Simchas Torah on the Upper West Side, where we sang nigunim for about 45 minutes and attracted a fairly large crowd … We did it in other places, maybe also in KlezKamp and KlezKanada, so that, over time, we built up some repertoire. I made some tapes for Michael, he listened to them, he made copies of recordings he had of repertoire that I didn't grow up with, but that was similar to the stuff that I grew up with that I liked, and this year, more than ever, it's gelled into an actual full-length presentation which we've performed three or four times.

While the Singing Table emerged from singing Hasidic repertory on a religious holiday, Sruli Dresdner is careful to differentiate their approach to nigunim from that of contemporary Hasidim. He notes, 'We don't present this music from a religious perspective, because that's not who we are, primarily – we present it as music'.

This comment encompasses both the Singing Table's musical aesthetic and their philosophical approach to the music. Musically, the Singing Table approaches Hasidic repertory as a preserved rather than a current tradition, seeking to perform traditional, Old World Hasidic repertory rather than that popular today in the Hasidic world, and to explore traditional performance idioms, reflecting the aesthetic values of Western classical music's historical performance movement rather than a direct engagement with contemporary Hasidic performance practice. Dresdner notes:

> One of the fights I have with Michael [Alpert] about that is, is this a living tradition or a dead tradition? He takes the more living tradition kind of thing, and he doesn't like to say this is what the Hasidim *used* to sing – but the truth is, in many cases, this *is* what the Hasidim used to sing, and they don't sing any more – even if they know it, they don't, it's not part of their active life.

This revivalist aesthetic in turn enables Dresdner to engage with the repertory he learned during his childhood while remaining at a distance from the current values – both musical and religious – of the Hasidic world. Adopting a historical performance aesthetic allows him to reclaim the musical repertory he values without the baggage of ultra-Orthodox religious practice. Nevertheless, despite this intentional distancing, working with Hasidic music has also led both Dresdner and Alpert to reassess their own relationships to the Hasidic world. Coming from a less strictly observant background than Dresdner (Alpert grew up around both secular and religious family members), Alpert observes that his romanticised imagery of the Hasidic world has been tempered by Dresdner's perceptions of religious fundamentalism in the Hasidic world. By contrast, it is perhaps the positive reception of the work of the Singing Table that has led Dresdner back towards a greater appreciation of the world in which he grew up. Alpert observes:

> There's a lot of things I appreciate about *khsidishe velt* [the Hasidic world] …
> but neither do I have as much *derekh erets* [respect] as I had ten years ago, for
> that world as a whole. And some of that has been, there's been a continuing
> move to the [religious] right. Some of it has been my friendship with Sruli, too.
> You know, it's very funny, because we've each kind of moved towards each
> other's perspective in some way, because, I mean, I've come to kind of agree
> with him that a lot of stuff in the *frum* world is really just out to lunch and has
> just gone way too far … and I've come to appreciate, I mean in the neutral
> sense of 'appreciate', portions of the *khsidish* world – and the *frum* world – as
> not just a bastion of traditionality, but as a place of some *meshugene* [crazy]
> fundamentalism. Whereas I think Sruli, in a way, has come back towards not so
> much a total rejection of that, and more towards seeing some [positive] things.
> And even though he always had the love of the music, he's finding his way of
> being more comfortable with all that, so that's an interesting thing.[13]

Frank London

A contrasting approach to the performance of Hasidic vocal music is adopted by Frank London and Lorin Sklamberg. These two musicians might reasonably be accorded a significant degree of credit for introducing and popularising Old World Hasidic music within the wider contemporary Yiddish music scene. While from the beginning Hasidic material played an important role in the repertory of the Klezmatics, London and Sklamberg have also released three recordings which present Hasidic material in new, contemporary musical settings: Nigunim (1998, with Uri Caine), *Zmiros* (2001, with Rob Schwimmer) and *Tsuker-zis* (2009, with Knox Chandler, Ara Dinkjian and Deep Singh). London explained:

> We focused on a certain repertoire, these East European Jewish religious songs
> … So, to find the repertoire, we did everything, we went to books, went to our
> family, went into a Hasidic community where we both hang out a lot, and asked
> people to sing songs; learnt songs at weddings, *tishes* [gatherings] and Shabbes,

---

[13]   Michael Alpert, interview with the author, Weimar, 31 July 2002.

going and hanging out; went into the archives at YIVO and other places, and found archival recordings – and bought lots of contemporary Hasidic recordings to learn songs.[14]

These projects, then, reflect a repertory-based approach, using fieldwork and archival material side by side to collect suitable musical material. Outsider and insider perspectives are combined here: while Frank London did not grow up in an Orthodox home, he later spent some time in a more strictly religious environment. Although, like Dresdner, he rejected this way of life, here, at least as a musician, London describes a certain fluidity in movement between the secular and strictly Orthodox worlds.

This fluidity of perspective is also reflected in London's approach to the religious context of this music. Whereas Dresdner's description of the musical goals of the Singing Table seeks to emphasise the disjuncture between his approach to nigunim as a musician and the religious life of contemporary Hasidim, London emphasises the perceived spiritual nature of Hasidic vocality but seeks to disengage this from its ultra-Orthodox context. This is not only a reaction to perceived religious fundamentalism; it is also a direct response to the dissatisfaction he feels with the way contemporary Hasidic recordings present this repertory.

Today's strictly Orthodox Jewish community supports a thriving popular music industry: indeed, these recordings – encompassing both traditional and new music – account for at least half the recorded Jewish music currently available in the USA (Kligman 2001, 106).[15] Produced and marketed within the Orthodox Jewish world, these recordings reflect the values of the community both in their musical content and in their packaging, bearing legends such as: 'Please do not play this CD on the Sabbath and Jewish Holidays. It is strictly forbidden by Torah and copyright laws to duplicate this tape for any purpose. Thank you' (Suki and Ding, n.d.).

While nigunim sung unaccompanied at religious occasions form the mainstay of Hasidic musical life, the majority of contemporary popular recordings of Hasidic material are commercial studio productions issued by specialist Orthodox record labels. Among those popular today – judging from the display in a Boro Park store – is *Shabbos Classics*, produced by major Brooklyn-based Orthodox music company Suki and Ding. Consisting of relatively traditional repertory, the musical items – a selection of nigunim, *zmires* and other religious songs – are attributed to various Hasidic sects. The album – one of a series of at least ten

---

[14]   All quotations in this section, unless otherwise noted, from Frank London, interview with the author, New York, 3 April 2003.

[15]   Within the religious Jewish community, the whole genre of Orthodox popular music is often referred to as 'Hasidic'. Many recordings of traditional Hasidic material form part of this genre, and several popular contemporary Orthodox performers come from Hasidic backgrounds; nevertheless, this music is also performed and consumed by other strictly Orthodox, non-Hasidic Jews (see Kligman 1994, 9, and Wood, 2013, for discussion).

'Classics' volumes – is marketed with images of community nostalgia: a Yiddish subtitle reads '*Heymishe shabbos* nigunim' (home-style Sabbath songs), and the title is superimposed over a sepia picture of an Old World Hasidic scene.

If the packaging of strictly Orthodox popular music reflects the religious outlook of this community, the performance style on these recordings also illustrates great differences in musical aesthetics between the Hasidic and Yiddish music communities. *Shabbos Classics* is typical: a soloist or men's choir (strictly Orthodox interpretations of Jewish law prohibit men from listening to women's voices), in both cases singing with high intensity throughout and fluently ornamenting the melodies, is accompanied by synthesisers playing in a light pop style, complete with synthesised drums and numerous piano glissandi and key changes. These recordings are often well produced; nevertheless, while the use of synthesisers and beats derived from pop music reflects the influence of wider American music culture, to an outsider to the Hasidic world, they sound kitschy at best, far from the historicist or contemporary musical aesthetics which have largely been adopted by world music artists including klezmer revivalists. As listening material, therefore, they are largely unappealing to those outside the strictly Orthodox community.

Frank London relates this difference in musical presentation to the different outlooks of the communities concerned:

> And here's the point: most contemporary Hasidic recordings, for my taste, for the last 40 years, are horrible. At best, at *best*, they contain great singing. And good songs, with abysmal accompaniment. And at worst it's downhill from there. But there's rarely been something where I felt the *music* had the same spirit as the song. So our whole point was to make the musical accompaniment – the instrumental accompaniment – have the same spirit and the same meaning, the same ethos as the sung music, which is a very deep music. So we tried to make it that way, to make music where the accompaniment didn't work against the meaning of the song, where the accompaniment is spiritual – it's not a disco track, you know – because for me, disco is not a spiritual thing ... And also, it didn't feel Jewish – the [modern Hasidic] accompaniments don't feel Jewish. So we wanted the accompaniments to feel Jewish. Because it's interesting: the Hasids want their accompaniment to feel hip and modern. We live in the hip, modern world. We don't have any need to do that, to prove it to anyone, we're not trying to do that. So we can go another way. So with these, we research, we find songs that we love. I think it's a great vehicle for Lorin's voice. I think he's right up there with the best of the Hasidic singers.

While London speaks of 'the same ethos as the sung music', unlike the Singing Table, London and Sklamberg do not seek to recreate either past or present Hasidic performance practice. Rather, they present the melodies in new settings, where individual arrangements are guided by their contemporary musical sensibility. London describes:

With me, with Lorin, we use any trick – we have no rules except going after a certain sound. So if it makes sense to have only the people in the room with the one mike, we'll do that. If it makes sense for each of us to play 15 parts, we'll do that ... On 'Avrom ben Shmuel' [1998 recording by London, Sklamberg, and Caine], Lorin's basically singing ... with himself in thirds. And then, on the high part of the song, which has the emotional lift, for just four bars, we add a third harmony and then it goes away. And it's almost subliminal, but it has this feeling of great uplift ... The third voice adds the colour, all of a sudden, and it comes away. Now, when you think about singing, you would never just all of a sudden go to a harmony for three notes and then stop. But it really made sense, and it just added that 'thing', it really went with the emotion of the song. So, yeah, we're always trying to do that.

While eschewing, then, Hasidic ideas of what constitutes 'hip and modern' music, London and Sklamberg's recordings nevertheless do fit into the hip, modern category of contemporary popular world music. Like many contemporary artists, they use a combination of traditional and innovative musical elements to market their music to an audience who are primarily outsiders to this repertory.

This transformation is achieved primarily through arrangement. Whereas the musical arrangements on Hasidic recordings are generally subservient to the vocal melodies, on London and Sklamberg's recordings the instruments do not merely accompany the vocal lines but rather play an active part in shaping each arrangement. This contrast is particularly evident in comparing their 1998 recording of the slow Lubavitch nigun, 'Eyli Atoh' ('You are my God', a verse from Psalm 118; the nigun is associated with the Alter Rebbe, the first Rebbe of Lubavitch), with the most prominent Lubavitcher Hasidic recording (*Chabad Nigunim, Volume 1*, 2000 [1960]).[16] The nigun has a rhyming binary structure: AB / CB. On both recordings, the complete nigun is performed three times. Both performers choose similar speeds; London, Sklamberg and Caine extend the final repetition of the nigun by repeating each of the two parts. The Lubavitch version is performed by a men's chorus, accompanied by accordion; the nigun is fully harmonised throughout by the chorus and accordion. The only variation between verses occurs in the distribution of voices: the first repetition features a soloist accompanied by the chorus humming, the second repetition is sung by all, and the final repetition is sung by a group of voices with hummed accompaniment, all voices singing again for the second part of the nigun.

---

[16]   This CD appears to be a reissue of the 1960 LP *Chabad Melodies, Vol. 1*. Rabbi Samuel Zalmanoff, dir. Collectors Guild CGL, 615 (publication details from Koskoff 2001, 205). On the Lubavitch recording, Eyli Atoh is rendered as 'Keili atoh', following the Orthodox practice of avoiding the use of names of God outside prayer. While this recording represents an older series of Lubavitch recordings, a similar performance style is used for the same nigun on a later Lubavitch recording: *Hisvadus Hasidit*, NOAM recordings, 2002.

By contrast, each repetition of the nigun is arranged differently in London, Sklamberg and Caine's version. Aside from Sklamberg's voice and London's trumpet, the album uses a range of keyboard instruments (accordion, piano, harmonium, electric piano, Hammond organ); the instrumentation varies throughout, providing contrast. The first repetition of 'Eyli Atoh' is sung by Sklamberg over long drone notes. A less ornamented version of the melody is picked out in the top range of the electric piano, and London's trumpet enters with a countermelody. In the second repetition the voice and trumpet countermelody continues, but the accompaniment is now harmonic and rhythmic, giving the nigun a different character. The first half of the final repetition of the nigun is instrumental, played by London on trumpet with accordion and piano accompaniment. This leads to a sense of climax at the second part of the nigun, when the voice re-enters; both London and Sklamberg vary the melody to reinforce this climax. Overall, the shape of this arrangement builds up rhythmic, textural and melodic intensity, giving a sense of structure which is absent from the Lubavitch recording.

While the overall texture of London, Sklamberg and Caine's recording is not a traditional one, their arrangement nevertheless incorporates several elements of traditional Hasidic vocal practice, including Sklamberg's vocal style, the playing of certain phrases in heterophony or harmonised in thirds, and the linking of phrases to avoid a drop in intensity. While these features sit relatively easily with a contemporary Western musical style, in other projects London and Sklamberg explore Hasidic soundworlds further. The opening number of the soundtrack to the film *Divan*, 'Lomir makhn a bayt' (Let's make a deal), is a Hasidic song featuring unaccompanied voices (London 2003); the heterophony of the first verse is expanded to complete asynchrony in the second, each voice singing the verse independently. 'Tepel', a nigun featured on the Klezmatics' album *Rise up!* (2003), and arranged by the band, briefly features a 'faux-Hasidic boys' chorus' (made up of band members' children), which directly imitates a sound typical of modern Hasidic recordings, an in-joke for those who recognise this reference.

Although as musical packages London and Sklamberg's Nigunim and *Zmiros* projects are idiosyncratic, reflecting the musical personalities of their creators, and representing arrangements and textures unlikely to be copied closely by other musicians, their creators see themselves as playing a dual role as both commercial musicians and transmitters of culture. That these recordings play a role in the dissemination of the repertory concerned outside the ultra-Orthodox world is particularly evident in the *Zmiros* project, which was linked with the creation of a new *bentsher* by the Edgar M. Bronfman Center for Jewish Student Life: Hillel at New York University.

Ranging in size from a fold-out card to a small book, a *bentsher* is a traditional textual medium for religious vocality. It contains the Hebrew text for the grace said after meals, usually supplemented by the texts for prayers said at home, and *zmires*, traditional songs sung at the Shabbes table. *Bentshers* are frequently produced either by individuals, to mark weddings, bar mitzvahs and other celebrations, or by organisations seeking to produce a booklet reflecting their own communal celebration of Shabbes. The new NYU *bentsher*, *Ain Sof* (Gershman 2001), is a particularly elaborate example: many songs are included, and traditional Hebrew texts are supplemented with artwork, stories and other material providing a commentary upon the texts and the Sabbath itself. In this context, then, the *Zmiros* CD – which was made available packaged with the *bentsher* and as a stand-alone recording – provided a further level of commentary, introducing both lesser-known Hebrew/Aramaic and religious Yiddish songs, and unfamiliar melodies for better-known songs. By presenting traditional Hasidic melodies in a musical idiom compatible with a contemporary aesthetic yet also preserving elements of traditional performance style, the Nigunim, *Zmiros* and *Tsuker-zis* projects – together with London and Sklamberg's other forays into this repertory, notably with the Klezmatics – make this older repertory available to wider audiences who might otherwise not have encountered it. I asked London whether the NYU students used the melodies he had recorded:

> I can't say yes or no. But certain songs have definitely insinuated their way into [the wider consciousness], you know, songs that were gone out, 'Shnirele Perele' (a religious Yiddish song recorded by the Klezmatics on *rhythm + jews* [1992]), clearly ... One thing Lorin and I try to do is just have really good taste about the songs we pick, because we're almost *curators* – we're not composers, we're curating, and so we try to pick songs that we think people would like ... On the new Klezmatics album, *Shteyt Oyf!* (2003), we have two – a nigun and a 'Yah Ribon' [an Aramaic *zemer*]. I'm sure people are going to sing those.

Teaching Nigunim: Hasidic Material as Performance Practice and Experience

The discussion above has focused on Hasidic nigunim as a vocal repertory, exploring the motivations of different individuals to engage with this material. Nevertheless, the Hasidic nigun cannot solely be defined in this way: an equally important defining aspect of the nigun is the manner in which it is performed. Indeed, performance practice itself can define the transition from a melody to a nigun. Not only can many klezmer melodies be sung as nigunim and vice versa, almost any melody, sung with appropriate style and intention, has the potential to become a nigun. One informant laughed that her brother and his friends, studying at a yeshiva (religious school) in Jerusalem, had fooled an old rabbi into singing the theme tune from the computer game 'Tetris' as a nigun, in which guise the melody then spread around the yeshiva world.[17] An appropriate performance style,

---

[17]   Fieldnotes, 23 March 2003. See also similar examples cited by Koskoff (2001, 184–5). Note that the Tetris theme tune she refers to is likely 'Korobeiniki', originally a Russian folk song, thus not wholly distant from the aesthetic world of East European Jewish music.

then, can be the key that turns a melody which may otherwise seems banal into a meaningful performance, in turn giving access to the perceived spirituality of this musical repertory.

Within Hasidic circles, the aesthetic criteria by which performance is judged may seem on the surface to have little to do with Western conceptions of musicality. Describing the singing of nigunim among the Lubavitcher Hasidic community, Ellen Koskoff observes that for Lubavitchers: 'the beauty or effectiveness of a performance has little to do with Western classical notions of musicianship (such as the ability to project one's voice or to sing in tune). Lubavitcher musical ability is, rather, defined solely in relation to one's closeness to the living or historical rebbes, to one's knowledge of hasides [Hasidism], and to the context in which one has learned the repertoire of nigunim' (Koskoff 2001, 143). Similarly, Asya Vaysman notes that '*hartsik*' (heartfelt) was the adjective most commonly used by her female Hasidic informants to describe a good musical performance (Vaysman 2010, 179).

Nevertheless, as in other religious communities where music-making is valued primarily as an aspect of religious practice rather than as an independent entity, a recognisable soundscape or aesthetic exists which characterises traditional Hasidic singing. It would be a mistake to identify Hasidic nigunim as representing a unified tradition of performance practice: both the repertory and its performance contexts are diverse, with a particularly great difference existing between material as performed on Shabbes and other Jewish holidays when instruments are not permitted, and that performed during weddings and holidays such as Purim, when instruments are permitted – the latter being closer to that most frequently found on modern Hasidic recordings.[18] However, a common aesthetic heritage for this group of repertories can be found in the soundworld of traditional Jewish prayer, which emphasises individual expression within a group setting.

The following discussion, then, explores the strategies used by contemporary klezmer musicians to construct a 'Hasidic' performance aesthetic within the context of musical transmission. In this context, issues of style come particularly to the fore: since the majority of those seeking to learn Yiddish music today have little experience of the soundscape of religious Judaism, those choosing to teach traditional Hasidic material within the klezmer scene and further afield must explicitly teach the performance aesthetic they seek alongside the repertory itself, finding a means to express the musical and experiential aspects of this performance tradition and to transfer performance practice steeped in religious context into a music-centred setting.

This process is illustrated by teaching that took place during a Yiddish music workshop, 'Klezmer Wochen Weimar', held in Weimar, Germany, during July and August 2002. This workshop was unusual for a number of reasons. It had a far

---

[18]   Since the operation of electrical equipment is also subject to certain restrictions within Jewish law, recordings may only be made on occasions on which instruments may be used; therefore it is particularly difficult to find Hasidic recordings of unaccompanied religious song as it would be heard on Shabbes.

smaller enrolment – around 40 students – than many other Yiddish music camps; classes extended over a full week rather than four or five days, enabling engagement with musical material at greater depth than is usually possible during such camps; and the material covered during the week was particularly geared towards its intended audience, advanced musicians from Germany and other European countries, who had significant experience of performing klezmer music, but relatively little knowledge and experience of traditional Judaism (most participants were not Jewish). The instructors explicitly aimed to break down frequently held stereotypes about klezmer and Jewish music, whether overused clichés of performance style, or romanticised imagery of East European Jewish musicians. Singing nigunim formed a substantial part of the week's activities, based around a plenary session held first thing every morning, during which an hour of nigunim and Yiddish dance served as a warm-up, both physical and musical, for the day ahead. These sessions were jointly led by Michael Alpert and Sruli Dresdner; other members of the teaching staff attended and frequently added their own comments to the discussion. The aim of these sessions was explicitly not only to teach repertory, but also to relate aesthetic principles covered during these sessions to wider areas of Yiddish music. Further plenary sessions looked in depth at certain aspects of Hasidic music. One was spent exploring the sounds of the Hasidic world, in particular, according to Michael Alpert, listening to modern Hasidic recordings with the aim of undoing romanticised perceptions of 'the Hasidic world and where it is musically'.[19] In another, ethnomusicologist Judit Frigyesi gave a lecture-demonstration entitled 'Speech Rhythm in Jewish Music', again exploring the acoustical space of the Orthodox Jewish world, but here relating the aesthetic of Jewish prayer to performance practice in song. Outside the core programme of the week, Hasidic material was included in some small-group performance classes, giving an opportunity for both singers and instrumentalists to explore details of styling in greater depth.

While these classes comprised the explicit teaching programme of the week as far as Hasidic material was concerned, the instructors also encouraged participants to identify with the perceived spiritual properties of Hasidic vocal music, albeit outside a traditional Orthodox Jewish setting. Towards the end of the week the majority of participants were involved in two strikingly contrasted performances of nigunim. The first was an impromptu singing session on the Friday night, during which the shared repertory of nigunim learned during the week was transferred to a performance context far more resembling a Hasidic *tish* (gathering) or Shabbes meal. Sitting outside a smart Weimar café, in which a scheduled klezmer jam session led by Alpert and Dresdner was taking place, a group of participants sang and pounded on a table strewn with drinks and the remnants of a meal. Although the predominantly non-Jewish character of the week meant that Shabbes was not differentiated from other days in the course programme, the Friday night atmosphere thus created – aided by a certain quantity of alcohol – gave an experience entirely different from the formal early morning singing sessions. The second nigunim

---

[19]   Michael Alpert. Teaching session at Klezmer Wochen Weimar, 30 July 2003.

performance took place during the final concert of the week; held on the grounds of Ettersburg Castle, just outside the former site of the Buchenwald concentration camp. The concert, which celebrated the achievements of workshop participants during the week, began and ended with all participants and staff on stage together singing nigunim. The performance was unaccompanied, and participants stood shoulder to shoulder and moved to the sounds of the nigun: even though this was a stage performance, this presentation echoed the physically cramped yet musically energetic performance space of a Hasidic *farbrengen*.

My post hoc comparison of recordings made at several points during the week reveals a striking development between the first morning teaching session and the final concert. During the course of the week, the sound made by the full group of participants moved from a classical choral timbre, from which Dresdner and Alpert's voices stand out in their intensity, use of ornamentation and phrasing, and in clearly being leaders who are followed by the rest of the group, to a richer heterophonic sound, within which other voices besides those of Dresdner and Alpert participate in ornamentation, and anticipate coming phrases. The physical involvement of the participants in the performance of nigunim also changed over the course of the week, from initially sitting on chairs in a circle and concentrating on vocal performance, to the formation of a dense group around a table or on stage, within which all participants constantly moved, swaying, banging on the table or stamping on the stage to mark the pulse.

This transformation was achieved via a number of different teaching techniques. Vocal repertory was taught entirely by ear, with no use of printed notation; musical points were made using a combination of musical examples (sung and sometimes recorded) and words. Judit Frigyesi related the aesthetics of Jewish music to wider sounds in the traditional Jewish world – the sounds of singing and the sounds of speech. Seeking to explore the 'acoustical space' of traditional East Ashkenazi Jewry, she observed that 'the sound that Orthodox, traditional Jews hear is the sound of reading, and the sound of reading is music'. She commented that the concepts of 'speaking' and 'singing' themselves differ substantially in a traditional Jewish environment from the way they are used in English, a point reinforced by Michael Alpert, who jumped in to comment that traditional Yiddish usage uses the verb *zogn* (to say) of a nigun – 'Nu, *zog* a nign' (Hey, *say* a melody) – rather than using the verb *zingen* (to sing) more commonly used for secular songs. This *zogn* might mean anything between melodic song and a rhythmic style of speech: not metric but not completely free. Frigyesi continued: 'Even the most metric is a little bit speech-like, and even the most speech-like speech is somewhat metric. And there is a constant play between these two things'.[20]

Traditional Jewish law mandates that prayer should take place in a group yet that within the group each member has the responsibility to pray as an individual. Coupled with the rhythmic flexibility described above, this leads in traditional

---

[20]   All quotations taken from Judit Frigyesi's presentation, 'Speech Rhythm in Jewish Music', Klezmer Wochen Weimar, 2 August 2002.

Jewish prayer to the heterophony described below by Jeffrey Summit. While the pace of the service is set by the prayer leader, who at times acts as a soloist, in between sections recited aloud, individuals proceed at their own pace:

> Such Jewish prayer often sounds like a cacophony of voices. Individuals proceed at varying speeds; rarely are two people chanting exactly the same words at the same time. Worshippers chant in an undertone, each choosing a comfortable key … At least in East European tradition, to daven [pray] is to sing, chant, move and sway. One must bring an emotional intensity and involvement to the recitation of the prayers (Summit 2000, 26).

Attempting to achieve this heterophony in a musical rather than a prayer context, Frigyesi taught the group of around 40 students to sing 'Sholem aleykhem' (Peace to you), a Hebrew *zemer* for Friday night, to a simple melody learned from an informant. She then encouraged the group to sing in their own individual speech rhythm, repeating the short song again and again. Gradually, individual performance speeds diverged, the beginnings and endings of each repetition of the song becoming completely asynchronised; at this point she declared, 'it starts sounding more like a Jewish sound'.

Individual variation to this extreme degree is more characteristic of certain parts of traditional Jewish prayer, rather than of nigunim and song, within which variation tends to occur on a smaller scale. Nevertheless, transferred from formal prayer to song, this aesthetic of heterophony forms the basis of the group performance of nigunim. While one or more individuals may take leadership roles, starting or stopping the group, or encouraging a change of speed or melody, the overall impression is of a mass of sound within which each singer simultaneously forms part of a coherent group sound and yet sings as an individual.

This performance aesthetic also impacts the way harmony and rhythm are conceptualised in this repertory. Although nigunim are frequently performed both within and outside the Hasidic world with a harmonic instrumental accompaniment, in many cases easy to realise even for those nigunim in modes other than the Western major and minor, the functional progression of the piece is primarily melodic rather than harmonic, with melodic tensions and cadential figures replacing the harmonic variation which might be expected in a similar Western melody. In traditional Hasidic vocal practice, musical timing is flexible both on a small scale, reflecting individual independence within the heterophonic aesthetic discussed above, and on a larger structural scale, representing a tendency to create musical excitement by singing before the beat. Following a demonstration of a nigun with Dresdner, Michael Alpert observed to students how while the nigun had a regular meter, the pulse was not always regular, in particular, climactic moments were frequently anticipated:

> Maybe it was obvious, but … it's not just kind of dah-dah-dah [*imitates strict rhythm*] all the way through. At those points, you tend to rush into those kind of

climaxes. [*sings*] … and it kind of comes sooner than you think, which is a very common principle in Yiddish folksong also, that gives it a special flow, and an urgency – if it just had a straight rhythm it would get monotonous and boring, but all of a sudden – [*sings*] da da DAAAA! – you know, it's already going on to the next stage. And then you get pulled along with it, which is a very beautiful thing.[21]

In practice, this anticipation either of climactic points or of new phrases can lead to entire beats being skipped, as illustrated in Example 5.1, transcribed from an unidentified Hasidic tape used by Kurt Bjorling at the Weimar workshop to illustrate aspects of tuning and style. Singing a triple-time melody, a boy soloist (transcription b) skips a beat in his approach to a cadence (compare transcriptions a and b), creating a strong sense of forward propulsion.

Example 5.1   Metric fluidity in *nigun* performance

Example 5.2   'Ma'arash'

Another common feature of the heterophonic performance of nigunim, combining both rhythmic and melodic heterophony, is the anticipation of notes, either in time or by sliding to sound the next pitch before the note arrives. Example 5.2 is transcribed from a performance of 'Ma'arash', a slow nigun, sung by Michael Alpert and Sruli Dresdner at the concert following the Weimar workshop (Dresdner begins, joined by Alpert from the second phrase. Extract notated in tempo; in performance pulse was flexible; // indicates a pause).

---

[21]   Michael Alpert. Teaching session at Klezmer Wochen Weimar, 30 July 2003.

Lines connecting with noteheads on the transcription indicate vocal slides between pitches. In all occurrences, upward slides rearticulate the previously sounded pitch, and downward slides anticipate the next. While the majority of slides – those notated on the stave itself – were sung by both Alpert and Dresdner, each singer also ornamented the melody in his own way, indicated by the symbols above and below the stave (those above the stave apply to Dresdner; those below the stave apply to Alpert). Here, an asterisk (*) indicates a note articulated early, a slash (/) indicates a slide, and a tilde (~) a mordent-like ornament. Glancing at the distribution of these symbols indicates differences in individual style: Dresdner more commonly accentuates notes by anticipation, and Alpert more commonly uses mordents. Within this pattern, the singers' individual ornaments tend to alternate, each responding to the other's choices.

While these examples illustrate elements typical of Hasidic vocality, Hasidic performance practice extends beyond what might conventionally be considered to be musical material: the experience of singing nigunim additionally combines both physical factors – singing is conceptualised as a whole-body rather than a purely vocal activity – and spiritual/emotional aspects, in the traditional performance context of this material. To illustrate the former during a morning singing session, Sruli Dresdner took a religious Hasidic story, creatively using this to make two broader musical points to the group of students:

I'd like to tell a little story – Hasidim tell lots and lots of stories. Anyway, this one is, I think, very much related to what we're doing, and to klezmer music – and maybe all music … One of the early Hasidic rebbes was a man by the name of Moshe of Kobrin … He said something I think very smart: he was once giving a talk, and he was telling the followers, the people around, about the importance of prayer. He mentioned one word that's repeated very often in the prayers, and he said, 'When you pray this word, all of your body, the whole top and every limb, every piece of your body should be inside the word'. And then somebody from the back of the room raises his hand, and he asks – he's a big man – he says, 'How can I get my big body into this little word?' And the rebbe responded, that 'for people who think like that, I can't talk to you'.

The first point, I think, is part of the reason why people like Alan [Bern] feel so strongly about a certain style of klezmer playing that he dislikes, is because of that, because the person is bigger than the notes. [*Sounds of agreement from the audience.*] And I think that's a very important part of this music – maybe all music – that you should put yourself into the notes and not the other way around. But the second point that I thought about this story for, is … move [the] body. The body is a very important part of this singing. So you can't sit like this and sing [*sits still and sings*]. You have to move, so move! [*Sings, swaying and stamping his foot, everyone joins in.*][22]

---

[22]   Sruli Dresdner. Teaching session at Klezmer Wochen Weimar, 30 July 2003.

Like Frigyesi, Dresdner explicitly links religious practices with musical points, implying that even if the goal of singing is not a religious one, understanding the religious context of this repertory will help musicians to make appropriate performance choices – especially in a context like this workshop, where self-consciousness and habit meant that students were reluctant physically to loosen up and move while singing.

This familiarity with Hasidic repertory and vocality in turn served as a way for the workshop leaders to introduce participants to what Frank London describes as 'going to that place' – the spiritual aspect of the Hasidic nigun. This was couched in musical, rather than Jewish-religious terms: participants were encouraged to enjoy the heightened spiritual/emotional state achieved through singing in a large group. Some time after the Weimar workshop, I discussed with Sruli Dresdner how this transformative experience had occurred during the two singing sessions – the Friday night singing session and the concert – at the end of the week, allowing many participants to make the link between the theoretical elements of the tradition discussed by their teachers, and their own performance experience. As our conversation, reproduced below, illustrates, this transformation not only extended to the students' relationship to Hasidic repertory, but also involved a change in Dresdner's own views about performing and teaching this material to German musicians. While the other teachers on the programme had spent considerable time performing and teaching there, this was Dresdner's first experience of teaching in Germany. Like many other American Jewish musicians, he initially approached the idea of German musicians playing Jewish music with ambivalence or even trepidation; however, this was overcome both by the positive reactions of workshop participants and also by Dresdner's own desire to present access to the spiritual component of this music as nonexclusive, based in the music itself rather than in religious practice:

> SD: At the beginning, I was a little nervous about how people would receive this, and it was a little weird for me, frankly, for obvious reasons. But it stopped being weird or scary very early on, because obviously the people who came to this conference were people who wanted to learn about Jewishness and Jewish life, and I think very much about Jewish spirituality. I think one of the things [where] the klezmer revival makes a mistake is if they try to cleanse this music of all religious iconography. It's not about being religious, or proselytising, or anything like that, but it's music that's spiritual in nature, and I think that a lot of people – including the German musicians that primarily made up that workshop – *are* drawn to it for the spirituality … You don't know for a few days if they're enjoying it or if they're just doing it, but it was obvious – I think at the beginning, maybe [they were just doing what they were told], but as they became more involved, they realised the spiritual power of this, and the power it has to bring people together, and I think they really enjoyed it. Did you have that sense as well?

AW: Yes, I think it made a difference on that Friday night when we were sitting around outside the cafe, singing, you know, an evening [singing] round tables, because I'd been talking with some people in the group, in the class [Dresdner's vocal workshop] – we'd been singing after your class – about this idea of sitting around the table and just singing as a group, and I think actually *doing* that, for a few people was like, 'Oh!' you know, 'that's it'.

SD: That's what it's all about.

AW: Yes.

SD: I agree with you that it really gelled that night sitting round the tables at the cafe, outside. But I thought it gelled a lot also at the concert performance, [AW: Yes!] when people were like, 'Oh!', you know, 'fifty of us can get together and sing these nigunim', and it just gave them a sense of belonging to something.

AW: I thought it was quite funny in a way, because if you listen to it on the CD [of the final concert], there's none of the atmosphere, and it just [sounds] like random people singing – to the audience it must have been quite bizarre!

SD: Although I hope I'm not going out on a limb – I think the audience at least saw the transformative power of it [AW: Oh, totally!] ... So, it was great ... it was really great. I feel grateful that the participants wanted to learn these melodies, cared to learn them. And I always feel this way ... that, separate from the klezmer repertoire, the Hasidic repertoire is appreciated in a different [way], and I think a lot of people want that difference, they want to learn these melodies. I don't want to pontificate too much on this and get myself into trouble, but you know, in some cases the klezmer melodies are contrived – that's of course true of Hasidic melodies also, but at least the ones that I think are really great I feel are much more organic than many of the klezmer melodies. And they're not there to show off any sort of virtuosity, it's just about being able to feel what you sing.[23]

While their personal backgrounds may be far apart, Dresdner's experiences with the German musicians, then, seem ultimately to echo his own approach to Hasidic material: the positive reactions of his students further reinforce the high value he accords to nigunim as a musical repertory, and the experiences of singing nigunim in the final concert echo his assertion that it is not necessary to make this music within an ultra-Orthodox religious setting in order to access its spiritual-emotional content.

---

[23]   Sruli Dresdner, interview, 2003.

Performing Hasidic Music to the Wider Jewish Community

While the teaching sessions outlined above operated within the musical-cultural cocoon of the klezmer scene, all the performers I spoke to were also actively involved in presenting their work with Hasidic repertory to a wider, particularly American Jewish, audience. Both a quest for work opportunities and a sense of recovering or preserving a lost, valuable Jewish musical heritage has led many musicians, such as the workshop leaders mentioned above, not merely to reproduce traditional Hasidic music for passive consumption but also explicitly to present this repertory as a functional, participatory music, capable of playing a role in contemporary non-Orthodox Jewish religious life.

Hasidic-style music is no stranger to mainstream Jewish worship: since the 1960s, 'neo-Hasidic' nigunim have become a popular component of synagogue services in denominations ranging from modern Orthodox to Reform and Reconstructionist (Slobin 1989, 195–212). This musical development has accompanied a movement towards a more participatory prayer style encouraging personal spiritual expression, and also reflects a wider fascination with Hasidism. If today's Hasidic community is distanced both physically and philosophically from mainstream American Jewish culture, Hasidism itself and the image of the Hasid had enormous influence on twentieth-century American Jewish thought and cultural imagery. Arthur Green writes that 'Hasidic influence or inspiration can be observed in virtually every field of Jewish creativity – in music, art, poetry and theatre. The impact of hasidism on the non-hasidic Jewish community in the twentieth century has been tremendous' (1996, 446).

The Hasidism inspiring those described by Green as 'altogether remote or estranged from Hasidic practice' (1996, 446) is largely linked with the early days of the Hasidic movement, rather than with today's Hasidic community. Nevertheless, musically, the Hasidic material most frequently incorporated into synagogue services has not been the music of early Hasidism, but rather more recent neo-Hasidic compositions that recast elements of the Hasidic nigun in a folk-pop style (Summit 2000, 95). The most popular – and prolific – composer in this style is Shlomo Carlebach (1925–1994), an Orthodox rabbi who used music as a means to reach out to 'hippie', disengaged Jewish youth, attaining vast popularity which has continued after his lifetime.[24] While incorporating some of the rhythmic features of Hasidic material, Carlebach's melodies are generally much simpler than traditional Hasidic nigunim, lend themselves easily to Western harmonisation, and do not include central Hasidic musical elements such as heterophony, traditional ornamentation or ABCB form. A few older Hasidic melodies have made their way into the mainstream synagogue repertory; however, again, these are primarily among the shorter and simpler of the Hasidic melodies.

---

[24]   His example has been followed by many recent Jewish songwriters, including the late Debbie Friedman (Reform) and Shefa Gold (Reconstructionist). See Kligman (2001) for discussion.

Seeking to introduce a wider variety of traditional Hasidic melodies to non-Hasidic audiences, Dresdner noted that, despite a high level of general interest in things Hasidic, the response from audiences is frequently ambivalent: while various non-Orthodox synagogues were happy to hire him for his Friday night programme, most of their members are simply not interested in sitting around all night singing nigunim Hasidic-style. This desire to engage with Hasidic musical material, yet ambivalent response when presented with the 'real thing', is not simply a case of casual misunderstanding, but is rooted both in the contemporary Jewish music scene and in the wider politics of representation of the Hasidic community among American Jews. These factors go some way to explain how, while this repertory is universally perceived as valuable in the abstract, crossing the border between a passive and an active engagement with traditional Hasidic music can uncomfortably challenge personal boundaries, both musical and religious/philosophical.

What began as a mystical sect, offering an alternative to the heavy scholarship of rabbinic Judaism accessible only to the learned, has become the community that, above all others, now stands in the popular imagination for the strictures of rabbinic law. The reluctance of both scholars and the wider public to engage with this transformation of the Hasidic community – exacerbated, perhaps, by the difficulty of penetrating the community as an outsider – has led instead to a perpetuation of broad-brushed stereotypes and idealisms. Introducing a collection of essays on Hasidism and observing an imbalance of material, Ada Rapoport-Albert writes:

> [Twentieth-century hasidic scholarship] has tended to concentrate on the early history of hasidism but has paid little attention to more recent or contemporary developments … Implicit in the scholarly concentration on early hasidism is the sense, on which there has been a virtual consensus, that while the movement had begun as a genuine spiritual revival, it soon degenerated into a vulgar personality cult, devoid of any original religious ideas but providing ample opportunities for an avaricious, imperious leadership to exploit its naïve following and to delude it with extravagant claims. This sense, which has led many scholars to conclude their histories of the movement in the middle of the nineteenth century at the latest, is now increasingly recognised to stem either from an idealised depiction of early hasidism that overlooks or misconstrues some of its features, or from a view of late hasidism which is blinkered by inapposite value judgements. In this latter view there is a failure to note not only such original thought as does continue to develop in the later stages, but also the numerous expressions of hasidic creativity and enterprise in various spheres of activity within the modern world (1996, xxiii).

Despite this lack of engagement by both scholars and others with the reality of contemporary Hasidism, beginning in the 1960s the Hasidim have become widely perceived to symbolise Jewish spiritual authenticity; as Peter Eli Gordon observes, 'Hasidism fascinates American Jews' (1990, 49). This thirst for things Hasidic, coupled with a willingness to blind oneself to the contemporary reality of Hasidism in favour of maintaining broad-brushed stereotypes, means that the gap left by scholarly research is frequently filled by romanticised imagery. As Gordon notes, 'Jews standing outside Hasidic life have often 'imagined' Hasidism. They have derided it or romanticised it, but they have rarely understood it' (1990, 49).

This popular fascination with Hasidism exists, then, almost entirely at arm's length, mediated by outside agents for consumption by the outside world. Jack Kugelmass (1997) describes how coffee-table books presenting images of Hasidic life frame these images with commentaries employing well-worn tropes, and popular books on Hasidic thought present decontextualised stories and soundbites, focusing attention away from ritual and observance and towards feel-good spirituality. Kugelmass uses the term 'folk ethnography' to describe his literature of coffee-table books, 'a corpus of material revealing the quests of American Jewry for self-understanding', collectible objects playing a role in 'the construction of collective selfhood' (1997, 39). In choosing the term 'ethnography', he implies a paradoxical 'us and them' relationship with the Hasidim portrayed: American Jewish collective identity is defined in the presence of, yet in opposition to, this Jewish other. Removed from the arm's-length portrayal of the picture book, musicians become at the same time performers of the imagined Hasid, and mediators between the Hasidic world and audience, which mediation extends to musical sound as well as imagery.

Nowhere is an 'idealised depiction' of Hasidic practice more evident than in descriptions of Hasidic vocal music. The characteristic sound of Hasidic nigunim has long been used as a musical symbol of Jewish authenticity. Mark Slobin identifies such an example in the score to *Fiddler on the Roof*. He writes:

> The composer Jerry Brock integrates snatches of Hasidic *nign* into the basic Broadway sounds of the score to provide authenticity, as in 'If I Were a Rich Man's' *yobba-dobba* and *biri-biri-bom*. It is typical of *Fiddler*'s period that its creators turned to the then-exotic Hasidic sound (this was around 1960, before the rise of Hasidim as the 'authentic' Jews among mainstream Jewish-Americans) as their ethnic point of reference (2002b, 473).

Again, however, this image of Hasidic sound is far from the reality of popular contemporary synthesiser-backed Orthodox recordings, and equally from the soundscape of traditional Hasidic performance practice, which, as described above, challenges a range of Western conceptions of normative music-making. Rather, in order to present Hasidic music to a wider audience hungry for a sound perceived to be authentic, it has been made musically compatible with the aesthetic norms of its audience. Similarly, involved in the musical arrangement and direction for various recordings of Hasidic material during the late 1950s and early 1960s, Velvel Pasternak recounts the difficulties he encountered in training a group of Lubavitcher Hasidim to sing nigunim in tune and time with an orchestra, and how he failed to teach them to follow the vocal harmonies he had composed, having instead to employ professional singers to sing the harmonies on the recording. Despite using these professional singers and spending 'several months of weekly rehearsals' (1999, 26) persuading the Hasidim to sing in a completely different way from that which they were used to, the resulting recording was hailed as 'one of the finest authentic Jewish recordings ever made' (1996, 33).

Ironically, then, while an extensive engagement with the contemporary Hasidic musical world, steeped in the ethnographic ethos which has underpinned the klezmer revival, has led today's Yiddish musicians to reassess stereotypes of the Hasidic world in their performance and teaching, in marketing traditional Hasidic music to the wider Jewish community these same musicians become performers of this popular imagined Hasidism. Music is a commercial enterprise, and stereotyped images remain the staple means of marketing re-created traditional Hasidic music to a wider audience. Sruli Dresdner's website advertises:

> Let us transport you to an Old World Hasidic Shteebl where you will experience the wondrously intense Nigunim that inspire the Hasidim to cleave to God and life!
>
> *Friday Night Hasidic Service*
>
> A beautiful, inspiring and interactive program that infuses the Friday Night liturgy with the soul and wisdom of Hasidic story, song and dance. In the tradition of the Tish, we will follow this intimate program with a lively Rikud – a spirited dance.[25]

Similarly, the cover image of London, Sklamberg and Caine's Nigunim disc, a reproduction of the painting *Alefbet-Lexicon* by Russian-Jewish artist Grisha Bruskin, contains elements associated with Hasidic spirituality – men in hats blowing a ram's horn, wrapped in prayer shawls, wearing *tefillin* (phylacteries) – and is covered in Hebrew lettering, the words disjointed and often illegible, suggesting a spiritual message yet beyond the grasp of the onlooker.

Hasidic Vocality as Yiddish Musical Utopia

In engaging with Hasidic material, the musicians discussed in this chapter illustrate a constant negotiation between the desire to make good music, the need to satisfy a paying audience and the challenge of Yiddish cultural continuity. Their performances of nigunim reflect values of mainstream American culture at the turn of the twenty-first century – a widespread interest in spirituality outside the framework of organised religion, and, musically, a quest for historically informed

---

[25]   http://www.sruliandlisa.com/hasidicnigunim.html, accessed 18 July 2003.

performance – at the same time widening a conception of Yiddish music which has generally focused upon secular rather than religious music.

In our wider map of musical Yiddishland, venturing into the Hasidic musical world might further be read as an encounter with Yiddish utopia. As the number of native Yiddish speakers and people who grew up in a Yiddish cultural environment dwindles within the secular world, the Hasidic community continues to grow, offering a tempting inroad into the future of the spoken language, and the perpetuation of cultural traditions based upon East European Jewish models.

This utopia is reflected in musicians' approaches to Hasidic repertory. As the Hasidic community has taken pains to preserve Old World cultural forms, Hasidic repertory and performance practice bear an aura of historical authenticity, a way to access the inaccessible past.[26] Like contemporary classical historically informed performances, the performances of Hasidic material discussed above extract the musical material from its original context even if 'corrupted' by present performance styles. Unlike Hasidic conceptions of authenticity based on religious practice or lineage, then, here this authenticity is located in the musical sound itself. Hasidic performance practice becomes a prototype for all Yiddish music performance; a warm up for the klezmer and Yiddish song ahead. Further, Hasidic musical practice read as musical archetype allows these musicians not merely to reproduce Hasidic music of the past or to critique current Hasidic performance practice, but also to open the possibility of multiple concurrent interpretations of this strand of Yiddish vocal music, in turn reinserting themselves into the lineage of this repertory as equally valid heirs and interpreters, and increasing their legitimacy as proponents of Yiddish culture.

This musical utopia is often elided with an utopic view of spirituality. Recreating traditional Hasidic performance practice under the rubric of historically informed performance provides a vehicle for musicians to experience something of the spiritual intensity of this music without buying into the religious values and practices of the strictly Orthodox Jewish community. In turn, this facilitates a kind of synthesis of progressive Jewish culture and traditional Ashkenazi religious musical expression largely unavailable within the institutions of formal Jewish religion in contemporary North America. In her essay subtitled 'Klezmer as Jewish Youth Subculture', Alicia Svigals observes:

> There are many people who wish they could be culturally Jewish, spiritual, and progressive all at once. They secretly long for a congregation that would be a cross between a B'nai Jeshurun – a synagogue on Manhattan's Upper West Side that boasts progressive politics, religious tradition, a big youthful crowd, and sappy liturgical music of the Israeli Europop variety – and one of those

---

[26]   Jeffrey Shandler has suggested that for some American and European Jews, visiting Hasidic neighbourhoods in Brooklyn has become 'another way of "going home"', playing a role related to that of Jewish heritage travel to Eastern Europe (1989, 22).

shuls [synagogues] deep in the heart of Brooklyn that features great *khazones* [cantorial singing] but most decidedly doesn't marry gay couples (2002, 214).

This re-imagining of spiritual space underscores a utopic vision of Yiddishland – musical practices enable the creation of a new, better Jewish world.

Nevertheless, beyond this vision of utopia, substantial ontological differences between the communities engaged with Hasidic repertories today remain. The value accorded to Hasidim as carriers of a vernacular Yiddish vocal tradition and the desire to experience the spiritual high associated with the singing of nigunim are balanced by the challenges the Hasidic community presents to the outside visitor in terms of its strict religious orthodoxy. As the two worlds continue into the Yiddish future, it seems likely that musicians will continue to turn to the Hasidic world for source material. Nevertheless, given the substantial move to the religious right of Jewish orthodoxy during the mid-twentieth century, a genuinely two-way musical relationship is still distant.

Chapter 6

Technology, the Sonic Object and the (Re)Construction of Yiddish Music

The preceding chapters explored the musical and discursive products of the encounters of American Yiddish musicians with two metaphorical 'border regions': one geographical – Central and Eastern Europe – and one cultural – the strictly Orthodox Hasidic community.[1] This chapter considers a third form of musical encounter, one particularly spurred by new music technologies: the encounter of contemporary musicians with the recorded Yiddish past. The fusion of 'past' Yiddish materials with 'contemporary' musical idioms is hardly a new phenomenon: seven or eight decades previously, Yiddish songs, already read as symbols of an archaic culture, were arranged in American popular styles such as swing for radio broadcast.[2] Nevertheless, during the first decade of the twenty-first century, newly available music technologies, coupled with reference to popular styles including hip hop, prompted a handful of Yiddish musicians to explore a relatively new arena of fusion, creating music that directly juxtaposes historical and contemporary recorded voices.

Recorded music – both commercial recordings of the early twentieth century and field recordings – played a foundational role in the klezmer revival from its inception, sometimes filling the role of absent musical mentors: the stylistic choices of their forebears influenced the aesthetic directions of many revival bands.[3] Later, following increased scholarly interest in Yiddish music, the availability of historic recordings increased greatly. Many more archival recordings were uncovered, catalogued and reissued; simultaneous developments in the cleaning of old recordings and digital duplication meant that material that previously had remained in specialist archives became readily available with little geographical constraint.[4]

---

[1]   A previous version of this chapter appeared as: Abigail Wood (2007a) '(De) constructing Yiddishland: Solomon and SoCalled's HipHopKhasene'. *Ethnomusicology Forum* 16:2, 243–70 (http://www.informaworld.com). I am grateful to Taylor & Francis Ltd. for permission to reprint material from this article.

[2]   A number of such recordings are presented on Yair Reiner and Henry Sapoznik's collection *Music from the Yiddish Radio Project* (2002).

[3]   See, for example, Lorin Sklamberg, cited in Chapter 3.

[4]   Examples include the 2004 release by the Vernadsky National Library of Ukraine of two CDs of 1910s–30s field recordings originally on wax cylinder.

These developments once more reconfigured the material culture of Yiddish music. While printed scores draw focus to processes of textual interpretation – the ways in which the musician brings out the sounds hidden within an encoded text – by contrast, in the recorded format, rather than a fixed text seeking interpretation, music becomes a sound object, a collectable, manipulable part of material culture. Each musical object encapsulates explicit, concrete historical referents, analogous to the images captured by a camera: 'photographed images', says Susan Sontag, 'do not seem to be statements about the world so much as pieces of it, miniatures of reality that anyone can make or acquire' (1973, 4).[5]

Sample-based music translates this material culture into musical form, facilitating the electronic juxtaposition of stylistically or temporally distant materials in a way that preserves their sonic diversity. The creative process focuses on manipulation and framing: the creation of a focused here-and-now from sonic shards reconstituted via montage. Embedding historical recordings within contemporary recordings enables musicians to juxtapose different 'miniatures of reality', placing historically distant voices in immediate conversation with the present. Technological innovation alone does not force dramatic change in the character and reception of art; nevertheless, the anthologising aesthetic made possible by new music technologies opens a rich discursive space.

Placing past and present musical voices on the same musical plane can collapse historical distance, articulating the continuity of expressive language and political cause. Among the songs that appear on the Klezmatics' 2003 album *Rise Up!* is Shmerke Katsherginski's 'Barikadn' (Barricades). The song, written in the 1920s, describes a family of workers going out to build and protest on barricades; it quickly spread throughout the Yiddish-speaking world. The track opens with a recording of Katsherginski himself singing a verse of the song; crackle and hiss help the listener to identify his voice as historical, a musical sample patched into the album. As the (present) band begins to play an accompaniment, we hear Katsherginski explain the provenance of the song in Yiddish, presumably from an archival field recording. The sample fades out as Lorin Sklamberg begins to repeat Katsherginski's first verse. As the song progresses, a second level of digital manipulation is used: an echo of Sklamberg's voice repeats each line of the song. At first the sound of the echo is thin and distanced, moving between far left and right in the mix, creating a disembodied effect. As the song progresses, the echo turns into a stronger, harmonised repetition of each line, giving a sense of upward momentum. While the crackle, hiss and spoken word broke the continuity of the opening of the song, creating a complicated sense of time and place, the progression of the manipulated voice through the song is a constant reminder that the musical here-and-now is also subject to manipulation. Both voices, then, assume an ambiguous, dislocated position – and it is this very dislocation that emphasises the reading that the meaning of Katsherginski's song is not time-bound: rather, the

---

[5]   See Buck-Morss (1989, 4) for discussion of the encapsulation of concrete historical referents within material culture.

sense of urgency and protest of Communist activism in Katsherginski's 1920s is relevant to the shaken political world of the Klezmatics' post-2001 New York City.

Sampling can also serve as a tool to domesticate historically and culturally distant sounds. In a contrasting sample-based project, American-Israeli remix artist Diwon (Erez Safar) released *The Beat Guide to Yiddish* in 2008, a mixtape of (mainly) Yiddish recordings.[6] Better known for his work with Sephardic and Middle Eastern music, Diwon's foray into Yiddish music represents an encompassing view of musical Jewishness by 'that Yemenite kid'.[7] While the download page advertises that Diwon 'mixes some of his own music into forgotten sounds from Eastern Europe', in fact the majority of samples here are not European, but are rather American Yiddish recordings. By contrast to the stark sonic juxtapositions of the Klezmatics' 'Barikadn', Diwon's compilation avoids challenging the listener with historic distance; rather, leading her into Yiddish soundspace via a stream of familiar kitsch. The mix opens with 'Mayn shtetele Belz' (My hometown Belz), a song composed in 1932 by Alexander Olshanetsky, and which became iconic of nostalgia for the Old World. This is followed by recordings by popular stars of the 1930s–40s like Sam Medoff, through the Barry Sisters, to contemporary ultra-Orthodox Jewish rapper Lipa Schmeltzer, whose sounds, though progressive in the strictly Orthodox music scene, are generally considered to be outside the 'secular' contemporary Yiddish music scene. Likewise, his inclusion of Hebrew popular recordings of a similar era (including a sped-up version of Hava Nagila) blurs the customary ideological Hebrew–Yiddish divide.

Within this mix, recordings from the early twentieth century, possibly European, form a third temporal level of the mix, counterposed both against today's beats and against 1930s American Yiddish recordings. These recordings peek through the texture: a few bars of instrumental music here; part of a song here. Tellingly, the last appearance of such a voice is superimposed with horror-film style power chords, disquieting a standard untexted Yiddish phrase ending in the original recording (ay ay ay AY– ay ay, 15:50–16:03), and turning it into a parody of itself, an over-melodramatic Gothic horror moment. So what is the role of Diwon's kitsch? While his reading tends away from a nuanced encounter with the past that he claims to represent, he affirms an American-Yiddish normalcy, giving the listener permission to engage with a range of Yiddish materials, and re-establishing them as part of the sound world of a young audience who are hungry not simply for Yiddish but for hip, contemporary Jewish sounds.

The remainder of this chapter explores the discursive spaces of sample-based Yiddish music further via a close reading of Solomon and SoCalled's *HipHopKhasene*. Structured around a traditional Old World Jewish wedding ceremony, *HipHopKhasene* celebrates the metaphorical 'marriage' of hip hop and klezmer music, consummated via a series of collaborative musical tracks involving a group of prominent Yiddish musicians and samples from historic

---

6   http://www.shemspeed.com/diwon/, downloaded 14 July 2010.

7   The title of a previous release.

Yiddish recordings. Here I explore the concept, construction and context of *HipHopKhasene*, focusing particularly upon the way that sampling allows the simultaneous expression of multiple musical and cultural voices, which are juxtaposed during the course of the album and emerge in surprising combinations. While Solomon and SoCalled's 'wedding' is a ludic construction, the moment of the fictional marriage of fiddle and microphone draws together and comments on a number of threads representing processes of change in contemporary Yiddish musical culture, particularly concerning the nature of Yiddish musical and linguistic fluency as a new generation of musicians arrives on the scene.

Constructing *HipHopKhasene*

Recorded in the summer of 2001 in London, and released on CD in 2003 by German world music label Piranha, *HipHopKhasene* was produced by two of the younger musicians on the international klezmer scene, violinist and ragga-jungle DJ Sophie Solomon from London, then a member of klezmer-fusion band Oi Va Voi, and musician-photographer-magician Josh Dolgin, aka SoCalled, from Montreal.[8] As an album, *HipHopKhasene* was reasonably successful. Distributed via the world music section of mainstream European music stores. *HipHopKhasene* received positive reviews both within Jewish music circles and in the wider music press; it was one of the editor's selection of top new releases in British world music magazine *Songlines* (Jul/Aug 2003), and was awarded the *Preis der Deutschen Schallplatten Kritik* in 2004.[9]

The text of *HipHopKhasene*'s liner notes draws the listener directly into the imagined location of the wedding: the liner notes to the Piranha release of the album are simply headed 'Yiddishland, August 24th 2001'.[10] Couched as an account of the *shidduch* – the love-match – between hip hop and klezmer, Sophie Solomon's letter from Yiddishland is strewn with references to people, places and events – 'slivo-filled singalongs with Sruli & co and pickled cucumbers by the half-light of an icy Lower East Side dawn'. By bringing the listener into the sensory world of the individual, to familiar memories and in-group references, Solomon paints an intimate picture of Yiddish cultural life; a contemporary, everyday world where people hang out and music is made. Nevertheless, this secure sense of space is disquieted by geographical ambiguity. Both the imagined wedding the album

---

[8]   SoCalled's recent work is discussed in depth by Smulyan, 2012.

[9]   See review by prominent klezmer commentator Ari Davidow here: http://www. klezmershack.com/bands/socalled/khasene/socalled.khasene.html, downloaded 6 July 2010.

[10]   As discussed in the introduction to this volume, the epithet Yiddishland has frequently been used by insiders to refer to the Yiddish cultural world; its frame of reference, however, varies. Here I follow Solomon's usage, using 'Yiddishland' to refer particularly to the contemporary Yiddish music scene.

portrays and the real-life production of the music are anti-geographical: the first takes place in an imagined cultural space, and the second reflects the recording-based musical techniques used: the musicians who appear on this recording – even those who played 'live' – were recorded in several separate locations.

Both Solomon and SoCalled came to *HipHopKhasene* not only as musicians involved in the klezmer scene but also as experienced creators of beat-based musics. Before *HipHopKhasene*, Josh Dolgin had been making beats for about ten years. He explained:

> I always played piano, and accordion later on, and played in gospel, salsa, blues, funk and rock bands, but hip hop really spoke to me and my peers and I wanted to be a part of it ... So I worked with lots of rappers and musicians, and started making beats with a four-track, keyboards, sound modules and a drum machine. Then I moved onto sampling. I had to start collecting sounds to steal, and I started buying cheap, discarded, weird vinyl records from Salvation Armies and garage sales. I was also kinda getting into klezmer a bit more by then, getting a bunch of CDs of revivalist ensembles. So in my vinyl hunting, I started to find Jewish records, and I figured, hey, I can't be sampling George Clinton and James Brown like everybody else, I've got to find my own voice, I've got to represent myself in this music – and myself isn't a Black American funky self, it's an alienated, rural Canadian Jewish self. ... Anyway, so these Jewish records ... were simply exploding with perfect little bits to loop and chop up. ... Then I went to KlezKanada, and that really opened my ears to the music and I got more into the theory and unique rhythms and modes and melodies that I wanted to incorporate into the beats.[11]

Dolgin began to give workshops on making beats at the Canadian KlezKanada camp, where he met Sophie Solomon in 2001. A member of London based klezmer fusion band Oi Va Voi, she too had been exploring the fusion of klezmer music with contemporary dance beats. Later that year, they met again at a gig hosted by Solomon at Tonic, then a Lower East Side venue with a regular klezmer slot. She recalls, 'We just kind of enjoyed working together, it was a good spark. And suddenly, I just had this revelation, I thought *Hip ... Hop ... Khasene!*'[12]

While the sound of the word made an intriguing title, the concept of using the wedding both supplied a structure to the nascent album and linked Solomon and SoCalled's project to parallel artistic enterprises undertaken throughout the history of recorded Yiddish music, themselves rooted in the changing role of music in the American Jewish wedding. An East European Jewish wedding encompassed instrumental music for both dancing and listening, alongside other Yiddish musical forms, including liturgical chant and *badkhones* – improvised rhyming couplets from the *badkhn*, or wedding jester. As European Jewish immigrants arrived in America, the traditional wedding ceremony developed both to accommodate new

---

[11]   Josh Dolgin, e-mail communication with the author, 6 January 2003.

[12]   Sophie Solomon, interview with the author, London, 16 December 2002.

musical tastes and to reflect the living conditions of Jewish immigrants in New York City and other American urban centres: few were able to hold the lengthy wedding rituals they had held in the Old World.[13] On the other hand, weddings also became a locus where connections to European Jewish traditions and rituals could be expressed freely: Hankus Netsky observes that 'for immigrant Jews (as well as other immigrant groups) weddings were a safe "new world" outlet for uninhibited, unbridled quasi-religious ritual expression' (2004, 110).

Reflecting this conception of the wedding ceremony as a symbolic expressive space, Alothe ritual itself became an object of performance. Mark Slobin notes that mock wedding records were popular among many ethnic groups in late 1920s America. He observes that 'on these landmark discs, authentic wedding folklore is mixed with parody to create a unique genre of entertainment' (1987, 99). If this affectionate parody reflected nostalgia for the Old World, other stylised renditions of Jewish wedding material brought it up to date with the listening preferences of contemporary American audiences. Theatre composer Sholem Secunda's 'Bridegroom Special' (Sam Medoff and the Yiddish Swing Orchestra, 1940) and Harry Ellstein's 'Die goldene khasene' (The golden wedding, Abe Ellstein Orchestra with Dave Tarras, 1940) are both klezmer wedding tunes played in swing style by a full big band; here wedding dances are transformed into slick recordings for radio airplay.[14]

The klezmer revival brought further redefinitions of Old World wedding material. Rather than an object of parody or nostalgia, the wedding ritual became a cultural text subject to academic research and historically informed performance. Several contemporary klezmer bands, echoing the performance aesthetic of the early music movement in classical music, have created programmes where the repertory and performance practice recreate as faithfully as possible a wedding that might have existed in a certain time and place in Eastern Europe, picking a little from each of the lengthy rituals to create a structured performance. One such example is Budowitz's album *Wedding Without a Bride*.[15] Bandleader Joshua Horowitz writes in the liner notes:

---

[13]   These changes, however, did not take place in a uniform manner. In his study of Jewish wedding music in Philadelphia, Hankus Netsky observes that while some Old World wedding dances died out by the 1920s (2004, 120) and some uniquely American customs were adopted (2004, 131), other Old World elements were 'still observed at some weddings chronicled as late as 1970' (2004, 138).

[14]   Both recordings appear on *Music from the Yiddish Radio Project*, produced by Yair Reiner and Henry Sapoznik. Shanachie SH 6057 (2002).

[15]   Other examples include The Joel Rubin Music Ensemble, *Beregovski's khasene* (1997); Sophie Solomon also mentions a concert programme by Khevrisa structured around the ritual components of a wedding. Hankus Netsky (2004) discusses the roles and practices of klezmer music at weddings at length.

> In this CD we are presenting klezmer music as close to the way it sounded in
> its original wedding day context as possible. Of course we couldn't include the
> 8-day wedding in its entirety, but we have been able to produce the main musical
> pillars of the celebration day in order to lead the listener through its various
> stages. So if you listen to the CD from start to finish, you will be taken from the
> escorting of the family, to the veiling of the bride, to hear the *badkhn* [master of
> ceremonies and wedding jester] and *klezmorim* [musicians] eliciting tears from
> both bride and groom. Then you will hear them march to the ceremony, after
> which the musicians will invoke the souls of the deceased parents, eventually
> marching away from the ceremony to the banquet (Budowitz 2000, liner notes).

While the concept of the hour-long wedding suite as presented on this and other
CDs and performances is clearly a contemporary abstraction shaped by the LP/CD
format, Horowitz ascribes musical 'work' status to the compilation:

> In working on this recording, we were surprised at how the wedding, from
> beginning to end, offered a complex and emotionally subtle work as a form on
> its own, as intricate as any classical symphony (Budowitz 2000, liner notes).

This transformation from folk-religious ritual to 'work' invokes a new conceptual
framework. As Lydia Goehr has observed, the concept of musical work status,
originally used from around 1800 to define the norms of the classical canon,
has now been transferred within Western thought to many other forms of music:
'nowadays, no form of musical production is excluded a priori from being
packaged in terms of works' (1992, 244). This recourse to the work concept is
frequently a response to criticism: Goehr notes that 'musicians of many sorts have
been forced or have felt a need to justify themselves to their critics by showing
some willingness for their music to meet the conditions of work-production'
(1992, 250). Nevertheless, while the work concept confers a certain respectability
and legitimacy upon the music it describes, it does so by aspiring to standards
derived from classical music; 'compliant performance, accurate notation, and
silent reception' (1992, 253). In the case of *Wedding Without a Bride*, this appeal
to 'work' status buttresses the album against the common post-war conception of
Yiddish as a humorous language (see Shandler 2006, 60), conferring instead an
aura of respectability and seriousness upon the project.

While such recordings offered a template for an album structured around the
wedding, for Solomon the historicised frame of the authenticity they claimed was
problematic:

> I was thinking a lot about Budowitz and Khevrisa, and all these bands, and Joel
> Rubin's *Beregovski's Khasene* ... And all these guys were going, 'We will now
> play for you the music for an authentic *shtetl* wedding'. And I was like, 'well,
> that's all very well, but ... what is it to reconstruct an authentic *shtetl* wedding?'
> ... To be truly postmodern – we refer everything to our locus and to where we

are and how we perceive life, so everything comes through the prism of our consciousness. So to pretend that we can be completely authentic just doesn't make sense! So I wanted to be as authentic as I thought I could be. … I was thinking, 'I would like to make an authentic wedding recording, but I want it to be a hip hop authentic wedding recording – a hip hop *khasene*'. And so, in the same way that I guess they went about it, having all these ritual elements to the performance, that was how I foresaw it, that we would construct the ritual in the same way, but that we would have points of reference that were relevant to us.[16]

Here Solomon uses the word 'authenticity' in two different ways. The first of these refers to that which has been termed 'historically informed performance' by John Butt and others.[17] Grasping an opportunity to play in this manner was appealing to Solomon:

I love playing authentically and I love the rich authentic sound, and I felt in Oi Va Voi [Solomon's London band] it was getting a little bit lost because it was being compromised by the fact that we wanted to be very cutting-edge, and I needed to rein in the desire to play authentically.

On the other hand, Solomon also relates authenticity to a form of personal integrity, acknowledging the performer's positionality, and acknowledging what she refers to as 'kind of layers of cultural history that have built up'.[18]

Rather than attempting to resolve the tension between these two approaches to authenticity, *HipHopKhasene* plays with their juxtaposition. The basic musical texture of the album layers computer-sequenced beats with live musical performances. While the backbone of Dolgin's beats is a percussive accompaniment, generally built from historical and contemporary samples of klezmer drummers, these musical collages also include harmonic materials that fill out the musical middleground, and decorative or extramusical samples which punctuate the live performance. While the majority of this material was pre-recorded, in some cases samples are 'played' live by a musician manipulating a sampler. Playing over these beats, Solomon and Dolgin are joined by a group of musicians who represent some of the most prominent participants in the first phases of the 'klezmer revival': clarinettist David Krakauer, singer/violinist Michael Alpert, *tsimbl* (cimbalom) player and ethnomusicologist Zev Feldman, and trumpeters Susan Hoffman-Watts and Frank London.

Vocal material is incorporated in numerous ways into *HipHopKhasene*, functioning in particular as a medium of commentary. The textual material is diverse: while the seven wedding blessings are quoted from the traditional prayer book, the *badkhones* is a spontaneous, improvised commentary on the wedding

---

16   Sophie Solomon, interview, 2002.
17   See Butt (2002) for discussion.
18   Sophie Solomon, interview, 2002.

proceedings. Even during instrumental numbers, the sense of dynamic ceremony is reinforced by vocal interjections, reminding today's listener that Old World klezmer music was not usually heard in a quiet, static concert context, and retaining the basis of the wedding ceremony as a live event, not just a programming device.

Musically, the marriage of 'hip hop' (represented by sample-based music) and klezmer is represented by a gradual convergence of these two soundworlds, which leads up, within the narrative of the album, to the wedding ceremony itself. This musical negotiation plays out over the first seven tracks of the album. Table 6.1 summarises this process, which will be explored in greater depth below.

Table 6.1   *HipHopKhasene*: construction and instrumentation

Track	Title	Construction/instrumentation
1	Introduction	Electronics only, no live instruments/voices
2	Dobriden	Live instruments only; no overt manipulation
3	Badd-khones	Live voice only, no overt manipulation
4	Freylekhs far di kale	Instruments play over pre-recorded backing track. Structure dominated by backing track
5	(alt.shul) Kale bazetsn	Track constructed around vocal performance. Structure dominated by live performers
6	Electro taxim	Live musicians play improvisatory piece, joined by electronically manipulated echoes
7	7 Blessings	Large-scale structure determined by liturgy. Small-scale structure negotiates between unmetred chant and metred beats; each sometimes capitulates to the other

The album opens with an introduction ('Introduction', track 1) fabricated by Josh Dolgin. Entirely electronic, this piece superimposes a whole range of wedding soundbites in English, Yiddish and French – pilfered from Yiddish films, old participatory records and other sources – over an equally kitschy riff played on piano, accordion and glockenspiel. This sets the scene for the wedding, throwing the listener into a Yiddish cultural world, and introducing a world of stereotypes concerning the meaning of marriage. Among the opening voices, we hear:

> 'Now iz a khasene, dos gantse shtetl freyt zikh' (Now is a wedding – the whole town is getting excited)

> 'Tomorrow you will say, "I do"'

'Everyone we knew was there – musicians too!'

'While there's a chance, I'm going to marry the very next bird who asks me'
(Solomon and Socalled 2003, track 1)

Even these four statements encompass a range of references: a nostalgic Old World wedding scene is set, with some irony, alongside a stereotypical Americanised wedding ceremony, symbolised by the quintessentially Christian 'I do', words alien to the Jewish wedding liturgy.

The introduction also establishes the important role of humour in the *HipHopKhasesne*. In creating surface-level comedy via the juxtaposition of culturally distant materials, Solomon and SoCalled echo conventions of hip hop humour. Patrick Neate observes that 'conceptually, hip hop has always understood postmodern irony; sampling the best beats and hooks from everything from old soul tunes to kids' TV themes and kitsch musicals' (2003, 18). Simultaneously, the juxtaposition of dissonant material locates *HipHopKhasene* within a long tradition of Yiddish dialect humour. East European Yiddish jokes and sketches mocked the accents of Lithuanian or Polish Jews. In America, this form of humour meshed with the 'dialect jokes' which were a stock feature of American vaudeville, mocking the heavy accents and clueless ways of new immigrants trying to find their way in the New World. These jokes formed an essential part of American Jewish humour during the first part of the twentieth century, from 1920s sketches about hapless immigrant Cohen to Mickey Katz's 1950s 'Yinglish' parodies of popular American songs.[19] The comedy effect of Katz's music, writes Herbert Gans, is achieved 'largely because of the incongruity between American culture and a more or less Yiddish language' (1953, 213). However, if Mickey Katz laughed at immigrants unable to shed their Yiddish accents, in 2003, Solomon and Dolgin laugh at those who might assume that hip hop and klezmer cannot be viable bedfellows. As Dolgin says:

> There's a lot of straight up humour. Like that introduction is a joke, you know … but then the 'Kale bazetsn' is a serious piece. But you can laugh too, because there's Yiddish on top of beats. But, like, get over it.[20]

Thus *HipHopKhasene* moves straight from this celebration of nostalgic kitsch into the sound world of historically informed Yiddish music. Musically, the 'Dobriden' (track 2, traditionally a piece welcoming wedding guests), represents the arrival of the second partner, klezmer, at the wedding ceremony. This track is a traditional instrumental piece, entirely acoustic and recorded live in one take, a double bluff to catch out any listeners who have already pigeonholed this wedding as anti-traditionalist. Following the separate introduction of the two 'wedding partners',

---

[19]   See Weber (2003, 134–9) and Kun (1999) for discussion.
[20]   Josh Dolgin, interview with the author, New York, 30 March 2003.

subsequent tracks draw upon both live and sampled musical materials. The push and pull of cultural forces also continues within this texture: while the technique Dolgin uses to create his beats is contemporary, the beats themselves are made from sound samples recorded from modern and historical klezmer drummers; traditional klezmer melodies are reworked into the *HipHopKhasene* ceremony.

An example of this musical construction is 'Freylekhs far der kale' (*Freylekhs* in front of the bride, track 4), a dance number based around a well-known klezmer tune, the 'Sadugerer Chusidl' from the repertory of the early twentieth-century bandleader Abe Schwartz, which is here played over a pre-prepared electronic backing track. The original melody has three contrasting sections, following an AABBCC form. Here this basic shape is retained, yet Solomon and SoCalled's version expands upon Schwartz's model, adding textural contrast. The A section is upbeat in style, the melody played by Solomon on violin and Krakauer on clarinet. By contrast, for the first repetition of the B section, while the backing beat continues, the live instrumentation drops back to violin and cimbalom, the most traditional of 'authentic' instrument combinations, and in a subtle jibe at authenticist performance, a faint voice saying 'fair enough, fair enough' can be heard under the texture.[21] Josh Dolgin's electronic track adds a middle 8 before the C section, during which Michael Alpert shouts comments relevant to the festive mood: 'Lomir ale trinken a lekhayim far mazl, far brokhe, parnose un hatzlokhe' (Let's all raise our glass: for luck, for blessings, for livelihood and for success). These shouted comments continue throughout the number; following two repetitions of the basic structure, the melody disintegrates into a musical frenzy to finish.

The role of wedding emcee is shared both by a live musician – singer Michael Alpert, who introduces the wedding in Yiddish ('Badd-khones', track 3) and by recorded clips of narration taken from early American Yiddish wedding recordings. These voices, first heard in the Introduction, serve to guide the listener through the ceremony: 'Here comes the *badkhn*, the wedding jester, who now takes over' ('Kale bazetsn', track 5); 'Now, in honour of the relatives and guests – a *freylekhs*!' ('Freylekhs fun der khupe', track 8). These samples play a dual role: on the one hand, they are amusing and kitsch, referencing a sound world of nostalgic American Jewish recordings from which first-generation klezmer revivalists specifically sought to revive themselves.[22] On the other hand, just as in the recordings from which they were taken, these vocal interjections address the real-life problem of cultural fluency: if it cannot be taken for granted that listeners will know the structure of a traditional Old World Jewish wedding, some form of guide is needed for the album to make sense.

If the structure of 'Freylekhs far di kale' is dominated by its electronic backing track, the focus of the following track, '(alt.shul) Kale bazetsn' (Old-school seating of the bride, track 5), moves back to the live musicians: this track

---

[21]   Sophie Solomon, interview, 2002.

[22]   Alan Bern. Session at Klezmer Wochen Weimar, 1 August 2002.

is constructed around vocal material performed by Alpert and Dolgin.[23] At this stage of the traditional wedding ceremony the bride was seated and veiled, and the *badkhn* would address her and the guests, improvising verses and commenting on the proceedings.[24] Solomon and Dolgin were interested in the parallel between the Old World badkhn and today's rapper, both of whom improvise material in idiomatic, culturally rich language. On this recording, two *badkhonim* appear. One is Michael Alpert, who sings *badkhones* in Yiddish – credited on the liner notes as The Real Slim Litvak, a play on rapper Eminem's Real Slim Shady. The other is SoCalled, Josh Dolgin, who raps in English.

Alpert begins, performing lively Yiddish linguistic and cultural fluency by traversing a number of registers of idiomatic Yiddish expression. He introduces the musicians with playfully 'Yiddishised' names: Dovidl Krokover for David Krakauer, Velvl Tsimbler – literally 'Wolfie the *tsimbl* player' – for Zev Feldman.[25] While he's The Real Slim Litvak on the liner notes, Alpert further compounds the linguistic play in Yiddish, converting this name into a traditional Hebrew form, introducing himself as Reb Slimke bereb Elye – Mr Slim, son of Mr Elye; similarly he calls Josh Dolgin '*der bal-microfon*', translated as 'the mike-meister', but constructed using a Hebrew-Yiddish linguistic device that already exists in several forms – *bal habayis* 'master of the house'. His *badkhones* embraces Jewish religious language, quoting Ecclesiastes: 'there's nothing new under the sun'; in naming musical instruments, he moves into klezmer argot, using the term '*verfli*' rather than the more common Yiddish '*fidl*' for a violin (see Rothstein 2002, 28).

Set against Alpert's *badkhones* is a rap by Josh Dolgin. Musically, the texture moves from the unmetred, melodic chant of the *badkhn*, set against an irregular, interrupted electronic drum beat, to the quick, metred speech of rap, set to a regular beat. Like Alpert, Dolgin deliberately juxtaposes contrasting registers of language: Solomon observed that this is probably the first time the word '*ketubah*' has been used in a rap; 'cimbalom' is presumably not far behind: 'Oy, I gotta party to crash, so let the cimbaloms bash, we've got glasses to smash, we can get trashed, so buffet it up, yo – it's all you can drink, say I do and do it all night – nudge nudge, wink wink'.[26]

Here, the ceremonial breaking of a glass during the Jewish wedding ceremony becomes merely the first broken glass of the evening (echoed literally later in the album, where a glass is heard to smash eight times in succession), and the *ketubah* (Hebrew, marriage contract), is 'outmoded and dated'. Dolgin's juxtaposition of 'youth' slang and Yiddish terminology stages a comedic cultural dissonance

---

[23]   *Kale bazetsn*: seating of the bride. *Alt.shul*: lit. old school/old synagogue, here a play on internet terminology.

[24]   A Yiddish word of Hebrew origin, the plural of *badkhn* is *badkhonim*; *badkhones* refers to the art of the *badkhn*.

[25]   Dovidl is a Yiddish diminutive of David. 'Zev' means 'wolf' in Hebrew.

[26]   Text by Josh Dolgin. Liner notes to Solomon and Socalled (2002).

that recalls several novelty parody numbers by white rappers, in which 'uncool' cultural elements are self-consciously inserted into rap textures.[27]

The '(alt.shul) Kale bazetsn' is followed by an instrumental track, 'Electro taxim', track 6, which serves as a bridge between functional parts of the wedding ceremony – the veiling of the bride and the wedding ceremony itself. Here, a new relationship between live klezmer performance and electronic techniques is explored: this is an unmetred, improvisatory piece played by cimbalom, accordion, violin and clarinet; while all the sounds here are played by acoustic instruments, electronic manipulation is used to overlay extra voices on top of the live performance.

The centrepiece of the album, however, is the recitation of the *sheva brokhes* – the seven Hebrew wedding blessings – by Michael Alpert ('7 Blessings', appropriately track 7 of the CD). This represents a different kind of vocal material, liturgical chant, which in turn presents a new challenge for the creative adaptation of ceremonial material into a sample-based medium. This track combines a 'live' recording with synthesised beats: the blessings were recorded unaccompanied, after which Dolgin superimposed a backing track around Alpert's recitation. Here Dolgin takes advantage of the fact that recitation, even if unmetered, has its own inherent sense of rhythm. The blessings are recited in the heightened speech rhythms of liturgical Hebrew chant; however, by chopping apart individual phrases and eliding their beginnings and endings, Dolgin is able to place accented syllables at the beginning of bars of his beat, building a metric structure around them. This, in turn, gives an overarching shape to the track: the seven individual blessings are joined into one item, which is shaped at the same time by electronic beats and the original Hebrew text.

While many of the vocal contributions to the *HipHopKhasene* attempt to reinsert a sense of live ceremony into the recorded medium, notably here, at the central point of the wedding ceremony, the illusion of the wedding ritual is explicitly broken. While Alpert recites the blessings in Ashkenazic Hebrew using a traditional *nusach* (melody), they were not recorded at a wedding, but rather as a decontextualised, on-the-spot soundbite. Working with a recording-studio mentality, Alpert sings the wrong melody the first time, stops, says 'That's not what I sing … "*Sheva Brokhes*": take two …' and starts again. Nevertheless, Dolgin chose to include the whole recording, including the false start. The inclusion of the mistake makes the hidden presence of the tape recorder explicit, and the listener's attention is directed back to the album as a montage of recorded sound. Though after this track the guests continue dancing (eight further tracks follow, including

---

[27]   This technique has frequently been use in comedy numbers by white rappers; recent examples include 'Weird Al' Yankovic's 'White and Nerdy' (*Straight Outta Lynwood*, 2006), evangelist Dan Smith's 'Baby Got Book' (2006; available for download from http://whiteboydj.com/babygotbook.html) and the much-parodied NBC Saturday Night Live short 'Lazy Sunday' (2005; available for download from http://www.nbc.com/Saturday_Night_Live/video/#mea=2921).

two remixes of previous tracks), the traditional Yiddish wedding ceremony has broken down; it returns to its former position as an Old World curiosity or a programming device for a CD, not a functional, modern-world ritual.

Deconstructing *HipHopKhasene*: Constructing a New Generation in Yiddishland

The reference to 'hip hop' in its title and the use of electronic beats self-consciously mark *HipHopKhasene* as the work of a new generation in the klezmer scene: both in its African-American context and outside, hip hop has predominantly been associated with the voice of disenfranchised, rebellious youth.[28] In adopting rap and hip hop conventions to critique the klezmer 'establishment', Dolgin and Solomon's work is closely aligned with a slew of other Jewish musical and cultural outputs that received wide media attention both inside and outside the Jewish community during the early 2000s. Judah Cohen suggests that 'newness' and a progressive Jewish intellectualism were dominant threads in the discourse of 'hipster' artists who 'promoted a narrative of meaningful deviation from what they perceived as the staid Jewish norms of previous decades, gaining attention and cultural capital in the process' (2009b, 2).

At first glance, in the case of *HipHopKhasene*, this 'deviation from staid norms' seems as much jest as serious gesture: indeed the intellectual, countercultural positionality adopted by Cohen's Jewish hipsters also resonates with the outlook of the first generation of the klezmer revival.[29] While on the surface Solomon and Dolgin self-consciously set themselves up as young rebels against earlier klezmer revivalists, through their fidelity to Yiddish cultural forms, and through affirming the musical voices of dominant performers such as Alpert, Feldman and Krakauer, they position themselves clearly within the boundaries of Yiddishland. Further, this is primarily a klezmer album, not a hip hop one. Title aside, Solomon and Socalled do not seek here to present themselves here as serious hip hop artists, neither do they particularly interrogate or parody hip hop culture itself, unlike, for example, the cover art of Israeli rapper Subliminal's album *Ha-or ve-ha-tsel* (The light and the shadow) which combines visual imagery drawn from hip hop culture with the provocative use of Jewish religious imagery, or ultra-Orthodox American Jewish rapper Lipa Schmeltzer's Yiddish track '*Gelt*' (Money), which parodies an MTV rap video.

Nevertheless the plurivocal aesthetic of hip hop combined with the mimetic possibilities of sample-based music allows Solomon and Socalled to articulate

---

[28]   See Ogbar (1999) for discussion.

[29]   It is clear from Tamar Barzel's work that the klezmer revival has consistently occupied an ambiguous space in relation to wider manifestations of 'radical' Jewish culture: some klezmer artists participated in avant-garde projects, while other figures, including Marc Ribot and John Zorn, sought to 'promote Jewish music beyond klezmer' (2010, 220).

a persuasive commentary on the construction of contemporary Yiddish cultural spaces. In laying out a map of shared sonic references, they present the listener with a comprehensive soundscape of today's klezmer world. Historical performers are quoted either in sound or by the attribution of tunes to them; the live performers appearing on the recording include some of the musicians who have been the most influential in recent decades. In juxtaposing diverse materials, *HipHopKhasene* gives a picture of a music culture in motion, capturing moments of creativity in a collage where the edges show and are confused. Josh Dolgin's irreverent microphone records everything – not just a polished exterior, but a cross-section of musical practice, focusing attention on the processes rather than the products of creativity. While the overall picture is complex and multi-layered, the choice of material is not arbitrary: what makes *HipHopKhasene* function successfully is its articulation of a coherent shared realm of cultural references; the juxtaposition of materials can both bridge and highlight the cross-generational void. The incorporation, rather than ironing out of imperfections, and the placing of ephemeral and formal materials side by side, dislodges illusions of vernacular Yiddish continuity, instead highlighting the fluid construction of cultural fluency within a music revival system.[30]

This distinction is key to the identity of a new klezmer generation. Ironically, through KlezKamp and its kin, the generation of Solomon and Dolgin has grown up with more exposure to traditional Yiddish music than was possible 30 years ago: both hip hop and klezmer are in some sense vernaculars to Solomon and SoCalled. This growth in expertise in Yiddish music is coupled with a sustained level of interest from those new to Yiddish culture. New klezmer festivals continue to spring up around the world, Yiddish summer programmes recruit increasing numbers of students, and other cultural organisations have observed a surge in interest. For those of Solomon and Dolgin's generation, then, words like *khasene* and *badkhones* don't need to be in inverted commas; neither is it a controversial or radical statement simply to play klezmer. Nonetheless, if few of the older generation of klezmer revivalists grew up knowing the Yiddish language from home, this number is still smaller in the next generation, as the network of events which constitute the klezmer scene itself becomes a primary context for the Yiddish cultural life of many of its protagonists. Changing patterns of fluency are reflected directly in the soundscape of *HipHopKhasene*. Michael Alpert performs his *badkhones* in Yiddish but Josh Dolgin raps in English.

HipHopKhasene, then, invites wider discussion of the relationship between music, identity and discourse and in revival movements. In drawing upon past or

---

[30] Shandler observes that today's imagined portrayals of Yiddishland tend to be ambitiously and extravagantly utopic: they 'defiantly expand the scope of Yiddish in the face of prevailing notions that its sphere is shrinking' (2006, 121). By presenting a broad range of cultural materials and smoothing over the cracks between Yiddish subcultures, musical performances often contribute to this portrayal of Yiddish culture which wilfully ignores the contemporary reality of its subcultural, postvernacular position.

culturally 'other' musical traditions, Chris Goertzen observes that 'each [revival] "revives" selected cultural goods in ways representing the modern needs of those sponsoring the revival, needs that may change as one set of sponsors succeeds another' (1998, 99). Nevertheless, discussion of the 'needs' of contemporary revivalists often focuses on ideological and musical considerations rather than upon the functional aspects of musical revivals and their relationship to wider aspects of an individual's musical life. Different uses of the 'traditional' label have frequently been discussed in the music literature, but rather less attention has been given to the extra-musical implications of such labels. Analytical terminology may even inhibit the contextualisation of musical phenomena in relation to practices rather than products: the term 'klezmer revival' suggests a narrow repertory-based view of this musical phenomenon, a view strongly contradicted by *HipHopKhasene*. Rather, in using sampling as an expressive technique to express postvernacular cultural affiliation, Solomon and SoCalled construct a young, contemporary Yiddish subjectivity which privileges the listening ear rather than the fluent tongue, and dismisses Yiddish utopias in favour of a place where real people hang out and make music. If ideological concerns have dominated both popular and academic discourse concerning revival movements, the present discussion suggests that the musical products of these within revival scenes may themselves offer an alternative picture, critiquing comprehensive ideological constructs in favour of highlighting an interactive, recursive flow between ideology and lived cultural space

Conclusion

In this volume, I have laid out a map of overlapping discursive and musical worlds, caught at the intersection between the infrastructures of a dwindling immigrant linguistic subculture now labelled 'postvernacular' and a new transcommunal music scene entangled in the wider aesthetics of revival. The institutions of American Yiddish culture have been adapted and reinvigorated, creating new contexts for the transmission and performance of Yiddish cultural materials. At the same time, the notion of a Yiddish song repertory has continually been reimagined: as linguistic performance; as material, printed canon; as a musical-aesthetic praxis; as a shared soundscape.

Indeed, it is remarkable that while the performance scene described in the past four chapters has often been defined by a linguistic denominator ('Yiddish') or by an attitude to the past ('revival'), its products have tended to be defined neither by an emphasis on linguistic fluency nor by overwhelming attention to older song forms. This observation was borne out in my interviews with several Yiddish cultural activists, including Michael Alpert, who reflected when we spoke in 2002 that very few of the many people he had taught in workshops and camps had really grasped the vocal technique and style of older Yiddish folk songs.

Likewise, Yiddish poet and songwriter Beyle Schaechter-Gottesman, born in 1920 in Vienna, and who grew up in Czernowitz (then in Romania), contrasted the enthusiasm of young Yiddish learners with the lack of linguistic immersion available:

> BSG: The times change so much – there are different epochs. I don't know … once, writers, songwriters used to lament that there were … [so] many Yiddish poets … relative to our small people, there were a lot of poets. Even the poets themselves used to … I was introduced to Glatshteyn, you know, the great poet Glatshteyn. Someone introduced me as a new poetess. 'Oh!' he said, '*another* poetess!'

> AW: And now …

> BSG: Today we don't have so many. But we have young people – there is a whole group, new, truly young people, who aren't born Yiddish speakers. It's difficult, but they have talent, and they experiment. It wouldn't hurt if they knew the language better, but that is the situation, they can't. We have a conversation group: every Friday we meet here, and we talk, simply talk. Because they learn here and they learn there, but they have no chance to speak. So every Friday we speak.

AW: Do many of the new Yiddishists write songs? Because I've seen a lot of poems [by young Yiddishists], but I haven't seen so many songs.

BSG: The fact is, no. They really don't, I don't know why. One needs to be a singer oneself [in order to write songs]. A new dimension.[1]

For some, the most potent response to this point of transition is to celebrate continuity, asserting that widespread Yiddish fluency is still within reach. Jeffrey Shandler observes that today's imagined portrayals of Yiddishland tend to be ambitiously and extravagantly utopic: they 'defiantly expand the scope of Yiddish in the face of prevailing notions that its sphere is shrinking' (2006, 121). In April 2003, I return to the Yidisher Filharmonisher Folkskhor – the Jewish People's Philharmonic Chorus – nearly two years since I sang for a season with this Yiddish choir. The small hall of the Sholem Aleichem cultural centre in the Bronx is packed with an appreciative audience. The programme includes old favourites alongside some challenging repertory, and I'm pleasantly surprised at how good the choir has become. The concert ends with a resounding rendition of 'Vaserl', a folk rock-style song written in the late 1970s by Yiddishists Perl Teitelbaum and Rukhl Schaechter. Comparing the Yiddish language to a frozen stream in winter, the song expresses raw optimism about its future. The strident chords of the final chorus resonate through the hall – the keyboard accompaniment so loud that the recording I'm making becomes distorted – and the song ends to rapturous applause: 'Stream, stream, don't give up yet: the frost will thaw, The spring is coming soon'.[2]

Nevertheless, notwithstanding this spirited assertion, elsewhere in the Yiddish music scene, alternative locations of meaning jostle for expressive space, challenging the primacy of mutually understood language in conveying the meaning of a song.

As musical material passes between performers, listeners and teachers, it comes to embody not only the material encapsulated explicitly in its text – its historical and cultural points of reference – but also what Daniel Neuman has termed 'immanent music history', 'a history not so much of music itself as of its creators or consumers' (1991, 269). In this way, songs, then, become flexible vessels for meaning, encouraging the constant re-reading of each musical text. For example, the words of 'Borsht' – a love song recorded by Brave Old World (*Beyond the Pale*, 1994) – tell the story of a protagonist from the town of Balta, who loves his sweetheart and tries to convince her that he is ready to marry her. The song describes a humorous kitchen table scene, where the intimacy of shared food is set alongside the intimacy of love: a lovesick suitor's compliments for the best borsht he has ever tasted are a prelude to extravagant declarations of love.

---

[1]   Beyle Schaechter-Gottesman, interview with the author, New York, 30 March 2003. Translation from Yiddish mine.

[2]   Fieldnotes, 1 April 2003.

Brave Old World's performance of this song and its subsequent reception, however, build a further collage of stories around this song. These include another kitchen table, that of Bronya Sakina, the Ukrainian Jewish immigrant at whose table Michael Alpert learned the song; the intimate musical relationship of the four band members, whose experience in musical styles outside the traditional Yiddish sphere informs their arrangement of the song; and that of the klezmer revival itself, which as a movement has created the conditions for this CD album to receive international distribution. Through this medium many listeners – many who will never hear the band perform live – will experience this recording, adding their own experiences to the mosaic of meanings it carries.

Through such open-ended constructions of meaning, the notion of a Yiddish listening public is itself reimagined. As Jocelyne Guilbault has observed, the concept of the 'local' has become crucial to cultural identification within the world music industry and beyond, generating in turn actions directed to the protection and promotion of local cultural capital and identity (2006, 138). Yet here, the boundaries of the 'local' are constantly renegotiated: the romantic nationalism of European Yiddishism continues to reverberate in the new 'Yiddishland' described here, but this imagined land is now coterminous neither with a linguistic nor an ethnic/religious community, but rather invites active affiliation and participation.

In focusing on Yiddish song as a 'local' musical practice, my discussion here of the contexts in which Yiddish song is performed, taught and recorded has necessarily been narrow in focus. Choosing to focus on the work of a small number of professional creative artists, whose work highlights creativity and is aimed at a transnational, perhaps global audience, I have overlooked other musicians whose role in the performance of Yiddish song in North America is no less significant. Synagogue cantors singing nostalgic Yiddish numbers, elderly Yiddish theatre actors now participating in a gala event, members of local klezmer bands and choirs, young people recording a grandparent's childhood songs, kids attending Workmen's Circle programmes, and all those who choose simply to open a Yiddish songbook are just a few of those others who daily reiterate the continuing relevance of Yiddish song to contemporary audiences. I have also cut fine cultural and geographical boundaries, excluding musicians in the Hasidic community and outside North America.

Nevertheless, within these wide contours of public engagement with Yiddish song, it is remarkable how frequently the individuals, institutions and ensembles cited in these chapters reappear, as venues, teachers, performers, arrangers, producers and recording artists, reinforcing the 'locality' of contemporary Yiddish music. A small group of highly visible individuals and their peers model a mode of cultural engagement that interlaces professional and affective relationships to Yiddish music; they form node points in a tight interpersonal network where personal connections – whether peer relationships or student–teacher relationships – support the processes of musical creativity. While today's Yiddish music has far greater public visibility than the number of people actively involved as performers, creators or culturally literate listeners, the close network that underpins the scene enables the simultaneous expression of global reach and local, intimate imagination, sustaining a 'local' cultural field whose discourse extends far beyond the musical sphere.

Yet this network does not remain static: a decade after the musical snapshots which opened the first chapter of this book, the musical scene depicted here continues to move onwards. At first glance, a decade into the twenty-first century, the flourishing klezmer scene seemed to have hit a downturn. Glancing at the album reviews section of Ari Davidow's *Klezmershack* website, the energetic flurry of new releases of the late 1990s and early 2000s slowed in the ensuing years to a smaller trickle, sales perhaps a victim of their own previous success. Nevertheless, at the same time song seems to have moved even further into prominence within the klezmer scene: remarkably, more than half of the tracks included in the 2011 second edition of the *Rough Guide to Klezmer* CD are vocal numbers.

Meanwhile, new paradigms of transcommunalism and transnationalism continue to emerge, stretching the imagined boundaries of 'local' musical practices. The musical encounters of the late 1990s and early 2000s discussed here were characterised by a performative cosmopolitanism: representing the remnants of an endangered culture, American Yiddish musicians embraced the world music industry and appeared on new stages in Eastern Europe, making them household figures among a much wider audience than a previous generation might have imagined. By contrast, the transnationalism of the 2010s has often been characterised by complex identities and cultural exchange, further propelling the Yiddish music scene away from a model of boundaried postvernacular linguistic or ethnic specificity towards new musical vernaculars. Changing power relations over the Atlantic Ocean have also realigned the Yiddish musical map: today musicians from Germany and the former Soviet Union now appear alongside their American colleagues as performers, composers and teachers.

The turning of generations in a close-knit music scene is marked with both sorrow and joy. Locality is bound up with intimacy; Adrienne Cooper's album *Enchanted: A New Generation of Yiddishsong* (2010) invokes this intimacy via the metaphor of familial relationships. In the collage of pictures that make up the CD inner cover, in the liner notes and in the voices in the CD itself, Cooper is surrounded by two sets of close relations. The first are her own family: we see sepia pictures of her parents and grandfather, samples of whose voices, preserved on a 1947 home wax disc recording, are carefully melded with Coopers own in the evocative song 'A Song Book: My Family'. Elsewhere, the voice of Cooper's daughter, Sarah Mina Gordon, weaves in and out of Cooper's vocal line. Interleaved among this network of relations, however, is a second kind of family, whose contribution is equally apparent: musicians, including Cooper's contemporaries Marilyn Lerner and Frank London, but now extending to a new generation – and including voices from further afield. Nearly two decades after her nervous first trip to Poland discussed in Chapter 4, Cooper thanks her 'Russian/ Moldovan/Ukrainian buddies whose joyful soulprints are all over this recording' (Cooper 2010, liner notes).

Enchanted was tragically to be Adrienne Cooper's last album; as I write these words of conclusion in December 2012, just a year after her untimely passing, dozens of members of her extended Yiddish family--including virtually all of the musicians whose work I have discussed here--gather on stage for a memorial concert in New York City. Tears meld with exuberance as Lorin Sklamberg, dancing with Michael Alpert, leads a spirited rendition of 'Ale Brider'; the concert ends with 'Sholem Lid' (Peace Song), a song which Cooper popularised in workshops and concerts, led by her daughter Sarah Mina Gordon. Some three dozen vocalists on stage link arms; clarinettists and trumpeters raise their instruments in frenzied improvisation, the intensity of musical experience invoking the intensity of personal and communal loss. Besides the hundreds of audience members attending the sold-out concert, a live stream of the event clocks up over two thousand views, echoing a further, more distributed community.

In the months following her passing, I had previously stumbled upon numerous smaller memorials to Cooper on the internet, among them a Facebook event announcing a memorial concert entitled 'Koved far Khane' (In Adrienne's Honour). But this time, the concert was not in New York; organised by a group of young musicians from Riga, Berlin and Munich, it took place in a Berlin club. Among those taking part in both concerts is Daniel Kahn – yet another face of the upcoming generation of American Yiddish song, whose career to date neatly illustrates emerging paradigms of imagination. Born in 1978 in Michigan and living in Berlin since 2005, Kahn performs dark political cabaret in Yiddish. His band, 'The Painted Bird' borrows the name of Polish-Jewish author Jerzy Kosinski's violent and controversial 1965 novel; among his masked co-performers, Kahn stands out as a radical and solitary voice. Amid Yiddish-American workers' songs of the early twentieth century, Kahn introduces material of his own, including biting commentary on difficult issues. Past and present concerns are here linked not by imagined community but by projections of moral ambiguity: in his 2009 CD, *Partisans and Parasites*, a plot by Jewish ghetto fighters to murder six million Germans in revenge for the Holocaust leads to difficult contemporary questions. Using the Yiddish protest tradition as a model for the expression of his own experiences, Kahn writes pointed songs in response to the wall in Israel/ Palestine and America's behaviour towards the victims of Hurricane Katrina in New Orleans. Kahn's oppositional ontology offers an alternative approach to the transgenerational spread of Yiddish song: here not a warm family scene, but an ongoing starting point for dissent.

These changing sounds of American Yiddish music do not so much define the present (or future) boundaries of the Yiddish local as invite us to continue to follow these musicians on their journeys. The breadth of the practices cited here challenges the longevity of the paradigms of heritage affiliation and named musical subculture ('klezmer') used by previous scholars to frame the musical scene discussed here. As we continue to think and rethink the Yiddish music scene, it is as well to remember that musicking is an everyday process: while the choice to sing in Yiddish may reflect many choices, ultimately creative expression is based not on a disembodied weighing up of cultural, aesthetic and linguistic politics; rather, these concerns are embedded within the day-to-day practicalities of making good music. The future directions of Yiddish song will depend on all of these artists and their continued engagement with Yiddish musical material, creatively working with, rather than being constrained by, ever-changing paradigms of fluency, locality, intimacy and cosmopolitanism.

Shoyn nito keyn nekhtn	*There's no yesterday,*
Nokh nito der morgn	*Tomorrow's not yet here,*
S'iz nor do a pitsele haynt –	*There's only a little bit of today,*
Shtert im nit mit zorgn!	*So don't disturb it with worries.*
Khapt arayn a shnepsl	*Grab a drink*
Kol zman ir zaynt baym lebn –	*All the while you're alive –*
Mirtseshem af yener velt	*God willing, in the other world*
Vet men aykh nit gebn![3]	*You might not get any.*

---

[3]   Khayim Zhitlovski. Text from Vinkovetsky et al. (1983, 124).

Bibliography

Abu-Lughod, Lila (1991) 'Writing against Culture'. In Richard G. Fox, ed., *Recapturing Anthropology: Working in the Present*. Santa Fe, NM: School of American Research Press, 137–62.

Adler, Israel (1995) 'À la recherche de chants perdus: La redécouverte des collections du "Cabinet" de musique juive de Moisei J. Beregovski'. In Vincent Dehoux et al., eds, *Ndroje balendro: Musiques, terraines et disciplines*. Paris: Peters, 247–67.

Amit, Vered, ed. (2000) *Constructing the Field: Ethnographic Fieldwork in the Contemporary World*. London: Routledge.

Arbeter Ring (1929) *Tzvey hundert lider* [Two hundred songs]. Chicago, IL: Arbeter ring gesangs fareyn.

—— (1930) *Workmen's Circle Camp*, commemorative booklet. Self-published.

Barzel, Tamar (2004) '"Radical Jewish Culture": Composers/Improvisers on New York City's 1990s Downtown Music Scene'. PhD diss., University of Michigan.

—— (2010) 'An Interrogation of Language: "Radical Jewish Culture" on New York's Downtown Music Scene'. *Journal of the Society for American Music* 4:2, 215–50.

Bastomski, Shloyme (1923) *Baym kval: material tzum yidishn folklor* [By the spring: material from Yiddish folklore]. Vilna: Farlag 'Naye yidishe folksshul'.

Behrend, Siegfried (1967) *Es brennt: Lieder aus dem Ghetto*. Hamburg: Musikverlag Hans Sikorski.

Benjamin, Sheldon (1988) 'Der Bobes Yerushe: A Boston Neuropsychiatrist Brings a Tape Recorder to His Grandmother and Preserves a Lifetime of Yiddish Music'. *Der pakn-treger/The Book Peddler*, Winter 1988/5748, 21–3.

Beregovski, Moshe, ed. Mark Slobin (1982) *Old Jewish Folk Music: The Collections and Writings of Moshe Beregovski*. Philadelphia, PA: University of Pennsylvania Press.

——, ed. Mark Slobin et al. (2001) *Jewish Instrumental Folk Music: The Collections and Writings of Moshe Beregovski*. Syracuse, NY: Syracuse University Press.

Bern, A. (1998) 'From Klezmer to New Jewish Music: The Musical Evolution of Brave Old World'. Originally published in *Mensh & Musik*, 1998. Downloaded from http://www.klezmershack.com/articles/bern.new.html, last accessed 7 May 2012.

Bohlman, Philip Vilas (1988) *The Study of Folk Music in the Modern World*. Bloomington, IN: Indiana University Press.

—— (2001) 'Ethnomusicology III: Post-1945 developments'. Downloaded from *Grove Music Online*, ed. Laura Macy. http://www.grovemusic.com/, accessed 14 January 2004.

Bohlman, Philip Vilas and Otto Holzapfel (2001) *The Folk Songs of Ashkenaz*. Middletown, WI: A-R Editions.

Bordin, Khanan (1999) *Vort bay vort* [Word by word]. Jerusalem: Hebrew University.

Boyarin, Jonathan and Daniel Boyarin, eds (1997) *Jews and Other Differences: The New Jewish Cultural Studies*. Minneapolis, MN: University of Minnesota Press.

Braun, Joachim (1987) 'The Unpublished Volumes of Moshe Beregovski's Jewish Musical Folklore'. *Israel Studies in Musicology* 4, 125–44.

Brenner, Frédéric (1996) *Jews/America/A Representation*. New York, NY: Harry N. Abrams.

Brown, Elicia (2001) 'Whose Klezmer Is It, Anyway? A Tour of Berlin's Fascination with Things Jewish Reveals Some Frayed Nerves and a Growing Sensitivity by a New Generation'. *The Jewish Week* (New York), 7 December 2001.

Buck-Morss, Susan (1989) *The Dialectics of Seeing: Walter Benjamin and the Arcades Project*. Cambridge, MA: MIT Press.

Butt, John (2002) *Playing with History: The Historical Approach to Musical Performance*. Cambridge: Cambridge University Press.

Cahan, Yehuda Leib (1912) *Yudishe folkslieder mit melodien* [Jewish folksongs with melodies]. 2 vols. New York: The International Publishing Co.

—— (Vilenski, L., pseud.) (1913) 'Yudishe folkslider' [Jewish folksongs]. *Der Pinkes* (Vilna), 355–66.

Cohen, Judah M. (2009a) 'Transplanting the Heart Back East: Returning Jewish Musical Culture from the United States to Europe'. In Jeremy Cohen and Moshe Rossman, eds, *Rethinking European Jewish History*. Oxford: Littman Library of Jewish Civilization, 221–44.

—— (2009b) 'Hip-hop Judaica: The Politics of Representin' Heebster Heritage'. *Popular Music* 28:1, 1–18.

—— (2010) 'Rewriting the Grand Narrative of Jewish Music: Abraham Z. Idelsohn in the United States'. *Jewish Quarterly Review* 100:3, 417–53.

Cohen, Judith R. (1995) 'Women's Roles in Judeo-Spanish Song Traditions'. In Maurie Sacks, ed., *Active Voices: Women in Jewish Culture*. Urbana, IL: University of Illinois Press, 182–201.

Cooper, Adrienne (1993) 'Notes from a Concert Journal'. *Jewish Folklore and Ethnology Review* 15:1, 11–13.

Cooperman, Bernard Dov (2006) 'Jewish Studies Professors and the Community: A Response'. *Shofar* 24:3, 136–40.

Dobrushin, Yehezkhel and Avraham Yuditzki (1940) *Yidishe folks-lider* [Yiddish folk songs]. Moscow: Farlag Der Emes.

Fader, Ayala (2009) *Mitzvah Girls: Bringing up the Next Generation of Hasidic Jews in Brooklyn*. Princeton, NJ: Princeton University Press.

Fein, Richard J. (1986) *The Dance of Leah: Discovering Yiddish in America*. Rutherford, NJ: Fairleigh Dickinson University Press.

Feingold, Henry L. (1996) *Lest Memory Cease: Finding Meaning in the American Jewish Past*. Syracuse, NY: Syracuse University Press.

Feldman, Walter Zev (1994) 'Bulgaresca/Bulgarish/Bulgar: The Transformation of a Dance Genre'. *Ethnomusicology* 38:1, 1–35.

Felman, Shoshana and Dori Laub (1992) *Testimony: Crises of Witnessing in Literature, Psychoanalysis, and History*. New York, NY: Routledge.

Fishman, Joshua A., ed. (1981) *Never Say Die! A Thousand Years of Yiddish in Jewish Life and Letters*. Contributions to the Sociology of Language, 30. The Hague: Mouton.

—— (1990) *Yiddish: Turning to Life*. Amsterdam and Philadelphia, PA: John Benjamins Publishing Company.

Flam, Gila (1992) *Singing for Survival: Songs of the Lodz Ghetto, 1940–45*. Urbana, IL: University of Illinois Press.

—— (1997) 'Singing Yiddish Songs in Israel'. *Musical Performance* 1:3, 1–7.

Fog Olwig, Karen and Kirsten Hastrup, eds (1997) *Siting Culture: The Shifting Anthropological Object*. London: Routledge.

Foucault, Michel, trans. Jay Miskowiec (1967, translation n.d.) 'Of Other Spaces: Heterotopias'. Downloaded from http://foucault.info/documents/heteroTopia/foucault.heteroTopia.en.html, accessed 18 March 2010.

Frankl, Hai and Topsy Frankl (1981) *Jiddische Lieder*. Frankfurt am Main: Fischer.

Freedman, Jonathan (2008) *Klezmer America: Jewishness, Ethnicity, Modernity*. New York, NY: Columbia University Press.

Fulbrook, Mary (1999) *German National Identity after the Holocaust*. Oxford: Polity Press.

Gans, Herbert J. (1953) 'The "Yinglish" Music of Mickey Katz'. *American Quarterly* 5:3, 213–18.

Gelbart, Matthew (2007) *The Invention of 'Folk Music' and 'Art Music': Emerging Categories from Ossian to Wagner*. Cambridge: Cambridge University Press.

Gershman, Sarah, ed. (2001) *Ain Sof: There Is No End*. Hoeboken, NJ: KTAV Press.

Gilbert, Shirli (2005) *Music in the Holocaust: Confronting Life in the Nazi Ghettos and Camps*. Oxford: Oxford University Press.

Ginzburg, Shaul M. and Pesach S. Marek, ed. Dov Noy (1991) *Yiddish Folksongs in Russia: Photo Reproduction of the 1901 St Petersburg Edition*. Ramat Gan: Bar-Ilan University Press.

Goehr, Lydia (1992) *The Imaginary Museum of Musical Works: An Essay in the Philosophy of Music*. Oxford: Oxford University Press.

Goertzen, Chris (1998) 'The Norwegian Folk Revival and the Gammeldans Controversy'. *Ethnomusicology* 42:1, 99–127.

Gold, David L. (1985) 'Jewish English'. In Joshua A. Fishman, ed., *Readings in the Sociology of Jewish Languages*. Leiden: Brill, 80–298.

Goldberg, David (1996) *Yidish af yidish* [Yiddish in Yiddish]. New Haven, CT: Yale University Press.

Goldsmith, Emanuel (1998) 'Yiddishism and Judaism'. In Dov-Ber Kerler, ed., *The Politics of Yiddish: Studies in Language, Literature and Society* (Winter Studies in Yiddish 4). London: Altamira Press, 11–22.

Gorali, Moshe, Gideon Almagor and Moshe Bick (1970) *Di goldene pave: yidishe folkslider* [The golden peacock: Yiddish folk songs]. Haifa: Haifa Music Museum and AMLI Library.

Gordon, Peter E. (1990) 'Imagining Hasidism'. *Tikkun* 5:3, 49–51.

Gottesman, Itzik N. (2003) *Defining the Yiddish Nation: The Jewish Folklorists of Poland*. Detroit, MI: Wayne State University Press.

Gradenwitz, Peter (1988) *Die schönsten Jiddischen Liebeslieder*. Ulm: Fourier.

Green, Arthur (1996) 'Early Hasidism: Some Old/New Questions'. In Ada Rapoport-Albert, ed., *Hasidism Reappraised*. London: Vallentine Mitchell, 441–6.

Gruber, Ruth E. (2002) *Virtually Jewish: Reinventing Jewish Culture in Europe*. Berkeley, CA: University of California Press.

Guilbault, Jocelyne (2006) 'On Redefining the "Local" through World Music'. In Jennifer C. Post, ed., *Ethnomusicology: A Contemporary Reader*. New York, NY: Routledge, 137–46.

Herzfeld, Michael (2005) *Cultural Intimacy: Social Poetics in the Nation-State*. 2nd edition. New York, NY: Routledge.

Heskes, Irene (1992) *Yiddish American Popular Songs 1895–1950: A Catalog Based on the Lawrence Marwich Roster of Copyright Entries*. Washington, DC: Library of Congress.

Hirsch, Eric D. Jr (1987) *Cultural Literacy: What Every American Needs to Know*. Boston, MA: Houghton Mifflin.

Hirshberg, Jehoash (1995) *Music in the Jewish Community of Palestine 1880– 1948: A Social History*. Oxford: Clarendon.

Homa, Bernard (1990) *Footprints on the Sands of Time*. Gloucester: Beaver Press.

Horowitz, Joshua (1993) 'The Klezmer Freygish Shteyger: Mode, Sub-mode and Modal Progression'. Manuscript pending publication, downloaded from http:// www.budowitz.com/Budowitz/Essays.html, last accessed 7 May 2012.

Horowitz, Linda P. (1988) 'Yiddish Choral Music'. MMus diss., California State University, Fullerton, CA.

Howe, Irving (1976/2000) *World of Our Fathers*. London: Phoenix Press.

Hurvitz, Nathan (1986) The Folk Defend Their Lore. Unpublished article, Joseph and Chana Mlotek archive. YIVO Add. 1142.

Idelsohn, Abraham Z. (1929/1992) *Jewish Music in Its Historical Development*. New York, NY: Dover.

—— (1932) *Hebräisch-Orientalischer Melodienschatz*. 10 vols. Leipzig: Friedrich Hofmeister.

Jacobson, Marion (2002) 'Newish, not Jewish: A Tale of Two Bands'. In Mark Slobin, ed., *American Klezmer: Its Roots and Offshoots*. Berkeley, CA: University of California Press, 187–205.

—— (2004) 'With Song to the Struggle: An Ethnographic and Historical Study of the Yiddish Folk Chorus'. PhD diss., New York University.

Jaldati, Lin and Eberhard Rebling (1966) *Es brennt, Brüder, es brennt: Jiddische Lieder*. Berlin: Rütten & Loening.

Janda, Elsbeth and Max M. Sprecher (1962) *Lieder aus dem Ghetto: Fünfzig Lieder jiddish und deutsch mit Noten*. Munich: Ehrenwirth Verlag.

Kaminsky, David (2001) '"And We Sing Gay Songs": The Klezmatics: Negotiating the Boundaries of Jewish Identity'. In Kay K. Shelemay, ed., *Studies in Jewish Musical Traditions: Insights from the Harvard Collection of Judaica Sound Recordings*. Cambridge, MA: Harvard College Library, 51–87.

Katsherginski, Sh[merke] (1948) *Lider fun di getos un lagern* [Songs from the ghettos and concentration camps]. New York: Congress for Jewish Culture.

Kettmann, Steve (1998) 'In Today's Berlin It's Hip to Be klezmer: The Playful Jewish Music is the Rage in Germany's Biggest City, and a Community Once Wiped Out Is Getting Back on Its Feet'. *San Francisco Chronicle*, 20 December 1998.

Kirshenblatt-Gimblett, Barbara (1973) 'Yivo Folksong Project: New York, Montreal, Toronto'. *The Canadian Journal for Traditional Music* 1, 1. Downloaded from http://cjtm.icaap.org/content/1/v1art3.html, accessed 30 March 2004.

—— (1988) 'Documenting a Song and Its Performance: A Questionnaire for Use by the Yiddish Song-zamler' (reprinted from the *Jewish Folklore and Ethnology Review*). *Der pakn-treger/The Book Peddler* 9–10, 23, 81–2.

—— (2001) 'Imagining Europe: The Popular Arts of American Jewish Ethnography'. In Deborah Dash Moore and S. Ilan Troen, eds, *Divergent Jewish Cultures: Israel and America*. New Haven, CT and London: Yale University Press, 155–91.

—— (2002) 'Sounds of Sensibility'. In Mark Slobin, ed., *American Klezmer: Its Roots and Offshoots*. Berkeley, CA: University of California Press, 129–73.

Kligman, Mark (1994) 'The Medium and the Message: The Recorded Music of Brooklyn's Orthodox Jews'. *Jewish Folklore and Ethnology Review* 16:1, 9–11.

—— (2001) 'Contemporary Jewish Music in America'. *American Jewish Year Book* 101: 88–141.

Klingenstein, Suzanne (1993) 'Visits to Germany in Recent Jewish-American Writing'. *Contemporary Literature* 34:3, 538–70.

Koskoff, Ellen (1978) 'Some Aspects of Musical Acculturation among Lubavitcher Hasidim'. *Working Papers in Yiddish and East European Jewish Studies* (New York: YIVO) 32.

—— (2001) *Music in Lubavitcher Life*. Champaign, IL: University of Illinois Press.

Kugelmass, Jack (1994) 'Why We Go to Poland: Holocaust Tourism as Secular Ritual'. In James E. Young, ed., *The Art of Memory: Holocaust Memorials in History*. New York: Jewish Museum with Prestel-Verlag, 174–84.

—— (1997) 'Jewish Icons: Envisioning the Self in Images of the Other'. In Jonathan Boyarin and Daniel Boyarin, eds, *Jews and Other Differences: The New Jewish Cultural Studies*. Minneapolis, MN: University of Minnesota Press, 30–53.

Kun, Jack (1999) 'The Yiddish Are Coming: Mickey Katz, Anti-Semitism and the Sound of Jewish Difference'. *American Jewish History* 87:4, 343–74.

Landis, Joseph C. (1981) 'Who Needs Yiddish? A Study in Language and Ethics'. In Joshua A. Fishman, ed., *Never Say Die! A Thousand Years of Yiddish in Jewish life and Letters*. Contributions to the Sociology of Language, 30. The Hague: Mouton, 349–68.

Lehmann, Heiko (2000) 'Klezmer in Germany/Germans and Klezmer: Reparation or Contribution?' Lecture presented at WOMEX, Berlin, 19 October 2000. Downloaded from http://www.culture-to-the-people.com/sukke/lecture.html, accessed 18 May 2012.

Leichter, Sinai (2000) *Anthology of Yiddish Folksongs: Volume 5, The Mordechai Gebirtig Volume*. Jerusalem: Magnes Press.

Lemm, Manfred (1992) *Mordechaj Gebirtig: Jiddische Lieder*. Wuppertal: Edition Künstlertreff.

Leuchter, Janet B. (2010) '"Provisions for the Journey": A Rarity from the Lost World of Yiddish Religious Song'. *Journal of Synagogue Music* 35, 120–44.

Lichtenstein, Murray H. (1984) 'Biblical Poetry'. In Barry Holtz, ed., *Back to the Sources: Reading the Classic Jewish Texts*. New York: Touchstone, 105–28.

Livingston, Tamara E. (1999) 'Music Revivals: Towards a General Theory'. *Ethnomusicology* 43:1, 66–85.

Loeffler, James (2001) Liner notes to London et al., *Zmiros*. CD recording: Traditional Crossroads. Pre-publication copy (personal communication).

—— (2010a) *The Most Musical Nation: Jews and Culture in the Late Russian Empire*. New Haven, CT: Yale University Press.

—— (2010b) 'Do Zionists Read Music from Right to Left? Abraham Tzvi Idelsohn and the Invention of Israeli Music'. *Jewish Quarterly Review* 100:3, 385–416.

London, Frank (2002) 'An Insider's View: How We Traveled from Obscurity to the Klezmer Establishment in Twenty Years'. In Mark Slobin, ed., *American Klezmer: Its Roots and Offshoots*. New York, NY: Oxford University Press, 206–10.

Mahmood, Saba (2005) *Politics of Piety: The Islamic Revival and the Feminist Subject*. Princeton, NJ: Princeton University Press.

Margalioth, Ayelet K. (1997) 'Yiddish Periodicals Published by Displaced Persons, 1946–1949'. D.Phil. diss., Magdalen College, Oxford University.

Margolis, Rebecca (2011) '*Hiphopkhasene*: A Marriage between Hip Hop and Klezmer'. *Studies in Religion/Sciences Religieuses* 40:3, 365–80.

Markovits, Andrei S. and Noveck, Beth S. (1996) 'West Germany'. In David S. Wyman, ed., *The World Reacts to the Holocaust*. Baltimore, MD: Johns Hopkins University Press, 391–446.

Michels, Tony (2005) *A Fire in Their Hearts: Yiddish Socialists in New York*. Cambridge, MA: Harvard University Press.

Mlotek, Eleanor G. (Chana) (1972) *Mir trogn a gezang: Favorite Yiddish Songs*. New York, NY: Adama Books.

—— (1978) 'Soviet Yiddish Folklore Scholarship'. *Musica Judaica* 2:1, 73–90.

Mlotek, Eleanor (Chana) and Malke Gottlieb (1983) *We Are Here: Songs of the Holocaust*. New York, NY: Educational Department of the Workmen's Circle and Hippocrene Books.

Mlotek, Eleanor G. (Chana) and Joseph (Yosl) Mlotek (1988) *Pearls of Yiddish Song*. New York, NY: Education Department of the Workmen's Circle.

—— (1995) *Songs of Generations: New Pearls of Yiddish Song*. New York, NY: Workmen's Circle.

Mlotek, Eleanor (Chana) and Mark Slobin, eds (2007) *Yiddish Songs from the Ruth Rubin Archive*. Detroit, MI: Wayne State University Press.

Mlotek, Joseph (1954) 'Ideological Changes in the Workmen's Circle Schools'. Unpublished research paper. YIVO archives, box WG1768.

—— (c. 1966) 'Mordechai Gebirtig – Troubadour of Our People: Program for Workmen's Circle Groups'. Lecture text, including songs. New York, NY: Education Department of the Workmen's Circle.

Mlotek, Mark (2006) 'Living a Secular Jewish Life'. In Barnett Zumoff and Karl D. Zukerman, eds, *Secular Jewishness for Our Time: A Three-Part Symposium by Three Generations of Writers, Educators and Cultural Activists in 1938–40, 1968–69, and 1998–2000*. New York, NY: The Forward Association, 264–70.

Móricz, Klára (2008) *Jewish Identities: Nationalism, Racism, and Utopianism in Twentieth-Century Music*. Berkeley, CA: University of California Press.

Mummert, Roger (1988) 'The Reblings: Yiddish Voices from East Germany'. *Der pakn-treger/The Book Peddler*, Winter, 9–10, 36–7, 82–3.

Neate, Patrick (2003) *Where You're At: Notes from the Frontline of a Hip Hop Planet*. London: Bloomsbury.

Netsky, Hankus (2004) Klezmer: Music and Community in Twentieth-Century Jewish Philadelphia. PhD diss., Wesleyan University.

Neuman, Daniel M. (1991) 'Epilogue: Paradigms and Stories'. In Stephen Blum, Philip V. Bohlman and Daniel M. Neuman, eds, *Ethnomusicology and Modern Music History*. Urbana, IL: University of Illinois Press, 268–77.

Ogbar, Jeffrey O.G. (1999) 'Slouching toward Bork: The Culture Wars and Self-Criticism in Hip-hop Music'. *Journal of Black Studies* 30:2, 164–83.

Ortmeyer, Benjamin (1996) *Jiddische Lieder gegen die Nazis*. Bonn: Verlag M. Webbe.

Ostow, Robin (1989) *Jews in Contemporary East Germany*. London: Macmillan.

Ottens, Rita, with Joel Rubin (2002) '"The Sounds of the Vanishing World": The German Klezmer Movement as Racial Discourse'. Proceedings of conference 'Sounds of Two Worlds: Music as a Mirror of Migration to and from Germany', Max Kade Institute for German-American Studies, University of Wisconsin-Madison, September 2010. Published online: http://csumc.wisc. edu/mki/Resources/Online_Papers/MusicConfPapers/Ottens-RubinPaper.pdf, last accessed 3 August 2010.

Pasternak, Velvel (1999) *Beyond Hava Nagila: Hasidic Music in 3 Movements*. Cedarhurst, NY: Tara Publications.

Rapoport-Albert, Ada (1996) Introduction to Ada Rapoport-Albert, ed., *Hasidism Reappraised*. London: Vallentine Mitchell.

Ratner, Leonard G. (1980) *Classic Music: Expression, Form and Style*. New York, NY: Schirmer.

Ray, Larry (2010) 'Migration and Remembrance: Sounds and Spaces of Klezmer "Revivals"'. *Cultural Sociology*, pre-publication copy available at http://kent.academia.edu/documents/0088/4785/Klezmer_paper.pdf, last accessed 3 August 2010.

Rogovoy, Seth (2000) *The Essential Klezmer*. Chapel Hill, NC: Algonquin.

Roskies, David G. (1999) *The Jewish Search for a Usable Past*. Bloomington, IN: Indiana University Press.

Rosmarin, Rachel (2000) *Mamma Used to Say: Pearls of Wisdom from the World of Yiddish*. Jerusalem: Feldheim.

Rothstein, Robert A. (2002) 'Klezmer-loshn: The Language of Jewish Folk Musicians'. In Mark Slobin, ed., *American Klezmer: Its Roots and Offshoots*. Berkeley, CA: University of California Press, 24–34.

Rubin, Ruth (1948) 'Yiddish Folksong of the Eastern European Jews'. Lecture text, including songs. New York: National Jewish Music Council.

—— (1967) 'Warsaw Ghetto Program'. Lecture text, including songs. New York: Education Department of the Workmen's Circle.

—— (1968) 'Yiddish Folksongs of Social Significance: Program for Workmen's Circle Groups'. Lecture text, including songs. New York: Education Department of the Workmen's Circle.

—— (1979) *Voices of a People: The Story of Yiddish Folksong*. Philadelphia, PA: Jewish Publication Society of America.

Salant, Yankl (2001) '1968 (or *Zumer-program* Year One)'. *Zumer in nyu-york* [Summer in New York] (YIVO Institute for Jewish Research) 1:1, 6.

Saminsky, Lazare (1934) *Music of the Ghetto and the Bible*. New York, NY: Bloch.

Sandrow, Nahma (1977) *Vagabond Stars: A World History of Yiddish Theatre*. New York, NY: Harper and Row.

Sapoznik, Henry (1988a) 'Collecting Yiddish folksongs: A Do-It-Yourself Guide for the Amateur Yiddish Song-zamler'. *Der pakn-treger/The Book Peddler* 9–10, 20–21.

—— (1988b) 'Bringin' It All Back Home: Klezmer Returns to Europe'. *Der pakn-treger/The Book Peddler* 9–10, 34–6, 82.

—— (1999) *Klezmer!: Jewish Music from Old World to Our World*. New York, NY: Schirmer.

Saxonberg, Steven and Magdalena Waligórska (2006) 'Klezmer in Kraków: Kitsch, or Catharsis for Poles?' *Ethnomusicology* 50:3, 433–51.

Schaechter, Mordkhe (1986/1995) *Yidish tzvey/Yiddish II: A Textbook for Intermediate Courses*. 2nd edition. New York, NY: Yiddish Language Resource Center of the League for Yiddish.

Schaechter-Gottesman, Beyle (1990) *Zumerteg/Summer Days: Twenty Yiddish Songs*. New York, NY: Yidisher kultur-kongres and the League for Yiddish.

Scherman, Nosson (1987). *Sidur ahaves sholem: The Complete ArtScroll Siddur*. 2nd edition, nusach Ashkenaz. Brooklyn, NY: Mesorah Publications.

Seroussi, Edwin (1995) 'Documenting Music in Israel'. In C. Berlin, ed., *Documenting Israel: Proceedings of a Conference Held at Harvard University on May 10–12, 1993*. Cambridge, MA: Harvard College Library, 153–66.

Shandler, Jeffrey (1989) *Going Home: How American Jews Invent the Old World*. Catalogue for exhibition at the YIVO Institute of Jewish Research, June 1989–February 1990. New York, NY: YIVO Institute of Jewish Research.

—— (1991) 'Pripetshik'. *Der pakn treger/The Book Peddler* 16, 42–3.

—— (2000) 'Beyond the Mother Tongue: Learning the Meaning of Yiddish in America'. *Jewish Social Studies* 6:3, 97–123.

—— (2002) 'Shopping for Yiddish in Boro Park'. *Der pakn treger/The Book Peddler* 40, 21–7.

—— (2006) *Adventures in Yiddishland: Postvernacular Language and Culture*. Berkeley, CA: University of California Press.

Sheramy, Rona (2007) 'From Auschwitz to Jerusalem: Re-enacting Jewish History on the March of the Living'. *Polin* 19, 307–25.

Silber, Laya (1997) 'The Return of Yiddish Music in Israel'. *Journal of Jewish Music and Liturgy* 20: 11–22.

Silverman, Jerry (1983/1999) *The Yiddish Song Book*. Lantham, NY: Scarborough House.

Slobin, Mark (1980) 'The Evolution of a Musical Symbol in Yiddish Culture'. In Frank Talmage, ed., *Studies in Jewish Folklore*. Cambridge, MA: Association for Jewish Studies, 313–30.

—— (1982) *Tenement Songs: The Popular Music of the Jewish Immigrants*. Urbana, IL: University of Illinois Press.

—— (1986) 'A Fresh Look at Beregovski's Folk Music Research'. *Ethnomusicology* 30:2, 253–60.

—— (1987) 'Fiddler off the Roof: Klezmer Music as an Ethnic Musical Style'. In Moses Rischin, ed., *The Jews of North America*. Detroit, MI: Wayne State University Press, 95–104.

—— (1989) *Chosen Voices: The Story of the American Cantorate*. Urbana, IL: University of Illinois Press.

—— (1993) *Subcultural Sounds: Micromusics of the West*. Hanover, NH: Wesleyan University Press.

—— (2000) *Fiddler on the Move: Exploring the Klezmer World* (American Musicspheres). New York, NY: Oxford University Press.

——, ed. (2002a) *American Klezmer: Its Roots and Offshoots*. Berkeley, CA: University of California Press.

—— (2002b) 'Unintentional History: Musical Moments in 1930s Yiddish Films'. *Yuval* 7, 468–80.

Slotnick, Susan (1976) 'The Contributions of the Soviet Yiddish Folklorists'. *Working Papers in Yiddish and East European Jewish Studies* 20. New York: YIVO Institute for Jewish Research.

Smulyan, Shayn (2012) 'The SoCalled Past: Sampling Yiddish in Hip-Hop'. In Lara Rabinovitch, Shiri Goren, and Hannah Pressman, eds. *Choosing Yiddish: New Frontiers of Language and Culture*. Detroit, MI: Wayne State University Press, 357-375.

Soloveitchik, Haym (1994) Rupture and Reconstruction: The Transformation of Contemporary Orthodoxy. *Tradition* 28:4. Reproduced at http://www. lookstein.org/links/orthodoxy.htm, accessed 18 May 2004.

Soltes, Avraham (1967) 'The Hebrew Folk Song Society of St Petersburg: The Historical Development'. In Irene Heskes and Arthur Wolfson, eds, *The Historic Contribution of Russian Jewry to Jewish Music*. New York, NY: National Jewish Music Council, 13–27.

Sontag, Susan (1973) *On Photography*. New York, NY: Farrar, Straus and Giroux.

Summit, Jeffrey A. (2000) *The Lord's Song in a Strange Land: Music and Identity in Contemporary Jewish Worship*. New York, NY: Oxford University Press.

Svigals, Alicia (2002) 'Why We Do This Anyway: Klezmer as Jewish Youth Subculture'. In Mark Slobin, ed. *American Klezmer: Its Roots and Offshoots*. New York, NY: Oxford University Press, 211–20.

Taussig, Michael (1995) 'The Sun Gives without Receiving: An Old Story'. *Comparative Studies in Society and History* 37:2, 368–98.

Tomlinson, Gary (1984) 'The Web of Culture: A Context for Musicology'. *19th Century Music* 7:3, 350–62.

Tumarkin, Maria (2005) *Traumascapes: The Power and Fate of Places Transformed by Tragedy*. Carlton, Victoria: Melbourne University Press.

Vaysman, Asya (2010) '"She Who Seeks Shall Find": The Role of Song in a Hasidic Woman's Life Cycle'. *Journal of Synagogue Music* 35, 155–83.

Vinaver, Chemjo and Eliyahu Schleifer (1985) *Anthology of Hassidic Music*. Jerusalem: Hebrew University of Jerusalem.

Vinkovetzki [Vinkovetzky], Aharon (1969) *Antologie fun yidishe folks-lider*. [Anthology of Yiddish folk songs]. Leningrad: [no publisher].

Vinkovetzky, Aharon, Abba Kovner and Sinai Leichter (1983–) *Anthology of Yiddish Folksongs*. 4 vols. Jerusalem: Magnes Press.

Waxman, Mordecai (1977) 'The Changing American Rabbinate'. In Gilbert S. Rosenthal, ed., *The American Rabbi*. New York, NY: Ktav, 165–88.

Weber, Donald (2003) 'Accents of the Future: Jewish American Popular Culture'. In Hana Wirth-Nesher and Michael P. Kramer, eds, *The Cambridge Companion to Jewish American Literature*. Cambridge: Cambridge University Press, 129–48.

Weinreich, Max (1952) *Shtudien vegn yidisher folklor fun Y.L. Cahan* [Y.L. Cahan's studies in Jewish Folklore]. New York, NY: YIVO Institute for Jewish Research.

Weinreich, Uriel (1949/1999) *College Yiddish*. New York, NY: YIVO Institute for Jewish Research.

—— (1968/1977) *Modern English-Yiddish Yiddish-English Dictionary*. New York, NY: Schocken.

—— (1971) 'Yiddish Language'. In Cecil Roth, ed., *Encyclopedia Judaica* 16. Jerusalem: Ktav, 789–98.

Werb, Bret (2008) 'Shmerke Kaczerginski: The Partisan-Troubadour'. *Polin* 20, 392–412.

Wertheimer, Jack (1998) *A People Divided: Judaism in Contemporary America*. Hanover, NH and London: Brandeis University Press.

Wex, Michael (1992) 'From the Memoirs of Yisroel (Israel) Wex, Yeshiva Beatnik'. Liner notes to Klezmatics, *rhythm + jews*. CD recording: Piranha.

Wohlberg, Max (2010) 'The Music of the Synagogue as a Source of the Yiddish Folk Song'. *Journal of Synagogue Music* 35, 6–34.

Wood, Abigail (2004) Yiddish Song in Contemporary North America. PhD diss., Cambridge University.

—— (2007a) '(De)constructing Yiddishland: Solomon and SoCalled's HipHopKhasene'. *Ethnomusicology Forum* 16:2, 243–70.

—— (2007b) 'Stepping Across the Divide: Hasidic Music in Today's Yiddish Canon'. *Ethnomusicology* 51:2, 205–37.

—— (2007c) 'The Multiple Voices of American Klezmer'. *Journal of the Society for American Music* 1:3, 367–92.

—— (2013) 'Pop, Piety and Modernity: The Changing Spaces of Orthodox Culture'. In Nadia Valman and Laurence Roth, eds, *The Routledge Companion to Contemporary Jewish Cultures*. London: Routledge.

Zalmanoff, Samuel, dir. (1961) *Chabad Nigunim, Vol. 2*. Nichoach-Lubavitch, N-5721.

Zalmanoff, Shmuel (Samuel), ed. (1985) *Sefer hanigunim*. 2 vols. New York, NY: Kehot Publication Society.

Zaltsberg, Ernst (1999) 'Moysey Beregovsky, Encyclopaedist of Jewish Folk Music in Russia'. *East European Jewish Affairs* 28:1–2, 141–5.

Zerubavel, Yael (1995) *Recovered Roots: Collective Memory and the Making of Israeli National Tradition*. Chicago, IL: University of Chicago Press.

Zim, Sol (1984) *The Joy of Jewish Memories Songbook: Nostalgic Melodies in Contemporary Settings by Sol Zim*. Cedarhurst, NY: Tara Publications.

Sound Recordings

A Tickle in the Heart (2003) *Klezcats*. CD recording: A Tickle in the Heart, Swing and Klezmer Trio Köln, [no number].

Alberstein, Chava and the Klezmatics (1998) *Di Krenitse* [The Well]. CD recording: Xenophile, XENO 4052.

Bobover Chasidim (n.d., reissue of 1961 recording) *Authentic Bobover Nigunim – Sung by Heimishe Bobover Chasidim*. Cassette recording: [no label or number].

Bogdanski, Majer (2000) *Yiddish Songs/Yidishe Lider: Melodies Rare and Familiar*. CD recording: Jewish Music Heritage Recordings, London, JMHR CD 017.

Brave Old World (1990) *Klezmer Music*. CD recording: Flying Fish, FF 70560.

—— (1994) *Beyond the Pale*. CD recording: Rounder Records, Rounder CD 3135.

—— (1997) *Blood Oranges*. CD recording: Pinorrekk, PRCD 3405027.

—— (2003) *Bless the Fire*. CD recording: Pinorrekk, PRCD 3405039.

—— (2005) *Songs of the Lodz Ghetto*. CD recording: Winter & Winter, CD 910 104-2.

Bresnick-Perry, Roslyn (1990) *Holiday Memories of a Shtetl Childhood*. Cassette recording: Global Village Music, C161.

Budowitz (2000) *Wedding without a Bride*. CD recording: Buda Musique, 92759-2.

Cooper, Adrienne (2010) *Enchanted: A New Generation of Yiddishsong*. CD recording: Golden Horn Records, GHP 034-2.

Di Goldene Keyt (1997) *Mir zaynen do tsu zingen!* [We're here to sing!]. CD recording: Di Goldene Keyt, [no number].

Gendler, Arkady (2001) *My Hometown Soroke: Yiddish Songs of the Ukraine*. CD recording: Berkeley Richmond Jewish Community Centre, [no number].

Jewish Music Research Centre, Jerusalem (1992) *Musical Traditions in Israel: Treasures of the National Sound Archives*. CD recording: National Sound Archives, Jerusalem, [no number].

The Joel Rubin Music Ensemble (1997) *Beregovski's Khasene (Beregovski's Wedding): Forgotten Instrumental Treasures from the Ukraine*. CD recording: Schott Wergo, SM 1614-2.

Kahn, Daniel and Painted Bird (2009) *Partisans and Parasites*. CD recording: Oriente Musik, RIENCD71.

Klezmatics (1988) *Shvaygn=Toyt: Heimatklänge of the Lower East-Side*. CD recording: Piranha, PIR20-2.

—— (1992) *rhythm + jews*. CD recording: Flying Fish, FF 70591.

—— (1994) *Jews with Horns*. CD recording: Piranha, PIR35-2.

—— (1997) *Possessed*. CD recording: Piranha, PIR1148.

—— (1998). See Alberstein, Chava.

—— (2003) *Shteyt oyf!: Rise Up!*. CD recording: Piranha, PIR1686.

Klezmer Conservatory Band (1985) *A Touch of Klez!* CD recording: Vanguard, VMD-79455.

London, Frank (2003) *Divan*. Soundtrack album to film by Pearl Gluck. CD recording: Frank London, [no number].

London, Frank, Lorin Sklamberg and Uri Caine (1998) *Nigunim*. CD recording: Tzadik, TZ 7129.

London, Frank, Lorin Sklamberg and Rob Schwimmer (2001) *Zmiros: Songs for Shabbat and Jewish Celebration*. CD recording accompanying *Ain Sof*. See Gershman (2001).

London, Frank, Lorin Sklamberg, Knox Chandler, Ara Dinkjian and Deep Singh (2009) *Tsuker-zis*. CD recording: Tzadik, TZ 8141.

Maxwell St Klezmer Band (1991) *Maxwell Street Wedding*. CD recording: Global Village, CD136.

Mikveh (2001) *Mikveh*. CD recording: Traditional Crossroads, 80702-4305-2.

Nichoach (2000) *Chabad Nigunim, Volume 1*. CD recording: Nichoach-Lubavitch, CDNCC 01.

Nirenberg, Mariam (1986) *Folksongs in the East European Jewish Tradition from the Repertoire of Mariam Nirenberg*. Cassette recording: Global Village, C117.

Reiner, Yair and Henry Spazonik (2002) *Music from the Yiddish Radio Project*. CD recording: Shanachie, SH 6057.

Schaechter-Widman, Lifshe (1986) *Az di furst avek*. [As you go away]. Cassette recording: Global Village, C111.

Schwartz, Leon (1993) *Like in a Different World: A Traditional Jewish Klezmer Violinist from Ukraine*. Cassette recording: Global Village, C109.

Schwartz, Teddi (1990) *Kumt arayn* [Come in]*: American Songs in Yiddish*. Cassette recording: Global Village, C141.

Solomon and SoCalled (2003) *HipHopKhasene*. CD recording: Piranha, CD-PIR1789.

Suki and Ding (n.d.) *Shabbos Classics 2*. CD recording: Aderet Music Corp, BH-5.

Andy Statman Quartet (1998) *The Hidden Light*. CD recording: Sony, SK 60814.

Various artists (2011) *The Rough Guide to Klezmer* (second edition). CD recording: Rough Guides, RGNET1252.

Waletzky, Joshua (1989) *Partisans of Vilna*. CD recording: Flying Fish Records, FF 70450.

—— (2001) *Crossing the Shadows: New Yiddish Songs*. CD recording: the composer, WM001CD.

Yugntruf (1977) *Vaserl* [Stream]. LP recording: Yugntruf, [no number].

Films

Broughton, Simon, dir. (1989) *Fiddlers on the Hoof*. BBC.

Daum, Menachem and Oren Rudavsky, prod. and dir. (1997) *A Life Apart: Hasidism in America*. DVD recording: First Run Features.

DuBose, Glenn and Don Lenzer, prod. and dir. (1995) *Itzhak Perlman: In the Fiddler's House*. Video recording: Angel.

Goldman, Michal, dir. (1987) *A Jumpin' Night in the Garden of Eden*. First Run Features.

Kempner, Aviva and Joshua Waletzky, prod. and dir. (1986) *Partisans of Vilna*. Video recording: European Classics.

Marshall, Cindy, prod. (1986) *A Life of Song: A Portrait of Ruth Rubin, Yiddish Folksinger and Folklorist*. Video recording: Ergo.

Waletzky, Joshua, prod. and dir. (1980) *Image before My Eyes*. Video recording: YIVO Institute for Jewish Research.

Index